A PORTUGUESE RURAL SOCIETY

BY

JOSÉ CUTILEIRO

GULBENKIAN RESEARCH FELLOW OF ST. ANTONY'S COLLEGE
OXFORD

CLARENDON PRESS · OXFORD
1971

Oxford University Press, Ely House, London W.1

GLASGOW NEW YORK TORONTO MELBOURNE WELLINGTON
CAPE TOWN SALISBURY IBADAN NAIROBI DAR ES SALAAM LUSAKA ADDIS ABABA
BOMBAY CALCUTTA MADRAS KARACHI LAHORE DACCA
KUALA LUMPUR SINGAPORE HONG KONG TOKYO

PRINTED IN GREAT BRITAIN BY
WILLIAM CLOWES AND SONS LIMITED
LONDON, COLCHESTER AND BECCLES

A PORTUGUESE RURAL SOCIETY

BY

JOSÉ CUTILEIRO

GULBENKIAN RESEARCH FELLOW OF ST. ANTONY'S COLLEGE
OXFORD

CLARENDON PRESS · OXFORD
1971

Oxford University Press, Ely House, London W.1
GLASGOW NEW YORK TORONTO MELBOURNE WELLINGTON
CAPE TOWN SALISBURY IBADAN NAIROBI DAR ES SALAAM LUSAKA ADDIS ABABA
BOMBAY CALCUTTA MADRAS KARACHI LAHORE DACCA
KUALA LUMPUR SINGAPORE HONG KONG TOKYO

PRINTED IN GREAT BRITAIN BY
WILLIAM CLOWES AND SONS LIMITED
LONDON, COLCHESTER AND BECCLES

Portugal: questão que eu tenho comigo mesmo

ALEXANDRE O'NEILL, *Feira Cabisbaixa*

FOREWORD

FORMALLY speaking, this book is based on materials gathered during some twenty months of field work carried out in a small region in the south of Portugal in 1965 and 1967. The facts that will be described and analysed, from the areas of plots of land to instances of adultery, were all recorded there, and in this respect the book is no different from most ethnographic monographs. Had I been English and learned Portuguese to visit this specific region for the sole purpose of doing field-work there I would not need to add the opening qualification. Since I am Portuguese, was born in the province where I have now worked, and, although not living there, had visited it many times before, the qualification is important.

Field anthropologists since Malinowski have tried hard to identify themselves with the exotic peoples they study. In Zande-land Evans-Pritchard regulated his household affairs with the help of Zande oracles. Claude Lévi-Strauss even speaks of a 'rebirth' of the anthropologist when he is in the field. The claims of deep and inside knowledge made by field anthropologists, and their misgivings about social sciences that employ methods not requiring the same degree and length of involvement with the people studied, stem exactly from this tradition of intensive field-work, implying a temporary identification of the observer with the observed. My problem, as could be expected, has been the opposite. In order to be able to observe and describe the life of some of my fellow-countrymen I had, as it were, to impersonate an Oxford anthropologist.

This raised a difficulty of method. Field anthropologists, whether they consider themselves scientists or not, work largely by induction. From the facts or cases that they observe, they induce general patterns of the society or of groups in the society they study. In the present case the mental process was indeed such when I was dealing with aspects that were remote from my previous non-professional experience, such as agricultural practices and labour relations. But in matters with which I had previously been more familiar, for the mere reason of being Portuguese, such as the workings of the administrative agencies, the relationship between the public and these agencies, many of the institutionalized forms of patronage, some aspects of family life, and, most of all, the corpus of moral and religious values and beliefs, an inductive approach was far less feasible. I tried, as far as possible, to work from facts to generalizations, and the book is presented in this way; but the process has not always been candidly described. Many generalizations had been, so to speak, acquired beforehand; the facts which in the book seem to lead to them were limited to verification by instances. This, so far as I can see, is unavoidable if the anthropologist is studying his own society.

It might be argued that no one ever does field-work with an open mind and that the difference, in this context, between myself and a foreign anthropologist would not be that I had preconceptions whereas he had not, but that he would have had different preconceptions.[1] The preconceptions of a native, however, are more firmly rooted in experience, and above all they are extensively ramified. They are bound to affect his research in a deeper, if more self-conscious way. Even when they are right, and allow him to concentrate more fully on important points, and to master information which only a long cultural acquaintance is able to select and make sense of, an important problem remains. The native will be quicker and more perceptive mainly with regard to details or isolated instances. Yet it will require a much bigger effort from him than from an outsider (ultimately perhaps even an impossible one) to be able to form an integral conception of a society of which, at least at some levels of experience, he is himself a part.

Even if he does form an integral conception of the society, his view will tend to be more distorted by emotional commitments than that of an outsider. These commitments would certainly help, were he to write a novel, a poem, or a political pamphlet. In an anthropological monograph the only legitimate commitments are theoretical. If, therefore, I appear to be emotionally attracted to or repelled by customs, factions, or people in the course of this book I can only say that I tried, to

[1] I leave aside two fallacies, current among social anthropologists: (a) that common sense and empiricism are synonymous, and (b) that empiricism has no ideological connotations. The discussion here is at another level.

the best of my ability, to avoid any deleterious effects of my emotions on my observations and judgement.[2]

A final point. The need to write a foreword about being a student of one's own society casts doubts on the epistemological status of social anthropology. If our inquiries met some elementary scientific criteria the respective nationalities of the observer and the observed would be irrelevant. Since they are not irrelevant, we are not, strictly speaking, scientists, and our analysis of social institutions lacks neutrality of observation, predictive capacity and certainty.

This is more a result of the complexity of the subject-matter than of our muddled thinking. Students of society may adopt one of two alternative procedures. Some isolate small and simple problems, and are able to establish sound relationships of cause and effect between elementary phenomena; the slow accretion of their works is one of the foundations on which a scientific general theory of society may one day be built. Others consider that to reduce their subject-matter to problems that may be dealt with in that manner is more frustrating at present than to risk less accurate descriptions and more provisional explanations of the complex problems that have long preoccupied moralists, philosophers, and historians of society. Most social anthropologists, including the present author, belong to this group.

In accordance with anthropological practice, names of people and places have been changed. I cannot, therefore, mention the names of those who confided in me during my

[2] Emotional responses to my presence were also of some importance. Societies are not homogeneous and a native is caught in a cross-fire of conflicting estimations more often than a foreigner. The different attitudes of the different groups of the society towards me were themselves evidence of local social tensions. A foreigner would have been classified in a group of his own, e.g. he would have been 'the Englishman' or 'the Frenchman'. A Portuguese had to be placed on one rung of the national ladder of prestige and social position. Except among those who became my close friends, attitudes towards me were marked by a basic ambivalence. This resulted from my own ambiguous position: I was a member of the upper group and yet I had elected to live in a village, and I spent most of my time with labourers and poor peasants. In this sense the poor and the rich alike had reasons both to trust and to mistrust me—opposite reasons in each respective case. I learned a great deal about the tensions of social stratification in Vila Velha only by observing the attempts to classify me as 'one of us' or 'one of them', an observation that could not possibly have taken place if I had been a foreigner.

field-work, though my debt to them will be obvious throughout this book. Some are good friends and often went out of their way to help me—I hope that they will forgive the anonymity in which I am forced to leave them here.

Of those whom I can thank I shall first mention Dr. Horácio Menano, who suggested that I undertake this study and helped me in times of doubt. Mr. Ruy Cinatti and Professor Jorge Dias guided my first approaches to the subject and from their discussions I benefited a great deal. Mr. Francis Huxley was a most stimulating teacher and I owe him more than our different types of anthropology might suggest. Dr. John Beattie and Mr. Luís de Sousa-Rebelo, who examined the thesis from which this book evolved, and Professor Raymond Carr, who read it at a later stage, contributed useful comments and suggestions. The structure of the chapters on land tenure benefited from discussions with Mr. Jean-Marc Fontaine. I am grateful to Dr. Rodney Needham who patiently read the manuscript and made many illuminating criticisms. My greatest debt, however, is to Dr. John Campbell, without whose friendly guidance and support (for more than five years) this book might never have been finished. None of them is, of course, responsible for any mistakes of fact or interpretation.

I wish to thank the Calouste Gulbenkian Foundation (Lisbon) and, particularly, Dr. José Ribeiro dos Santos, Director of the Foundation's Department of Science, who took a direct and gratifying interest in this project, for a grant that allowed me to carry out most of the work. The Warden and Fellows of St. Antony's College, who elected me to a Research Fellowship and thus enabled me to complete this book, also receive my thanks.

My friends, Andrés, Jonathan, Max, Peter, and Vivienne, formerly students of St. Antony's College, helped me in the physical task of putting together the manuscript of the first draft of this book. I owe the compilation of the tables to Mr. José Tolento. Professor Frederico George had the map and graph expertly made for me by his staff. Mrs. Susan Chapman typed the manuscript with great care and good humour. My brother, João Cutileiro, and Mr. Gérard Castello Lopes (a born anthropologist if ever there was one) took the photographs while visiting me during the course of my field-work.

Mrs. Suzette Macedo contributed many invaluable editorial suggestions and strove to correct my efforts to write in a foreign and illusive language. Whatever reads well in this book the reader owes to her—the remainder I had left beyond rescue.

During these last few years my wife and her children have bravely endured a life of travel, separation, discomfort, and uncertainty, and I dedicate this book to them with apologies.

J. P. C.

St. Antony's College, Oxford
Spring 1970

PREFATORY NOTE

SOME of the social, economic, and administrative bodies discussed in this book will not be familiar to the English reader. Several of them will have to be mentioned in the text before they can be dealt with and explained at length. The purpose of this Prefatory Note is, therefore, to provide a brief description of those bodies for the reference of the reader.

ADMINISTRATIVE BODIES

Câmara: local government body which corresponds roughly to the English town council.

Junta de Freguesia (or simply *Junta*)*:* local government body, subordinate to the Câmara and having jurisdiction over a smaller area.

SOCIO-ECONOMIC BODIES
(also described as Corporative Bodies)

Grémio da Lavoura: state-controlled organization, membership of which is compulsory for landowners. The intended function of the Grémio is to protect the landowners' interests and to implement and co-ordinate central agricultural policy at local level. The Grémio developed from a voluntary organization called the *Syndicato.*

Casa do Povo: state-controlled organization, membership of which is compulsory for landowners and labourers. The main functions of the Casa do Povo are to assist labourers generally and to handle unemployment problems.

SOCIAL BODIES

Misericórdia: lay brotherhood which functions as a local welfare agency.

KEY FOR IDENTIFICATION OF THE SOURCES REFERRED TO IN THE TEXT:

C.m.	Minutes of the Câmara
C.P.c.	Casa do Povo correspondence

C.P.m.	Minutes of the Casa do Povo
G.c.	Grémio correspondence
J.c.	Junta correspondence
J.m.	Minutes of the Junta
LN I LN II LN V	Local newspapers
M.m.	Minutes of the Misericórdia
S.c.	Syndicato correspondence

CONTENTS

LIST OF PLATES

(Photographs I, II, IX, X, and the photograph used on the dust-jacket are by Mr. João Cutileiro; photographs III, IV, V, VI, VII and VIII are by Mr. Gérard Castello Lopes)

INTRODUCTION

I

THE people whose institutions are analysed in this book live in five villages and a small town in the south-east of Portugal, close to the Spanish border. The settlements, together with some nine thousand hectares of land around them, form a basic division of Portuguese administration, the *freguesia.* The town is smaller than two of the villages but its past importance (as a military outpost and as the administrative centre of an area four times the size of the present freguesia) accounts for the fact that the parish church and administrative bodies are still located there.[1] The town, from which the freguesia takes its name, will be called Vila Velha in this study.

The town, villages, and fields do not differ in any striking way from other towns, villages, and fields of Mediterranean Portugal.[2] It is a country of wheat fields and olive groves, with a few isolated farm-houses, most of the population living close together in the settlements, which are clearly visible in the distance on account of the immaculate whiteness of their houses. Like some of the other towns in the province of Alentejo, Vila Velha is built on top of a hill and is encircled by a medieval wall. The surrounding villages are on the plains, two of them situated at the foot of the hill on which Vila Velha is built.

Each of the villages and the town constitute a neighbourhood with its own shops, taverns, post-office, and, with two exceptions, schools. Three of the villages have churches, although services are not held regularly. The freguesia has only one cemetery, situated just outside Vila Velha. All bureaucratic matters that can be dealt with locally must be settled in Vila Velha. If there is a

[1] I have translated *aldeia* as village and *vila* as town. These distinctions have to do with administrative importance, historical traditions, and sometimes—but not always—size. The urban space of a *vila* is generally better organized in a conspicuous way around a square where the most important civic, religious, and social buildings are found. An *aldeia* often has a much more disorganized urban space.

[2] The geographical distinction between a Mediterranean and an Atlantic Portugal has been pointed out by Orlando Ribeiro. See *Portugal, o Mediterrâneo e o Atlantico*, 2nd edition (Lisbon, 1963).

local doctor he lives in the town, but the pharmacy is in one of the villages. Each settlement is thus independent from the others in many aspects of its day-to-day life, but not in all.

The villages and the town are within walking distance of each other and the individuality of their respective populations—as testified by the existence of long-standing local families—is qualified by frequent intermarriage. Since marriage to people from outside is much rarer, the freguesia may be seen as a relatively self-contained web of interconnected kinship groups.[3] As a result of these intermarriages, land owned by local residents is scattered throughout the freguesia. Men living in one village or in the town[4] may have plots near any of the other villages. On their daily journey to and from their plots they meet people from the other villages through which they may even pass. Large estates, mostly owned by outsiders, encircle the villages like an outer belt. The labourers and sharecroppers who work on these estates are exclusively from the freguesia and, except in very rare cases, do not engage in agricultural work elsewhere. Although the villages each have different patron saints, the saint of Vila Velha is the patron of the whole freguesia and is by far the most popular. Accents vary slightly within the freguesia, but there is a generally recognizable way of speaking which can be distinguished from the accents of adjoining freguesias. To the untrained ear all the accents fall within the general mode of speech of the southern hinterland of Portugal.

The people of the freguesia are familiar with Vila Velha's historical traditions, and local rivalries are forgotten when they come into contact with the outside world. Away from home, people do not describe themselves as being from 'village A' or 'village B,' but as being from Vila Velha. There is, therefore, a feeling of identity with economic, familial, and religious roots, reinforcing the common denominator of local residence.[5]

During the course of my analysis I will sometimes have to leave the freguesia itself and make excursions to Vila Nova, a

[3] The information that supports this claim is confirmed by an analysis of the parish marriage register between 1945 and 1965.

[4] Except when I need to specify, I shall avoid this cumbersome distinction in the text, and write 'villages' for 'villages and town'.

[5] The coincidence of these factors with an established administrative division makes for the availability of quantitative and statistical data which would otherwise have to be extrapolated or dispensed with.

town of some five thousand inhabitants ten miles from Vila Velha.[6] These excursions correspond to the physical excursions that the people of the freguesia themselves have to make in order to conduct a wide range of their affairs. Some administrative and economic offices, the town hall, the landowners' association, the tax bureau, bank agencies and shops, far bigger than any found in the freguesia, are in Vila Nova, as are the residences of most of the owners of the freguesia's big estates.

II

Land and weather provide the natural background to economic and social life. In Vila Velha both leave much to be desired, and because of their shortcomings, the traditional crops rarely provide a good harvest. The solemn and austere beauty of the scenery gives great aesthetic satisfaction, but it betrays the underlying barrenness of the land.

The freguesia is divided into two topographically distinct zones: a flat zone, known as the *terras mansas* (literally 'mild lands') or *campas* ('fields'), corresponding to a granitic geological structure, and an undulating zone, known as the *terras ásperas* (literally 'harsh lands') or *dobradas* ('hilly land'), corresponding to silurian schists.[7] The *terras mansas* occupy not more than 30 per cent of the whole area, encroaching on the *terras ásperas* in two separate places: to the west and to the south of the freguesia. The rest is made up of *terras ásperas*.

The silurian schistose zone has a much thinner layer of arable land than the granitic zone. The soil is drier and stonier, and these features, together with the unevenness of the surface, are responsible for the lack of sustained fertility of these lands. The deeper layer of reddish granitic soil is more fertile, but the freguesia's best land is found in the zones of transition from the schist to the granite. The *barros*, or clay soils, of this area are

[6] Vila Nova is the head of the *concelho*. Concelhos are administrative divisions which comprise several freguesias. Several concelhos form a distrito. Vila Velha was the head of the concelho until 1851.

[7] The two most conspicuous features of the landscape are in the undulating zone: the hill of Vila Velha (289 m.) and a stretch of small hills, known as the *serra*, (278 m.), bordering the northern limit of the freguesia. The flatlands lie at an altitude of between 180 m. and 200 m.

rich, red, and deep, and their freedom from stones makes farming easy, but they occupy only a very small proportion of the whole (about 10 per cent), mainly to the north-west of Vila Velha.

This 10 per cent of better land would provide good conditions for irrigated farming of a more intensive type (although this has not been tried on any significant scale) and, even with the dry-farming methods at present employed, it always produces the best crop in the freguesia. The granitic soils (covering about 20 per cent of the area), less deep and more stony than the *barros*, with a few stretches of better quality soil, are suitable only for dry farming. They do not require unusually long fallow periods, but high productivity cannot be expected. Nevertheless, they are still considered good lands in local terms. The remaining 70 per cent of the land has a shallow mantle of dry and stony soils with rocks frequently exposed on the surface, which are of very low fertility. Dry farming with very long fallow periods is the only use to which this land is put at present.

Apart from the quality of the soil, rainfall is a most important natural factor. The region is subject to great irregularities of rainfall, both in terms of its distribution throughout the yearly crop cycle and of the total recorded each year. The rains come mostly in the cold months, between November and March. By then many crops are in their rest cycle but the cereals sown in autumn, which are of great importance in the region's economy, begin to sprout very early. The cereal crops are thus vitally affected by variations in rainfall during the winter months.

April is a month of great irregularity. Since it is then that cereals need rain for the grain to develop, the quality of the harvest hinges on the April rains. 'April', peasants often say in moments of despair over its unpredictability, 'is the cruellest month'. Their despair is understandable: a dry April ruins the crop, and even two nights of frost before the rains come may be enough to decrease substantially the amount eventually harvested.[8]

[8] During this century, rainfall in April has varied in different years from 0·0 mm. to 106·8 mm. For a technical discussion of rainfall in the province of Alentejo, cf. J. A. Marques Tapum, unpublished thesis on agricultural engineering (Lisbon, 1950), Chapter III. For a brief summary of the effects of the irregularities of rainfall on cereal cultivation in Portugal, cf. Mariano Feio, 'Clima e ocupação agrícola de Portugal', *Geographica*, i. 1 (Jan. 1965), pp. 4–9.

The hot, dry period of the yearly cycle lasts from May to September. Rainfall is extremely low in these months: there have been years when not a single drop of rain fell between April and October. October is a very irregular month and, if there is heavy rainfall, cereal seeds may be washed away or sowing delayed.

Within the general Mediterranean pattern of hot, dry summers, and cold, wet winters, this region is subject to unpredictable climatic conditions, which vary considerably from year to year; and this, combined with the poor quality of the soils, contributes to its low productivity.

The crops which these ecological conditions permit do not differ from those found in many other regions of the European south. Wheat and the lesser cereals, rye, oats, and barley, olives and acorns, have been the traditional products of the land. The raising of sheep and pigs has provided an important complement to the economy as has, albeit to a lesser extent in recent years, the rearing of goats, mares, and cows.

Farming is extensive since large areas are needed to make the concerns profitable. Around the villages and the town, and situated between these and the large estates, are zones of smallholdings, most of whose owners also work for the big estates as labourers or sharecroppers. There is no artificial irrigation except in the small vegetable gardens, called *hortas*, which also contain a few fruit trees.

Both historical circumstances—traceable as far back as the Christian reconquest of the twelfth and thirteenth centuries when the southern part of the country was divided into large estates which were granted to noblemen and to the religious and military orders—and ecological conditions have determined the type of crop planted and the farming methods used. These have had a direct effect on the social structure of the region. They have contributed to the low density of the population, which is composed mainly of landless or near-landless labourers and sharecroppers. Because of the nature of extensive farming, with its labour needs unevenly distributed throughout the year, there are many months during which landowners cannot provide labourers with employment, a situation which further emphasizes the rigidity of social and economic stratification.

III

The freguesia's population has fluctuated over the last hundred years. The figures below are taken from the official census records published since 1864.

Census Year	*Population*	*Census Year*	*Population*
1864	1,300	1920	1,769
1878	1,410	1930	2,161
1890	1,563	1940	2,526
1900	1,557	1950	2,455
1911	1,909	1960	2,161

The increase found up to 1940 corresponds to the over-all trend in Portuguese population growth. The decrease in population since 1940 has accompanied the introduction of mechanization on some of the large estates, and, since the late fifties, reflects the progressive decline of farming, which has led many people to leave the land for better opportunities elsewhere. The process is still under way. In December 1965 the resident population numbered 1,597, distributed among 571 households. The distribution by settlements was as follows:

Settlement	*Households*	*Number of people*
Vila Velha	89	292
Village I	41	122
Village II	59	162
Village III	49	121
Village IV	144	376
Village V	136	354
Scattered Farms	48	119

People in the freguesia make their living from the land. Even those who do not rely directly on farming, such as shopkeepers, tavern owners, and craftsmen, are still dependent on the outcome of the agricultural year. Only about forty local men are free from this contingency: these are the workers in the paper-mill built in 1950 on the southern outskirts of the freguesia.

The majority of the active male population is engaged in agricultural work, as labourers or sharecroppers (*seareiros*). Most of them are landless, but about two dozen men are wealthy enough to be in a position where they do not have to work on somebody else's land, and can employ other men to work on their own concerns. The men in this group are known as *proprietários*. The larger estates are nearly all owned by people living in Vila Nova. These rich owners of large estates are called *lavradores* or *latifundiários*,[9] and although they do not live in the freguesia, they are not faceless absentee collectors of rents. The gulf between them and most other local men, however, is as wide as the difference between the respective sizes of their holdings.

IV

Historically, Vila Velha is part of a wider society and has been subject to a large number of outside influences. Indeed, it could not be considered as anything but a segment of that wider society, the 'back yard' of an old civilization, marked by all its historical accidents. The first traces of man's presence in Vila Velha are dolmens belonging to a megalithic culture which was not restricted to this area. The Roman and Arab occupations also left their mark, and Christianity, as it spread, became the local religion. The establishment and consolidation of the Portuguese state gave Vila Velha its present language and integrated it into Portugal's economic, administrative, and legal systems. These have contributed much to shape social life. It is not my concern, however, to outline the cultural history of Vila Velha and trace the origins of its institutions. When a peasant says that he is going to draw water from his well, it is irrelevant to the present purpose that he is speaking in a Romance language about a technique made possible by Arab technology. Like ethnic characteristics, such things are taken for granted here; they represent the slow accretion of cultural traits through the centuries, and fall outside the scope of this analysis.

Some recent historical events, however, must be considered in a different light. Political, economic, and technological factors have brought about radical changes in the last 130 years and certain fundamental aspects of the present social life of Vila Velha are a direct outcome of these factors.

Ownership of land, as it is understood today—who owns land and on what terms—owes its present pattern to the re-shaping of the legal, administrative, and economic framework

[9] I shall call them latifundists in this book. The notion of *latifundia* varies from region to region. In Alentejo anyone owning estates of more than five hundred hectares is described as a *latifundist*.

of the country that took place during the decades that followed the formal overthrow of the *ancien régime* after the civil war ended in 1834. The Liberal parliamentary monarchy was replaced by a parliamentary republic in 1910, which gave way to the Corporate State in 1926. These political changes did not affect the basic characteristics of landownership laid down by Liberal legislation.[10] The main purpose of this legislation was to make land free and unencumbered (*livre e alodial*) in order to assert full individual property rights and increase production. This purpose was achieved. Large areas, previously in the hands of religious orders, noble houses, the Crown, and the local community itself (communal lands), many of them left completely uncultivated or hardly farmed at all, came on the market. By the end of the century the characteristic features of land tenure under the *ancien régime* had disappeared altogether, and had been replaced by the system that prevails today. This system did not promote a more even distribution of resources among the rural population: one group of latifundists was replaced by another. But it created the present pattern of social stratification or, one might say, the present class structure of Vila Velha.

The predominance of wheat among local crops was also stimulated from the outside. At the end of the nineteenth century government protection and the introduction of chemical fertilizers gave an unprecedented boost to wheat cultivation in

[10] The main measures of the Liberal regime affecting ownership of land were:

(1) The monasteries and religious orders were abolished and their land was put up for sale by public auction. Part of the Crown-lands in the hands of the nobility was sold in the same way.

(2) The system of entailment, whereby only the eldest son inherited the family patrimony (*morgadio*), was abolished, and property has since been divided in equal shares among all the direct heirs, male and female alike.

(3) The complicated system of taxes and other dues, payable on land properties to the Crown, noblemen, municipalities, and the Church, was greatly simplified. Many of these taxes, including the church *dízimos* ('tithes'), were abolished. The system of taxation was centralized and streamlined.

(4) Legislation, designed to promote the partition of communal lands, which had been initiated during the *ancien régime*, was carried further, and almost all communal lands were eventually divided.

These measures took some time to implement. In Vila Velha it was only in 1839 that the local authorities were asked to provide a list of holdings owned by religious orders in the concelho as a preliminary to their public auction. The freguesia's communal lands were not partitioned until 1874.

Portugal, which was further stimulated by the active support given by the Government to wheat farmers since 1929. The central place of wheat in local farming created patterns of work and unemployment which were of great sociological significance, both when wheat farming was at its zenith, and when it began to decline.

In recent years increasing industrialization in and around Lisbon and the demand for cheap manpower in western European countries have attracted large numbers of formerly ill-paid rural labourers and a progressive depopulation is taking place.

Other factors, particularly those of a political nature, have also helped to shape many of Vila Velha's present-day features. These will be mentioned in the course of this study. However, the changes in land tenure brought about in the middle of the nineteenth century, the emphasis on wheat cultivation from the end of the century onwards, and, in the last decade, the possibility of either moving to the industrial areas or emigrating, have been the most important recent contributions of the outside world to the social life of the freguesia.

PART ONE

LAND TENURE—SOCIAL STRATIFICATION

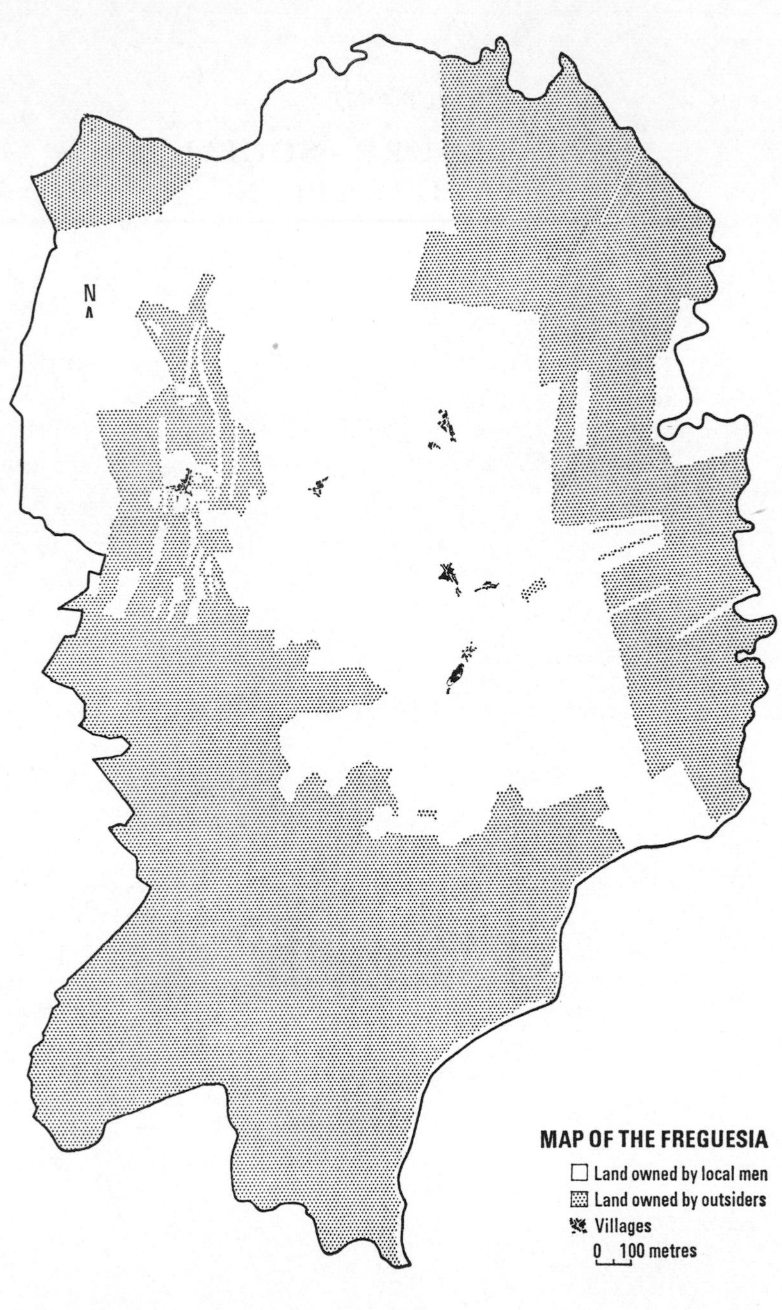
N
MAP OF THE FREGUESIA
Land owned by local men
Land owned by outsiders
Villages
0 100 metres

I

THE EMERGENCE OF THE PRESENT PATTERN OF LAND TENURE

LAND tenure is the key-stone of the social stratification of Vila Velha. At the end of the *ancien régime* about one-sixth of the land in Vila Velha was communal. There were estates belonging to the House of Bragança, to absentee noblemen, and to monasteries. A few estates belonged to local landowners who also rented land from members of these groups.[1] Around the villages there were clusters of smallholdings belonging to local peasants. One of these clusters was a result of a partition of land belonging to the House of Bragança which was carried out in the sixteenth century.[2] The land of these plots is comparatively fertile. A second cluster of smallholdings occupies some of the most fertile land in the freguesia and must also have been the result of a partition. This can be inferred from the neat geometrical pattern of the boundaries and from the description of these holdings in the book of accounts of the Misericórdia. I was unable to establish the date when the partition took place; but it was certainly completed before 1820.[3] Both the estates owned by outsiders and those belonging to local men were smaller than the big estates of today: the largest probably did not exceed three hundred hectares.[4] The fallow periods were

[1] There is no land property record for that time, nor is there any record of ordinary taxes. Unless otherwise stated, my evidence, both for the end of the *ancien régime* and for the changes that took place in the nineteenth century, comes from a book recording a war tax (Livro de Dízima de Guerra) collected in 1828, from the property deeds of some of the modern estates, from lists of taxpayers for 1852, 1878, and 1909, and from oral tradition.

[2] I owe this point to the Portuguese historian, Dr. José Pires Gonçalves, to whose knowledge of medieval Alentejo, from its ecology to its political history, I am also indebted.

[3] The smallholders are mentioned in a book of accounts of the Misericórdia for 1820.

[4] Although several could be owned as a single holding by the same owner, they were generally rented out in separate lots to local men and constituted viable independent units whose tenants were described as *lavradores* and independently taxed. Livro de Dízima de Guerra, 1828.

longer than today, and some parts of the estates were never farmed. The commons were mostly left uncultivated and used for grazing.

By the end of the nineteenth century the picture was very different. Land, freed by Liberal legislation, had changed hands, and the traditional groups of latifundists—the Crown, the nobility, the religious orders, and the community through its ownership of communal lands—was replaced by a new group of landowners of non-aristocratic origin. Some of these men were already prosperous under the *ancien régime*;[5] others began making their money at that time. Taking advantage of the new legal status of land property, they established the main agricultural 'houses' (agricultural enterprises run by one family through several generations) still found today. With changes due to the consolidation or division that followed the hazards of inheritance in each generation, these 'houses' were already well established by the end of the century, and the families who own them now, almost all related through marriage alliances contracted over the last four generations, have clearly differentiated themselves in terms of wealth and political influence from the rest of the plebeian population from which many of them originally came. In each of these families there is a recent ancestor known to have begun the consolidation of the family's present fortunes. Several factors contributed to the accumulation of wealth: inheritances,[6] hard work, profiting from the facilities provided by the clearing of hitherto uncultivated scrub land and the lending of money at high interest.

The concentration of landownership may be illustrated by the case of the two wealthiest families who own land in the freguesia. As well as other estates, 'family A' owns, as a single holding, land formerly belonging to eight estates of about eighty hectares each, held by different owners in the first half of the nineteenth century. One of 'family B's' estates (covering about 500 hectares) also comprises land formerly belonging to seven

[5] Indeed the richest family in the freguesia can be traced to one of the richest men in Vila Nova at the end of the *ancien régime*. The amount of land owned by the family increased dramatically during the nineteenth century. Under the *ancien régime* local men were rich in the local context: their wealth could not be compared to that of some noble houses and religious orders.

[6] Of one of these ancestors it is told that, when he stood witness at a trial and was asked his occupation by the judge, he replied, 'Heir!'

I. Street in Vila Velha

II. Carrying water

different estates, although five of them had already been consolidated and were owned by an absentee count at the end of the *ancien régime*.

Changes in ownership of land in the freguesia did not take place only at the level of the latifundists. The main local proprietários come from families who consolidated their land during the second half of the nineteenth century. Some were independent landowners, others began as managers of the big estates before they became landowners in their own right. Some families have since lost what they had, others have managed to keep, and even increase, the amount of land they own.

Today's landowning families, whether latifundists or local proprietários, were all established in the relative positions they now occupy by the beginning of this century. None of the latifundist families, however, can claim ancestors who would have had comparable wealth in 1828. Between the 1840s and the end of the nineteenth century a great reshuffle of property took place; but the conditions that made it possible disappeared, as did the social mobility that accompanied it.

The most socially significant, but not necessarily the most quantitatively important, change in land property patterns was that brought about by the partition of the commons. All other changes which altered the characteristic features of the *ancien régime* would have directly affected only the upper groups of society. The new rich owners usually farmed their land themselves,[7] whereas previous owners rented or leased it out; but to the labourers and sharecroppers who made up the majority of the population this could only mean a change of employer and not *per se* a change of conditions. The partition of the commons, however, affected their livelihood in a drastic way.

There were two commons (or *Baldios*), those of Coutada and Maxoa. The respective areas, as assessed when they were partitioned, were: 517 hectares and 1,035 hectares. They had been given to the people of the parish by the Royal House of Bragança, and they were managed by the local authorities.[8]

[7] In other parts of the province many of the new latifundists rented out their land. José da Silva Picão, writing at the end of the nineteenth century, states that this is the typical situation in Alentejo. See *Atravéz dos Campos—usos e costumes agrícolo-alentejanos*, 2nd edn. (Lisboa, 1947), p. 1.

[8] Reference to this donation was explicitly made by the Junta on 26 May 1852 and 19 March 1854. The terms on which the people of Vila Velha owned these

Sometimes a committee of local men dealt with the management of the commons, but they were appointed by the authorities, not chosen by the people themselves.[9]

From the end of the *ancien régime* till 1874 the commons seem to have been used in the following ways: parts of them were used for free grazing of sheep and goats (*gado miúdo*) by the local residents.[10] Tracts of land (*folhas*) were time and again set aside for allotment among residents (a minimum period of six months' residence as an independent householder was required to qualify for the lots)[11] to be cleared by burning the scrub for ploughing and sowing.[12] In 1864 the Câmara collected one-eighth of each plot-holder's harvest.[13] This may have been the customary share during the whole period. These allotments were frequent but not necessarily periodical. Among the duties of the Committee appointed in 1861 to supervise the commons was the allotment of plots 'whenever it deemed best'.[14] Residents were sometimes allowed to grow melons, and possibly other crops, in parts of the communal land that had not been allotted.[15]

In one of the commons (the *Coutada*) the local residents were allowed to graze cattle and mares (*gado grosso*) in fixed quotas per household and on a certain payment in kind.[16] The post of communal shepherd was auctioned every year until the partition.[17] Olive branches grafted on 'wild olive trees' (*zambujeiros*) were owned by those who had grafted them and not by the community.[18]

communal lands are not stated, however. But all evidence suggests that, although their management was entrusted to the organs of local government, their legal owners were 'the people', i.e. the heads of families living in the parish. They were proper communal lands, not municipal lands.

[9] Such was the case in 1861. J.m. 24 Aug. 1861.

[10] The animals sometimes trespassed in zones where they were not allowed and this gave rise to protests. C.m. 3 Sept. 1841; 4 Dec. 1841.

[11] J.m. 15 Feb. 1852.

[12] This was an 'ancient custom' (*costume antigo*) which the Câmara considered a contribution to the public good and public peace (*o bem público e o socêgo dos povos*). Cm. 7 Mar. 1840.

[13] J.m. 21 May 1864.

[14] J.m. 20 Aug. 1861.

[15] C.m. 21 Jan. 1843; 4 Feb. 43; 11 Feb. 1843; J.m. 15 May 1854.

[16] In 1852 the payment was about half a bushel of wheat (one and a half *alqueire*) per head for horses and about a third of a bushel of wheat (one *alqueire*) per head for cattle. (J.m. 14 July 1852 and 29 Aug. 1852.)

[17] The last auction took place in 1873. J.m. 3 Aug. 1873.

[18] This was respected after the partition (C.m. 26 Jan. 1873). Today many plots of land in the freguesia have olive trees that do not belong to the owner of the land.

These practices aroused no protests and were probably considered to be within the terms of reference laid down by the statute of the commons. But the decades before the partition witnessed a progressive encroachment of private on public rights. This sometimes took the form of a conflict between rich landowners and peasants and labourers.

The first encroachment came from the leasing out of small plots to private individuals which took place at least as early as 1814. A man applied for a plot and the *foro*[19] was generally determined by auction. These plots, therefore, became, for all practical purposes, private property. There were not many, and the lack of any protest against this practice seems to indicate that, after cereals were harvested, the grazing rights remained public.

Grazing rights were the main source of problems. '*Vaîne pâture*' in private property, if it ever existed locally, was no longer found by the end of the *ancien régime*.[20] The main grazing area was therefore provided by the common lands. This grazing area was vital for those who kept animals and had very little land or none at all, but was also convenient for the big landowners. By the middle of the nineteenth century these big landowners lived—as their heirs do now—outside the parish, most of them in Vila Nova, and would not therefore qualify as users of this land. However, they did use it, sometimes legally. In order to raise money, the Junta or the Câmara sold grazing rights for a given period to some of the landowners in parts of the commons. These sales led to protests.[21] In 1837 a buyer of grazing rights ceded his claim because he could not count on the co-operation of the population which continued to graze animals on the area. But this is the only recorded instance of such a withdrawal. In other instances the big landowners simply allowed their flocks to graze on the commons without any form

[19] *Foros* are forms of quasi-emphyteutic tenure. Raymond Carr, discussing the Galician *foros*, says that the 'nearest English equivalent is, perhaps, copyhold tenure.' *Spain 1808—1939* (Oxford, 1966), p. 9n.

[20] For a discussion of the general problem of 'open fields' and '*vaîne pâture*' in the southern hinterland of Portugal cf. Albert Silbert, *Le Portugal Méditerranéen à la fin de l'Ancien Régime*, 2 vols. (Paris, 1966.)

[21] C.m. 31 Aug. 1842; J.m. 26 May 1832. The exclusive right to supply fresh mutton to the freguesia was also put up for auction and the successful bidder was entitled to graze a certain number of sheep on the commons (300 in 1857, cf. J.m. 27 July 1857).

of contract. The Câmara—drawn from among these big landowners—was not very active in suppressing unauthorized grazing. In 1862, when protests were lodged against this practice, the Câmara ruled that unauthorized flocks should be removed with the proviso that this be held over until *after* the cereal harvest, seven months later, when the big landowners would in any case have enough grazing land on their own estates.[22] Infraction of the rules took another form with cattle and mares. The number of heads per household without grazing rights was restricted. However, many poor residents who did not own any cattle or mares, took those of rich landowners as theirs. This form of abuse seems to have been widespread in 1873.[23]

There were other problems raised by the commons which do not fall into the rich/poor dichotomy but are also instructive. Residents frequently took sheep and goats on the *coutada* where they were not allowed to graze.[24] There were also complaints against the way in which lots for cereal cultivation had been apportioned—complaints that always suggested that some had been favoured by the authority responsible for the division (Junta, Câmara, or Committee) against the legitimate rights of others.[25]

This type of problem throws light on the favouritism associated with the allotment of grazing rights and plots for cultivation on the commons, but its main importance for our present purpose is to show clearly the conflict that arose between private and public or individual and collective interest as a result of the existence of common lands. Nowadays, when labourers and peasants speak of the commons, they tend to idealize a system from which they, and not the rich landowners, had benefited and in which the rights of all were generally respected. They thus over-emphasize the positive contribution of the commons to their livelihood. The destiny of the communal land after

[22] C.m. 2 Jan 1862.

[23] C.m. 6 July 1873.

[24] The first recorded instance for the period under study is the Junta minutes for 3 Nov. 1841. They became even more frequent after the partition of 1874 had drastically reduced the area of communal grazing land (J.m. 15 Oct. 1878; J.m. 9 Feb. 1879; C.m. 14 Jan. 1884; C.m. 9 Jan. 1893). The remaining area could not feed more than four cows and four mares (J.m. 15 Oct. 1878). In 1912 it was decided to allow sheep and goats to graze on it freely, thus sanctioning *de jure* what was happening in practice (C.m. 8 Jan. 1912).

[25] J.m. 7 Mar. 1840; 20 Apr. 1842; 15 Feb. 1853; C.m. 23 Feb. 1856; 8 Feb. 1874.

partition is cited by labourers and peasants to prove partition itself a Machiavellian plot engineered by the big landowners.

A government decreee issued in 1869[26] stipulated that the partition of communal lands should take place when a majority of the heads of the families concerned should request it. In 1872[27], 204 resident heads of families officially signed a petition to the Câmara asking that, since the commons had been set aside for the exclusive use of the people of the freguesia from time immemorial, 'the said commons be divided among them on a strictly equal basis'.[28] A list of those entitled to land was drawn up and the *partidores* ('apportioners') were chosen. After an attempt had been made to prevent, or at least restrict, the partition through a counter-petition to the Government signed by fifty-three residents,[29] the division was finally made in 1874, sixty hectares being set aside to remain as common grazing land. The final list of those entitled to land as a result of this division contained the names of 382 heads of families, but, because there were still appeals to be considered, each of the two commons was divided into 410 different plots (*courelas*).[30] The *foros* were not auctioned off but were determined by the expertise of three landowners.[31] Each head of family was entitled to one plot from each common. On 8 November 1874 a ceremony was held in the Câmara and lots were drawn from two ballot boxes. To ensure that all would be conducted in strict fairness, a child of ten drew the lots for heads of families who could not be present.

When the proceedings were over, the former common land was fairly divided among all the residents, and the poorest of them now had at least two plots, one in each of the commons. Landless labourers had disappeared from the freguesia.

This situation lasted for only a short time and problems arose very soon after partition. Those concerned asked for a new assessment of the value of the *foros*, since they considered the existing charge 'excessive, unequal, and unfair'. The Câmara refused,[32] and asked those who had not yet done so to pay their *foros*, threatening them with the loss of their land.[33] This could

[26] 28 Aug.

[27] 19 Mar.

[28] C.m. 12 May 1872.

[29] C.m. 26 Jan. 1873.

[30] C.m. 3 May 1875.

[31] C.m. 28 Oct. 1874.

[32] C.m. 20 Dec. 1874.

[33] C.m. 1 Jan. 1875.

not have proved very effective, because five months later edicts for the same purpose and embodying the same threats were published.[34]

As might be expected, the system broke down. The Câmara minutes reveal some of the steps in the process. In 1884[35] a resident in one of the villages, notified by the Câmara to come and pay his *foros*, stated that, although he had been allotted a plot, he had never made use of it, nor had he yet paid any *foros*, and he suggested that the Câmara should take it in payment of his debt—a suggestion which the latter proceeded to follow. In 1892,[36] 1895[37] and 1903[38] the minutes mention the public auction of plots for which the *foros* had not yet been paid. In other cases the Câmara did not need to take direct action. Plots changed hands; landowners bought them from sharecroppers and labourers, and progressively consolidated the divided land. In 1907 the wealthiest latifundist had 166 plots in one of the commons registered under his name.[39] By 1914 only 69 of the 820 original plots remained.[40] As late as 1930 some of the remaining *courelas* in the old commons were bought and consolidated by a local landowner. Labourers had become landless again, having lost in the process the facilities that the commons had formerly provided.

People in Vila Velha often say that 'the rich stole the land of the poor', and it is likely that the Câmara, composed of wealthy landowners, was aware of what the ultimate result of the partition would be. They were local men who were fully aware of local conditions, not distant bureaucrats in central government, and they must have known that the size of the plots and the location of some of them, the poor quality of the land, and the meagre resources of those who had acquired them would render the project impractical, unless most of the plots were consolidated in bigger holdings. Indeed, a Câmara minute[41] of 1856 alludes to the unsuitability of the communal land for most farming purposes.

The fact that a majority of the local resident heads of families —204 out of 382—asked for partition would seem to indicate

[34] C.m. 23 May 1875.

[35] C.m. 17 May 1884.

[36] 30 May.

[37] 18 Feb.

[38] 11 May.

[39] C.m. 3 Apr. 1907.

[40] *Secção de Finanças*, Vila Nova 'Old Record of Land' (1914).

[41] 1 June

that even some of the 'poor' were willing to see it carried out. Given the relative strength of rich landowners and poor peasants and labourers, however, it is more than likely that many of the latter were persuaded, or even bullied, into supporting the partition. I am not basing this assumption simply on an oral tradition which seems to confirm it, but on observation of relationships between 'rich' and 'poor' at present, which will be abundantly illustrated throughout this book. The protest lodged by fifty-three residents against the partition may be seen in the same light. The Junta engineered the protest and fought unsuccessfully for its acceptance. The Junta's interests were twofold: first it considered the desirability for the ordinary people of the continued existence of communal lands, and secondly it hoped to be entrusted with their management and, once more, to be able to provide better administration and welfare from the income.[42] The position of the Junta was obviously closer to the long-term interests of local residents than that of the Câmara. But the Junta of Vila Velha was, as it still is, made up of small landowners whose power was less than that of the big landowners who sat on the Câmara of Vila Nova. In a few cases there may have been conflicting loyalties amongst the residents—some signed both the petition for partition and the protest against it.[43] But, on the whole, the power of the big landowners was far more conspicuous than that of the members of the Junta, and they carried the day.

Other factors may have contributed: some of the small local landowners must have seen the opportunity to increase their holdings (as indeed some of them eventually did). Even landless, or near-landless, men may have wished to possess land, and hoped that luck would give them plots in the more fertile zones. But the poor were as aware of local agricultural conditions as the rich, and many must have known that they could not count on long-term benefits from the land and, in some cases, not even on a short-term benefit, as the quick re-sale of plots indicated. Indeed, it is said that some of the plots were sold for a glass of wine.

[42] These advantages were clearly expressed in two minutes for 1863 (17 Sept.) and 1864 (27 Dec.) as well as in the petition to prevent, or restrict, the partition of the common lands.

[43] C.m. 6 July 1873.

The partition of the commons was important on several counts:

First, it contributed to the concentration of land in a few private hands. Other measures of the Liberal regime were also important in this respect. The new latifundists of the province own land which previously belonged to religious orders or aristocratic landowners or was entailed. But in the parish of Vila Velha the comparatively large extent of the commons made them an important factor in accounting for concentration in terms of area.

Secondly landless residents were deprived of a potential source of income. They could no longer afford to rear a few head of livestock,[44] or to sow cereals or other crops for subsistence.

Seasonal unemployment became an issue important enough to be mentioned in Câmara minutes only after the partition of the commons. Other factors may, of course, have played a part here. One of them is population increase. According to official censuses the population increased by 38 per cent between 1864 and 1911 and by 81 per cent between 1864 and 1940.[45] However, since agricultural productivity also increased, a more even distribution of resources could have prevented the misery associated with unemployment.

But the greatest single factor in the increase of productivity was the introduction of chemical fertilizers at the end of the last century, and the use of fertilizers implied that more capital would be needed for any agricultural concern to be viable. The commons could provide the land, but they did not provide the capital. However, had they remained undivided, they could have been a stimulating factor for co-operative enterprises, which have been so remarkably difficult to foster in the freguesia—and, for that matter, in the concelho as a whole.[46] It is therefore

[44] In 1910 a local newspaper complained that, by drastically reducing the area available for grazing, the partition of the common lands had led to constant problems of trespassing involving animals of the poor and the land of the rich (LN II, 35, 10 Feb. 1910). In 1912 a group of rich landowners (C.m. 24 Oct. 1912) lodged a collective complaint with the Câmara. With the stricter enforcement of by-laws governing these matters, that followed the establishment of the Republican Guards in 1911, the numbers of livestock owned by all but the very rich substantially decreased.

[45] The totals increased from 1,380 in 1864 to 1,909 in 1911 and 2,526 in 1940.

[46] Cf. Agostinho Carvalho, 'A aldeia alentejana da Granja de Mourão', in *Agros*, xlvi. 4 (1963), pp. 269–326, for an illustration of how the common lands provided the basis of a co-operative movement in the province of Alentejo.

legitimate to associate their partition and its consequences with the appearance of seasonal unemployment as a constantly recurring scourge for local labourers.

Thirdly the Junta was deprived of an important source of income. The partition is often referred to when the Junta complains of the financial difficulties that make it unable to act as an efficient organ of local government. This has contributed both to a limitation of benefits for the community—in terms of better roads, improved water supplies, and, up to 1947,[47] better health services—and to a greater dependence on the Câmara and other higher administrative authorities.

The fourth main consequence of the partition is of a different nature. It is expressed in values and attitudes, not in the material facts of land division, work opportunities, or local government budgets. It may be summed up in the phrase 'The rich stole the land of the poor.'

Labourers and peasants often question the legitimacy of the latifundists' ownership of land. Although under present political conditions this doubt is mostly expressed in private talk, all significant agitation by labourers in the country, notably the rural strikes of 1911–12 and 1962,[48] has taken place in Alentejo and not in the other provinces. The Communist Party is alleged to have found more support in this province than in any other rural region, and the Alentejo labourer is generally reputed to be morally more independent of his master than labourers and peasants in other provinces. This reputation is in part accounted for by the prevalent doubts about the legitimacy of the present distribution of land which is sometimes denied altogether.

In Vila Velha such beliefs are connected with the process by which the common lands were divided. This is cited as an example of how the rich, because they can manipulate laws and government institutions, give legal colouring to an immoral and selfish appropriation. The legitimacy of their ownership is of course also questioned on other grounds and for other reasons.

[47] In that year a *Casa do Povo* was established in Vila Velha. The functions of this body are described in the chapter on political structure.

[48] Peasant political agitation in the south of Portugal during the first decades of this century, apparently much less important than in neighbouring Andalucia, was never properly reported. Portugal did not have a Diaz del Moral. For the Spanish case see: J. Diaz del Moral, *Las agitaciones campesinas andaluzas—Cordoba* (Madrid, 1929).

But the commons provide a local and well-remembered illustration of the exploitation of the poor by the rich. This does not mean that peasants in the villages are constantly talking about the partition and the wickedness of the rich in promoting it. The partition took place almost a hundred years ago, and there are more urgent and pressing problems in their present-day lives. Nor do they claim that communal land as such should be put back to communal use. They have never done so explicitly, and they do not advocate it when discussing in private the unfairness of their world. The partition of the commons is important because it supplies them with a neat and well-recorded instance of what they consider to be their exploitation by 'the rich'—the wealthy local men and the central government which supports them. According to personal inclination and level of political consciousness this 'exploitation' is regarded by individual peasants as part of a conspiracy that will be overcome one day, or as part of an inherent order of society which they have to live with as best they can. Things have become more complex in recent years, since opportunities in the outside world combine with local economic difficulties to bring about a progressive devaluation of land. These economic difficulties are associated with the fortunes of wheat cultivation.

II

THE ROLE OF WHEAT

Except for the almost complete disappearance of vineyards and beehives at the end of the last century and the limited introduction of maize some thirty years ago, the freguesia's economy has been based, probably since the Roman occupation at least, on the same agricultural products—wheat, oats, rye, barley, olive oil, and wine—and on animal husbandry: sheep, goats, cattle, mares, and pigs. The relative emphasis on each activity has, however, varied with time, the main oscillations being between a predominance of animal husbandry and one of cereal farming. At present, the freguesia is apparently reaching the end of a period during which particular emphasis has been given to the cultivation of wheat. This period began in the last decades of the nineteenth century.[1]

Wheat had traditionally been the main cereal crop: it is the first local product mentioned in the *Geographical Dictionary* of 1758 and Vila Velha falls well within the wheat bread area of Portugal,[2] but the dramatic expansion of wheat cultivation that

[1] In 1874, immediately before the partition of the commons, about 300 head of cattle and 60 to 80 horses and mares were grazed on the commons. This was before protectionist legislation for wheat growers and the introduction of fertilizers. In 1965 there were fewer than a score of cattle and not many mares in the freguesia. The number of cattle is now increasing.

[2] The use of maize bread (from the sixteenth century onwards) was restricted to the north-west of the country and rye bread was eaten over a wide area extending from the north-eastern province of Trás-os-Montes to the northern districts of the Alentejo. As far south as Vila Velha it coexisted with the wheaten loaf. After the expansion of wheat cultivation and the more widespread marketing of wheat bread (made of both national and imported wheat), rye bread ceased to be baked locally. This change in eating habits had class overtones. The wealthy had eaten wheat bread since time immemorial, while the poor—or rather those who had to work as labourers on the big estates—were given rye bread as part of their wages in kind. By the end of the last century, the first operators of steam threshers in the province received loaves of wheaten bread instead of rye bread as their 'bread wage', to distinguish them from ordinary labourers (José da Silva Picão, *Atravez dos Campos—usos e costumes agrícolo-alentejanos*, 2nd edn. (Lisboa, 1947), p. 356, n. 2). Rich landowners, opposing the import of foreign wheat, tried to support (on ecological and medical grounds) the consumption of rye and maize bread in the

took place between the 1880s and the 1930s had important results which deeply affected the social life of the freguesia and indeed of the entire southern hinterland of the country. A combination of political measures, economic circumstances, and technological improvements led to this expansion.[3]

Technological improvements were of great importance. In 1883 chemical fertilizers were introduced into Portugal for the first time,[4] and in 1895 they had reached Vila Velha. Orders for fertilizers placed that year with the Landowners' Association (Syndicato Agrícola)—of which all local latifundists and many proprietários were members—amounted to 35,500 kg.; the quantity had increased ten times by 1898[5] and continued to rise.[6] Chemical fertilizers are now in general use.

Important mechanical improvements also took place. Late in the second half of the nineteenth century metal-frame ploughs were introduced[7] and gradually replaced the traditional wooden ploughs, which are sometimes still used to perform certain tasks. The first carts with metal in their wheel axis were introduced on the great estates at the turn of the century, and five to ten years later they were in general use. The first threshing machine used in the freguesia was probably the machine lent by the Government to a very rich landowner in 1899.[8] Before World War I, the three main 'houses' had acquired steam threshers, and a few others soon followed suit. Mechanized threshing became widely accepted. In 1921 a local newspaper advertised for hire a steam thresher owned by one of the pro-

rural areas and among the rural groups where they were traditional ('Relatório sobre farinhas, cereais e legumes' in *Documentos Relativos ao primeiro Congresso Agrícola celebrado em Lisboa em Fevereiro de 1888* (Lisboa, 1888), p. 16). In 1911 strikers in the Alentejo province demanded that wheat bread should replace rye bread in their wages in kind, and this was eventually done.

For many years now the local bread has been made of wheat, and other cerals are used to supplement wheat only in the cheaper loaves. Indeed, the word for bread (*pão*) is used to denote the wheat crop.

[3] Facts were, of course, unique, but they are illustrative of a general trend, and it is not possible to understand them independently of a wider canvas.

[4] Miguel E. O. Fernandes *A cultura do trigo pelos adubos químicos no Baixo Alentejo* (Lisboa, 1899), p. 9.

[5] S.c. 8 Sept. 1898.

[6] S.c. 7 Aug. 1918.

[7] LN II, 503, 9 Mar. 1919. This is written in the obituary of a 'progressive' landowner. In the same issue the newspaper reports the recent unloading in the port of Lisbon of the first agricultural tractors ever to arrive in Portugal.

[8] S.c. 11 Apr. 1899.

prietários in the freguesia,[9] and by 1965 only two or three small landowners threshed their wheat in the traditional manner. Another important change was the substitution of mules for oxen which began around 1920: mules are both cheaper and much hardier than oxen. Such technical improvements favoured the general expansion of farming that was taking place.

Newly cleared land was planted with cereals, vines, and olive trees, and the wilderness of uncultivated scrub began to retreat before these efforts. In 1857 a regulation of the Câmara forbade the location of beehives within a thousand steps of the vineyards and olive groves, as well as within a thousand steps of the villages as had been stipulated before.[10] Honey, an important traditional supplementary crop, was a typical product of unfarmed tracts of land and was bound to disappear as this land came under the plough. In 1866 thirty-nine citizens asked the Câmara to relieve heads of families of the traditional obligation of handing in six sparrow heads to the Câmara every year. Their request was granted.[11] The numbers of these birds was doubtless diminishing with the retreat of the scrub, and the duty had become both onerous and meaningless. But by the end of the century the wilderness was still far from being conquered. In 1888 the prize given by the Câmara for killing an adult wolf was worth more than ten times a labourer's wage.[12] In 1898 and 1899 a Vila Nova newspaper carried leading articles regretting the lack of rationality in local agriculture (a perennial complaint) and 'the great areas left wild' (*maninhas*).[13] In 1898 an official letter from the Landowners' Syndicato mentions the clearing of land then taking place.[14] Old men in the freguesia still remember vast areas of scrub subsequently used for cereal farming. It was the expansion of wheat cultivation that led to the clearing of all arable land in the freguesia (and, for that matter, in the province as a whole).

This expansion took its most dramatic form after the promulgation of the law of 1899[15] which, together with other minor measures, provided effective tariff protection for national

[9] LN II 615, 5 June 1921.

[10] C.m. 8 Apr. 1857.

[11] C.m. 25 Feb. 1866.

[12] C.m. 29 May 1888.

[13] LN I, 5, 27 Nov. 1898; 58, 3 Dec. 1899.

[14] S.c. 29 Oct. 1898.

[15] Law of 14 July 1899; regulated on 21 June 1900; preceded and followed by legislation to the same purpose but less bold passed in 1889, 1892, 1893, 1905, and 1911.

wheat. This law came after years of pressure by landowners on successive governments. The fight, which reached a climax with the '*Congressos Agrícolas*' of 1888 and 1889, had begun in 1857 with the debate over the introduction of free trade after some decades of protectionism. It took several forms—from theoretical considerations on the disadvantages of free trade to direct lobbying of ministers. The [Royal] Central Association of Portuguese Agriculture, which still exists, was founded in 1864 to support the struggle.

A detailed study of the movement has yet to be written and is outside the scope of the present work.[16] But three general points are of importance to the understanding of Vila Velha today.

First landowners in a cash-crop economy are largely dependent on government economic policies. Governments are thus constantly being harassed with requests from landowners on all sorts of matters, even during periods of consistent protectionism. The period between 1857 and 1899 was not characterized by protectionist policies, and feelings, aroused at local level against the central administration which failed to protect the economic interest of the landowner, were thus even more bitter at that time. Mistrust of government and bureaucrats, still found today, increased during the period.

A second point, closely related to the first, is the problem of the relations between town and country, or rather, between rural areas and urban areas. Government was by location, and often by composition, urban, and landowners felt that many of the policies they disliked (both before and after 1899) were designed to favour consumers in the great urban centres at the expense of the rural producers. Hostility to Lisbon, both as the centre of government and as a city—which still exists today—was prevalent in the 1857–99 period.

The third point is the opposition between agriculture and industry. The landowners' struggle in the years 1857–99 was

[16] Many books, pamphlets, and newspaper and periodical articles were published at the time in support of the landowners' case. Cf. Visconde de Coruche, *A agricultura e o paiz* (Lisboa, 1868); id., *A questão monetária dos cereais* (1894); D. Luiz de Castro, *Chrónicas Agrícolas* (Lisboa, 1890). Cf. also the proceedings of the agricultural conferences of 1888 and 1889 and the reports and petitions arising from them in which the landowners' case is expounded and debated in considerable detail. For a more general survey of agricultural life in Portugal in the last decades of the nineteenth century, cf. B. C. Cincinato da Costa, and D. Luiz Castro (eds.) *Le Portugal au point de vue agricole* (Lisbonne, 1900).

not a fight against government as such but a fight against the millers for the Government's favour. Flour mills were established in Portugal in the middle of the nineteenth century and soon became very important industrial concerns. They dominated the market, and many traditional wind or water mills were forced to close down. Through the extension of credit facilities they controlled bakeries in the main towns. Cheap imported wheat was of great importance to them and, as a group, they benefited most from free trade in cereals. They continued to flourish after 1899, although their power was curbed, and only since 1933 has the government managed to fix wheat prices and create an official organization—the National Federation of Wheat Producers—as sole legal buyer of wheat. Until then industrial millers and their agents were always the scourge of local wheat growers. The landowners' hostility to industry—which is based on their fear of losing manpower and their awareness of its development and success, while their own wealth and political power have declined—was stimulated by their protracted conflict with millers.

The law of 1899, while it secured a fixed price for wheat, did not make provision for agricultural credits. Now a cash-crop economy of this type could also be called a credit-crop economy. The summer harvest pays for the debts contracted during the year, and the autumn preparations for the new crop have sometimes to be financed with borrowed money. If not then, money will almost certainly have to be borrowed in any case before the harvest.

Traditional credit facilities seem to have been seriously lacking. There is no reference to any communal granary (*Celeiro Comum*) in Vila Velha, although there were several in the province between the sixteenth and eighteenth centuries. Lay brotherhoods did lend money, and the richest of these, the Misericórdias, did so in a regular way at moderate rates.[17] The amounts available for lending were not very large and, in any case, Liberal legislation impoverished the Misericórdias.[18] In 1907 the total amount lent by the Misericórdia of Vila Velha

[17] Records of some of the loans with interest of not more than 7 per cent are to be found in the books of accounts of the Misericórdia.

[18] In 1892 (17 Apr.) the minutes of the Misericórdia record its regret at the shift from their traditional sources of income to government bonds (*Inscrições da Junta de Crédito Público*).

was 60,000 reis.[19] It has now ceased to act as a money-lender.

In 1911 a *Caixa de Crédito Agrícola* ('a credit co-operative') was created by the Landowners' Association of Vila Nova[20] but its contribution was negligible. Private credit was therefore necessary to fill the need for loans. Fertilizers made higher capital investment necessary in cereal farming, and cereal farming appeared to be the obvious way of becoming wealthier in the years after 1899. As a result interest on loans rocketed. In 1911 a local newspaper reported that interest of 27 per cent was being charged.[21] In the 1920s interest of up to 35 per cent was being paid in the private money-market. At all levels of society almost anyone who had money to spare lent it either directly or, more often, through local brokers. Many peasants had to abandon sharecropping for lack of capital, and a few of the usurers increased their property with land from unpaid mortgages. The question of credit together with the issue of a fair price for wheat became the two acute problems facing wheat growers. High interest rates contributed to the virtual disappearance of prosperous sharecroppers, seriously afflicted small and medium landowners, and even the very rich were not unaffected. Constant complaints to the Government are found again and again in the Syndicato's correspondence throughout the first decades of the century: unfair taxation, the difficulties of relations with industrial millers, the high cost of fertilizers, the inefficiency of the railways, the unfavourable prices of agricultural products, etc. In 1927 the situation had, according to the Syndicato, reached the verge of complete collapse: '. . . the landowner is more and more convinced that the cultivation of wheat is the main cause of his ruin, not only because bad weather can destroy the harvest at any time, but also because measures of direct support have not yet been put into practice.'[22]

Measures of direct support were taken after 1929 with the wheat campaign.[23] This established an adequate price for the

[19] João Henrique Ulrich, *O crédito agrícola em Portugal* (*sua organização*) (Lisboa, 1908), pp. 292 f.

[20] Legislation passed by the republican government that year aimed at stimulating co-operative credit associations.

[21] LN II, 87, 11 Feb. 1911.

[22] S.c. 3 June 1927.

[23] The *Campanha do Trigo*, as it was aptly named after Mussolini's similar measures in Italy, had the avowed purpose of making the country self-sufficient in wheat production. After the 1934 harvest there was a surplus, exported in spite of difficulties

III. *Proprietário*

IV. *Seareiro*

crop, with a state-controlled federation of wheat growers as sole buyer, provided subsidies for its cultivation, and facilitated government loans at unprecedentedly low interest rates.

In the freguesia no suitable land remained still unfarmed at the time,[24] and to increase production many landowners reduced the number of years during which, in the traditional rotation of wheat, the land should be left fallow. Some of them uprooted holm-oaks to provide more suitable land for wheat. Even the sixty hectares which had been kept as communal land and which had traditionally been used for grazing, were mainly devoted to wheat cultivation in a rotation system after 1914.

In 1932 the price of wheat was so much higher than that for oats—which were sown the year after wheat in the traditional rotation system—that many landowners planted wheat again on the same land. The Syndicato estimated an increase of 15 per cent in the quantities sown in relation to the previous year due to this factor alone.[25] A record crop was harvested in 1934. When people talk about 1934, they say that in that year, 'even the stones bore wheat'—an exaggeration not far from the truth. The enthusiasm for wheat was so alarming that in 1935 the Government passed legislation to restrict sowing to suitable land, but nobody paid much attention,[26] and in 1936 landowners' associations in the province urged their members to observe the traditional fallow periods in the crop-rotation cycles instead of shortening them, as was becoming the rule.[27] None of these stipulations was implemented in the freguesia, and in 1951 the experts who wrote the report on an official agricultural survey of the concelho were very explicit in their views:

> It is absolutely necessary to reduce cereal cultivation (mainly wheat) in those soils where its production is uneconomical . . . for, if present tendencies continue and even less suitable areas are cultivated, the time will very soon come when the entire top soil will have disappeared as the result of erosion. This phenomenon is beginning to make itself felt, especially on land with very little top soil. The main causes are the impoverishment of the soil, the topography and nature of the landscape, climatic conditions, and the cultivation techniques employed.

raised by the buyers on the quality of the grain. But this was exceptional. To the present day, wheat has been imported every year.

[24] S.c. 12 May 1932.

[25] S.c. 5 Dec. 1932.

[26] LN II, 173, 29 Oct. 1935.

[27] S.c. 8 Sept. 1936.

It was only in the early 1960s, however, that landowners began taking measures in this direction. The economic viability of wheat was definitely viewed with serious misgivings by the richer landowners who keep more accurate accounts. Between 1959 and 1965 an average of ninety-two producers declared their wheat crop annually to the Grémio, although it is estimated that between 190 and 200 people grow wheat every year.[28] The quantity of wheat declared to the Grémio[29] has decreased between 1959 and 1965, and the latifundists were mainly reponsible for this reduction. The following table shows the number of kilos harvested by the ninety-two producers who declared their crop to the Grémio and by the two wealthiest latifundists.

Wheat Harvests 1959–1965

Year	*All Landowners*	*Latifundist I*	*Latifundist II*
1959	1,818,785	1,034,035	148,442
1960	1,536,698	755,350	165,897
1961	737,030	228,553	116,148
1962	1,217,359	445,007	110,011
1963	861,884	281,522	34,587
1964	655,071	251,981	25,570
1965	907,194	314,774	28,517

(Compiled from the Records of the Grémio da Lavoura of Vila Nova.)

In the autumn of 1965 the wealthiest latifundist gave up growing wheat altogether. It is still grown on his estates by sharecroppers, but these are becoming increasingly difficult to find. If the

[28] In principle, all wheat growers, landowners, tenants, and sharecroppers have to declare their wheat and sell what they do not consume to the Grémio. What generally happens, however, is that only those who sell their wheat bother to declare the size of their crops. Although the position of the others is illegal, they have never been molested on this account, both the Grémio and the Câmara considering that they are doing no harm and that their transgression is relatively innocent. It would have seemed unduly harsh to try to prosecute and fine them. Their individual yields rarely exceed their own consumption. Generally they have their wheat threshed by one of the two threshing machines hired out to the freguesia, as do many other small producers. The owner of the machine does not register this threshing (an evasion regarded as a favour by the wheat producer), but, by failing to do so, he is also evading taxation. These small 'illegal' producers mill their wheat in the two water-mills that still function in the freguesia.

[29] This wheat excludes not only that mentioned above but also some wheat grown by latifundists with land in the freguesia whose centre of operations is in an adjoining one, where it is declared, and includes some wheat grown in adjoining freguesias by latifundists whose main estates are in the freguesia of Vila Velha.

present trend continues, the quantities of wheat produced will be even more reduced in the future.

There seems to be a periodical need for increasing government support to wheat growers, and such support does not seem to be forthcoming in the present crisis. Landowners have asked again and again for an increase in the price they are paid for their wheat, and, although some small changes have been introduced, they have not seemed to them satisfactory. Latifundists have been mechanizing their concerns since the 1940s and are using tractors, harvesters, and harvest threshers wherever conditions permit. Some of them have engaged agricultural experts who have experimented with new strains of wheat, increased the quantities sown per hectare, and tried new combinations of fertilizers. All these efforts have failed to achieve results that are substantially different from the poor performances obtained by the more traditional methods of less wealthy landowners.

In the present economic context, state support has probably reached its limit: higher wheat prices would mean a rise in the price of bread, and bread is the staple food of most of the poor population in the country. Besides, yields have been so consistently low over the years[30] that the advisability of continuing to support wheat cultivation, in regions that now seem to be utterly unsuited to it, is scarcely questioned. The failure of wheat cultivation is important because emphasis on it has been a predominant factor in the local agricultural structure. Vineyards destroyed by phylloxera at the end of the last century were not replaced by resistant stock[31]. Also in the second half of the last century olive oil was replaced by paraffin as fuel, and began to suffer from the competition of other edible oils. Only in the

[30] See Appendix III.

[31] An 'anti-phylloxera commission' was formed in Vila Velha and held its first meeting on 9 June 1893. In the meeting of July 23, the President stated that it was impossible to fight the disease and advised the uprooting of the indigenous grape-vines and their replacement by 'American' ones. This was done in several parts of the concelho but not to any extent around Vila Velha. In fact there are plots known as vineyards X or Z where olive-trees and not vines are to be found now; and many houses in Vila Velha and the villages still have an *adega* (outhouses for keeping the wine press and the wine) which is used today to store other kinds of produce or has been converted into a dwelling house. In 1893 the situation was so serious that the commission met four times in one month (a remarkable achievement by local standards) and created sufficient momentum to lead to the establishment in 1895 of the 'Syndicato', a permanent association of landowners (Grémio de Lavoura Archives, *Proceedings of the Anti-phylloxera Commission Meetings*).

last thirty years have olive-trees been planted again on a substantial scale, particularly by proprietários; but they cannot take the place of a successful cereal crop, and scarcity of manpower is now making the harvest of olives more expensive.[32] As we have seen, many holm-oaks were cut down to facilitate cereal cultivation, and, since acorns were traditionally used for fattening pigs, the number of pigs raised dwindled. When a severe epidemic known as 'African plague' struck the province in 1961, most of the pigs in the freguesia succumbed and have not yet been successfully replaced.

Sheep raising was also affected by the emphasis put on wheat culture. In 1934 the Landowners' Association stated that 'the noticeable drop in live-stock husbandry was attributable to the fact that many tracts of land had been used for the expansion of wheat and other cereal cultivation, with a corresponding decrease in grazing land',[33] and the situation did not improve for many years. The only owners of sizeable flocks at present are the big landowners, and since the early 1960s the two main latifundists have been giving new emphasis to building them up. But the quality of grazing land is poor and the wool very rarely fetches good prices. A switch to sheep raising is not the solution to their present problems, let alone to the problems of those who own less land.[34]

[32] As with wheat, the bulk of the freguesia's olive production is concentrated in very few hands. Quantities vary, but in a good year the total may be estimated at about two million kilos. Between them, the two main latifundists produce about 1,250,000 kilos. Another latifundist and four of the local proprietários produce between twenty and sixty thousand kilos each. About three hundred people take olives to the olive press every year, but only about one hundred produce a saleable surplus above the needs of their households. The olives not retained for home consumption or sold for processing are pressed to make olive-oil and *bagaço* (the solid part that remains after pressing, used for animal feed). There is one industrial press in the freguesia, and the two richest latifundists have their own presses, which were in use until 1962 and 1964 respectively, but have remained idle since then. Most of the harvest is sold to buyers who come from outside. Olive-trees require even less continuous labour than wheat: every six years the land around them is cleared of weeds and the main branches are pruned. In the autumn the olives are gathered by small groups of women under the direction of a man.

[33] C.m. 28 Feb. 1934.

[34] One of these two latifundists has about 5,000 head of sheep, the other 2,600. Two other latifundists have flocks of about a thousand sheep each, three local proprietários have flocks ranging from 100 to 300, and several people have small flocks rarely exceeding some 50 or 60 head of sheep. There are some landless shepherds who graze their own ewes, as well as those they rent or take as shares for rented grazing land. Some small proprietários tried, on a small scale, to emulate the

Forestation is often suggested by both landowners and agrarian economists as the only real alternative left for most of the land in the freguesia. But afforestation is a long-term project, too expensive to be adopted by private landowners, and the Government has so far not seen fit to promote and support it. Wheat cultivation will probably continue to dwindle in the next few years, while landowners, struggling to pay their debts, seek the support of inadequate government subsidies each year and hope that a favourable April will bring a bumper harvest.

big estates and, after some years of very bad crops, reverted to sheep husbandry with small flocks of some two or three dozen sheep, only to switch back to cereals after coming up against the difficulties of finding suitable grazing land. Local experts estimate that, with present prices for wool and milk, flocks of less than one hundred sheep will not pay for the grazing land and the wages of a shepherd. The difficulties of making a profit from sheep have been further complicated by two facts: (i) Since schooling became compulsory, children—the cheapest form of labour—cannot be employed as shepherds. (ii) Only the latifundists have proper equipment for shearing and can sell their wool at the auctions organized by the Grémio.

The wool produced by other sheep farmers is dirty and not acceptable to the Grémio. It fetches lower prices from merchants who come to buy it *in situ* in April or early May.

III

THE VALUE OF LAND

IN a poorly industrialized and traditionally agricultural country such as Portugal, land was an investment offering security not otherwise to be found. Mistrust of other forms of investment, with the exception of urban real estate, was widespread until very recently. In the provinces of the south this preference for investment in land has varied with the fortunes of wheat cultivation over the last hundred years: it increased after the end of the nineteenth century,[1] reached its peak in the 1940s, and has declined sharply since the late 1950s.

When the commons were divided in 1874, eagerness to qualify for lots was intense. Everyone wanted to secure some land. A provisional list of heads of families had been drawn up by the parish priest in 1872[2] and further applications began to be lodged immediately—in some cases people hastily married in order to become heads of families, in others bachelor sons went off to live in separate houses, obviously to substantiate their claims to constitute an independent household. By 1874,[3] forty-seven applications of this kind had been made. One man, who did not qualify as the head of a family, invoked his position as a rural policeman to substantiate his claim; another the fact that he had served in the army for several years in Africa and 'now expected the motherland to give him his well-deserved recompense'.[4] Competition expressed itself in the opposite way as well—six people, who were included in the list, had to be removed, after others had complained and cast doubts on their status.[5] These cases involved poor people trying to obtain a small

[1] In the years before protection there was a decline in land values. In 1887 an important landowning concern (*Companhia das Lezírias*) estimated a decrease of 27 per cent in the rents of land between 1882 and 1886. A credit organization (*Companhia do Credito Predial*) acknowledged the decrease in value of landed properties and attributed it to the importing of cheap foreign cereals. *Documentos relativos ao primeiro congresso agrícola etc.* (Lisboa, 1888), pp. 66–8.

[2] C.m. 25 July 1872.

[3] C.m. 8 Apr. 1874.

[4] C.m. 13 Sept. 1874.

[5] C.m. 19 Apr. 1874.

plot of their own, but land was highly prized at all levels of society for many decades.

In 1899 three of the province's latifundists (one of them was the wealthiest landowner in the freguesia and the concelho at the time and also one of the richest men in Portugal) advertised the sale of several large estates which they had recently inherited from a common relation. The caption in the local newspaper read: 'Good Opportunity for Capital Investment in Alentejo', and the body of the advertisement clearly stated that the sale was due to the difficulties of dividing the inheritance equally among themselves.[6] Mortgaging an estate to buy another was a frequent practice in the decades immediately before and after the turn of the century. Although credit was generally available at high rates of interest, people borrowed money to buy land, and others bought land out of the interest on money they had lent. The inflation that followed World War I further emphasized the advantage of land as a valuable asset. An advertisement in 1920 proclaiming the sale, in small lots of about five hectares each, of a big estate adjoining the freguesia is indicative of the prevalent mood. The text states that the salvation of Portugal lies in wheat, and that buying these lots is not only a profitable, but also a patriotic, enterprise.[7]

As we have seen, the interest charged on private loans reached its highest peak between 1900 and 1929. And although the period was for many a time of crisis, land continued to be the standard for measuring stable wealth. A good illustration of this is provided by the decision of a local latifundist, temporarily in financial difficulties, who sold the charter of a small bank owned by his family rather than any of his estates—a decision that he now openly regrets.

The official credit facilities established since 1929 considerably reduced the number and importance of private loans. In the first years of the new system, cheap public credit was used to pay for the expensive private loans that had been contracted before the scheme came into operation, and the State soon

[6] LN I, 48, 24 Sept. 1899.

[7] LN II, 572, 23 July 1920. Experience had shown that in comparatively fertile land more money was to be made out of the sale of a big estate when it was divided up into small lots than when it was offered as a single unit. Between the end of the last century and the early 1950s, several estates in the province were thus divided up and sold by their owners, although none of these was in the freguesia.

became the greatest creditor. With the new rates of interest, land was put up for sale less often, and between 1940 and 1950 its value was higher than ever.

Since the late 1950s the accumulated debts resulting from these credit facilities[8] and the low prices of agricultural products have brought about a new crisis and the price of land has begun to drop.

It was possible to trace the prices of two plots—one of about four hectares and the other of five hectares—which had changed hands recently. The first fetched 22,000 escudos (£315) in 1959 and only 12,000 escudos (£171) in 1965, the second 45,000 escudos (£643) in 1950 and only 10,000 (£143) in 1965.

The drop in land values is reflected in the fluctuations in rents. The local Misericórdia owns a small plot with olive-trees and rents it out for periods of three years. Records of the annual rent for this plot were kept in the Misericórdia minutes and the figures have fluctuated as follows: 1942—200 escudos; 1951—300 escudos; 1957—511 escudos; 1960—300 escudos.[9]

A further illustration is provided by the land belonging to the Junta. For rotation purposes this land is divided into three sections (*folhas*). The so-called *Folha do Convento* was rented out in 1959 for a total of 14,269 escudos to sixteen different tenants, but in 1965 it was rented out for only 4,875 escudos to fourteen tenants. Rents from the *Folha do Pocinho e Tanque* amounted to 25,674 escudos in 1958 and to 14,700 escudos in 1964.[10]

In 1965 landowners estimated that, on average, land in the province was worth between one-half and two-thirds of its value in the early 1950s. The drop in prices is particularly marked in land used exclusively for cereals, i.e. without vines, or olive- or cork-trees.

A new wave of financial difficulties, accompanied by some bankruptcies, hit the freguesia in 1962. The only big estate

[8] Moralists and civil servants are often haunted by the belief that money borrowed by landowners for wheat cultivation is diverted to consumption. This belief accompanies another, also widely held, that very little of the rents or profits collected by latifundists is reinvested in their estates and the bulk is spent in an ostentatious way. For a violent diatribe against these alleged practices cf. Santos Garcia, *Estado da Economia Agrícola da Região de Evora—Causas e Efeitos* (*separata do Relatório da Caixa de Crédito Agrícola Mútuo Eborense relativo a 1935*) (Evora, 1936).

[9] M.m. 7 Oct. 1942; 21 Oct. 1951; 9 Sept. 1957. For 1960 there is a verbal arrangement.

[10] Junta. Proceedings of the public auction of communal land held 1958, 1959, 1964 and 1965 on 1 January.

recently sold fetched what was considered to be less than half its value fifteen years ago. It was sold by public auction after the bankruptcy of its owner, and had to be put up for auction twice before it found a buyer. Another latifundist was in the process of handing over his land to creditors at the end of 1965. The two wealthiest local proprietários are known to be in severe financial difficulties, and one of them was being sued for debt in 1964. Several others are also in trouble, and this is reflected in the increasing length of time they take to pay their taxes and official association fees—delays for which they eventually have to pay fines.

This trend is not confined to the freguesia alone. Its expression in a wider area (covering three concelhos) is seen in the increase in the number of lawsuits brought by creditors against debtors in the court of Vila Nova between 1955 and 1965. The table below shows this increase:

Year	*Lawsuits*	*Year*	*Lawsuits*
1955	7	1961	5
1956	0	1962	24
1957	6	1963	41
1958	9	1964	40
1959	6	1965	61
1960	2		

(Compiled from the records of the court of Vila Nova.)

Some of the debtors are shopkeepers, rather than landowners or sharecroppers, but their cases are the direct result of the difficulties of the latter.

There is widespread scepticism about the future of local agriculture. For the labourers and sharecroppers, factory employment, migration, and emigration are the obvious solutions. For the landowners the problem is more difficult: the alternatives are to persist in a ruinous activity or to sell their land. But selling the land, unless desperately pressed by creditors, is a very difficult decision to take now that land prices are so low. Some of the successful migrants have sold the small plots they owned: the rents, or shares of the crop, they were receiving were so small that the lump sum received from an untimely sale seemed a better alternative.

This is a reversal of traditional custom. The very few earlier migrants who managed to make some money, either in Lisbon or in Portuguese Africa, traditionally invested money in land at home whenever a suitable plot could be found. If they could not come back to work the plot themselves, it was entrusted to some close relative or rented out. Of those who have been leaving the freguesia since the 1950s, only one has, to my knowledge, bought land.

Land is ceasing to be the most solid asset, the standard against which other wealth is measured, the security that men strive to keep or acquire. A great change in the traditional outlook is rapidly taking place and no one is really immune from it.

IV

LAND DISTRIBUTION

OWNERSHIP of land, however, still provides a charter for social stratification. It still determines the main social groups of the population, or, as local people say, the main social classes.

The tables below give precise figures of the way land is distributed. Most landowners are individual persons. The Junta de Freguesia owns the remnants of the old commons (sixty hectares), and the parish church owns twenty-three plots making up a total of sixteen hectares.

Distribution of land in the freguesia

	Area	*Number of landowners*
	Less than 1 ha.	166
1–10 ha.	1 to 2	58
	2 to 3	44
	3 to 4	36
	4 to 5	31
	5 to 6	16
	6 to 7	20
	7 to 8	17
	8 to 9	9
	9 to 10	5
Total number owning less than 10 ha.		406
10–50 ha.	10 to 15	29
	15 to 20	11
	20 to 25	1
	25 to 30	4
	30 to 35	6
	35 to 40	5
	40 to 45	3
	45 to 50	2
Total number owning between 10 and 50 ha.		61
50–100 ha.	50 to 60	4
	60 to 70	2
	70 to 80	0
	80 to 90	3
	90 to 100	0
Total number owning between 50 and 100 ha.		9

Distribution of land in the freguesia—cont.

	Area	*Number of landowners*
100–500 ha.	100 to 200	9
	200 to 300	1
	300 to 400	1
	400 to 500	1
Total number owning between 100 and 500 ha.		12
	Over 500	3

Distribution of agricultural holdings

Classification by size	*Number of Landowners*	*Number of agricultural holdings*	*Total area of holdings (ha.)*
Less than 10 ha.—very small	406	1,166	992·4565
10– 50 ha.—small	61	450	1,271·4065
50–100 ha.—medium	9	77	592.4325
100–500 ha.—large	12	123	2,575·2200
Over 500 ha.—very large	3	19	3,472·2700
Totals	491	1,835	8,903·7855

(Source: based on data compiled from records of the Instituto Geográfico Cadastral, Lisbon).

The geographical pattern of distribution is shown in Map 1. Small properties are more concentrated around the town and villages, giving way to an outer belt of big estates. Since the boundaries of these estates often extend beyond the administrative limits of the freguesia, the difference between the area occupied by big estates, centred in the freguesia and employing local labourers, and the area occupied by small plots is even bigger than the map would indicate.

As it is, the areas shadowed on the map correspond to areas owned by latifundists who live elsewhere. They account for 54 per cent of the area of the freguesia. Some small plots are also owned by outsiders, as a result of family relationships and accidents of inheritance, and are rented out to local men. But these are few and of no significance for the present purpose.

Of some 480 resident landholders only twenty-six have enough land to provide them with a living and do not need to find employment on other men's land as sharecroppers or workers, or to engage in other activities. They are called proprietários and own 21 per cent of the land. The remaining 25 per cent of the land is distributed mainly among small landowners who also work as sharecroppers, although other people, particularly craftsmen, shopkeepers, and a few labourers, own some small plots.

Most labourers either own no land at all or own plots that are too small or too stony for farming.

These differences in the areas owned by the different groups are an obvious indication of sharp economic stratification. But since land is of varying fertility, an analysis of 'taxable incomes' is a more useful guide. 'Taxable income' does not correspond to real income: it is estimated by the tax bureau on the basis of an assessment of the value of the land and assets of each landowner.[1] These values are deliberately underestimated, but the criterion applied is fairly uniform, and taxable income can be used an as indicator of the degree of economic stratification, if not of its absolute value.

The latifundists receive 55 per cent of the 'taxable income' from land and the proprietários 23 per cent. The three wealthiest latifundists receive between them a total of 42 per cent. If only the freguesia is considered, two of the local proprietários have 'taxable incomes', which are apparently higher than those of all but the three leading latifundists. The proprietários do not own land elsewhere, however, while the latifundists do, and, if the income derived from their other lands is taken into consideration, all latifundists are well ahead of the proprietários. Only 22 per cent of the total income falls to the remaining resident heads of families.

Areas owned and 'taxable incomes' are very explicit indicators, but cannot replace real incomes as the ultimate indicators of economic stratification. The latter are, however, impossible to establish with adequate accuracy, in the absence of detailed agrarian economic surveys. Such surveys have to be carried out by expert economists and not by anthropologists. In the next section which describes the main population groups determined by landownership, rough estimates of these real incomes, based on a schematic and limited survey and on personal information from some of the landowners, are given. They are intended as a guide to absolute values which will make the relative values of

[1] It is called in Portuguese *Rendimento Colectável.*

'taxable incomes' more significant, and not as an accurate assessment of the financial situation of the landowners which would satisfy agrarian economists.[2]

[2] For a detailed analysis of real incomes in a similar region, cf. Agostinho de Carvalho, op. cit.

V

SOCIAL GROUPS

LATIFUNDISTS

ELEVEN latifundists own land in the freguesia.[1] They form the smallest and wealthiest group and stand well apart from the rest of the population, first and foremost in the amount of wealth they possess. Besides land in the freguesia, all of them own land elsewhere, in some cases amounting to several thousand hectares. Their estates are much better equipped than those of the other landowners and even under present conditions they employ many more labourers than any other group. Almost all the modern agricultural machinery used in the freguesia is owned by them: they own 17 out of 20 tractors, all 3 harvester-threshers, 2 out of 3 binders and reapers, and 3 out of 5 threshing machines.

Their incomes vary from year to year as do those of all landowners in the province. In a reasonably good year the wealthiest might have a net income of about £20,000 and the less prosperous about £4,000 at 1965 costs and prices. With the exception of two estates in the southern part of the freguesia, which are rented out by their owners, the land owned by these latifundists is farmed through a mixed system of direct farming and sharecropping. They do not live in the freguesia; most of them live in Vila Nova, a few in other towns in the province, or in Lisbon. Some of their houses rank among the finest in Portugal in size and furnishing, and they are amongst the largest householders in the country in the number of servants employed. Outwardly most latifundists are indistinguishable from other members of the Portuguese upper or upper-middle classes: they dress and speak like city dwellers, although some of them retain a southern accent. They do not have the weather-beaten look of the peasants. None of them works the land with his hands, nor has had to do so during his youth. When they

[1] Four of them are particularly important to Vila Velha because of the relative size of their holdings there. Others have their main estates elsewhere.

marry locally they marry into their own group. With three exceptions (two of them are men living in other concelhos who have inherited land in the freguesia) they are all related by kinship or marriage. These relationships are emphasized in the forms of address used among themselves, whereas humbler relations tend to be forgotten.

The latifundists' kinship web extends far beyond the concelho: they have family and relatives by marriage all over the province and in Lisbon, and much of their social life is nowadays spent with outsiders, not only to the freguesia, but also to Vila Nova. All this sets them apart from the people of the freguesia. They appreciate the contrast and like to stress it. Historically they are a new group and their wealth is fairly recent, but they make an effort to dissociate themselves, in more than strictly financial terms, from those who are, in the final analysis, of the same stock as themselves. Formal education has been one of the techniques used for this purpose since the middle of the nineteenth century.[2] Landowning families arranged marriages with university graduates and encouraged their children to obtain university degrees. Professional men who came to the provincial towns as doctors, lawyers, judges, or administrators and married rich heiresses, conferred on the families into which they married, if not a *noblesse d'épée* at least a *noblesse de robe*. They also provided a personal link between local landowning interests and the central administration in Lisbon, which was staffed and controlled by their former fellow-students at Coimbra. Many latifundists now have university degrees and their sons—unless they show absolutely no aptitude for the art of reading and writing—are invariably sent to university.[3]

In recent years, however, the university has become more open and is suspected of left-wing tendencies, while the latifundists have moved politically to the right since the 1920s. Moreover with the decline of agriculture, a university degree

[2] The prestige of formal education is well attested by the prominence given by local newspapers to the academic feats of wealthy local boys. The results of their examinations from primary school to university are reported with glowing congratulations.

[3] In Portugal attendance at a university depends on the financial capacity of the student's parents and gaining a degree both on the former and on the persistence of the student. Of an abnormally unintelligent doctor it was once said that the surprising thing about him was not that he should have managed to qualify but that he should have been able to learn to read at all.

began to be regarded as a practical weapon, to be used in the eventuality of having to earn a living, rather than as a way of emphasizing social distance from the rest of the population and consolidating privileged connexions. For this latter end some latifundists—although by no means the majority—have taken another line. They try to include themselves in the aristocracy,[4] by tracing their descent from some noble forebear. For this purpose genealogical trees are commissioned from an amateur heraldic expert in Evora who always manages to graft the latifundist families on to some respectably old branch of an aristocratic tree—in one case that of a Moorish king of the twelfth century. One man changed the spelling of his name to give it a more aristocratic touch. Signet-rings with coats of arms are worn with doubtful propriety. 'Genealogy,' a latifundist once said, 'is a marvellous science. You only need to lie once.'

These efforts are more effective among the latifundists and their friends than among the rest of the population who are not so sensitive to the prestige value of aristocratic descent and remember the plebeian and rustic origins of most of these men. But the distance between the present relative social positions of latifundists and the population at large is not abolished by these memories. The manager of one of the freguesia's wealthiest latifundists told me that he was a distant cousin of his employer's—'But I would not dare tell him so', he added.

The latifundists feel the need to be different, even if they cannot establish categories that would conclusively sanction these differences and be accepted by all. One of the reasons they cite to justify the employment of estate managers is that 'they know how to talk to them (the labourers) and we don't'. The avoidance of any form of manual labour is, of course, closely related to this attitude. The grandson of one of the latifundists had his school satchel carried to school by a servant. When a latifundist with a reputation for meanness had one of his sons drive a tractor on his estates, this was commented upon by his peers as a ridiculous state of affairs, totally unbecoming a man in his position. The behaviour of an eccentric latifundist who

[4] Aristocratic titles were abolished in Portugal in 1910. But the descendants of titled persons still print their titles on personal cards, letter-paper, and in telephone directories. They are addressed by these titles in all but official matters. Titles in Portugal are like guineas in England. They exist, and yet do not exist, and convey the flavour of a particular way of life.

insists on dressing in the rural fashion, retaining the local accent, and going to labourers' cafés where he gets drunk, provoked the comment from someone of this group: 'if his sons take after him, two generations from now members of the family will be born with tails.'

The latifundists' efforts to emphasize the distance between themselves and the rest of the population stem from a need to justify their ownership of land and their prominent position, regardless of the accidents of recent history. For this aristocratic rank, if accepted within the natural order of society, would be the most formalized justification. Their insecurity is exacerbated during critical periods such as 1936–9 (the years of the Spanish Civil War) or 1945, 1949, 1951, and 1958 (election years in Portugal when there was some political agitation). In 1937 a latifundist was shot by a lunatic. In the hours between the murder and the arrest of the murderer all the latifundists lived in acute fear of an impending communist uprising. During the 1949 and 1951 elections some of them reported men they suspected of being Communists to the Guards. Even at other times, however, they are prone to moments of political fear: I heard much more talk of communism among them than among any other group. They have a strong awareness of themselves as a group and a permanent, if often concealed, hostility to labourers. In a remarkable synthesis of fear and self-assertion they even call them *moujiks*. Labourers criticise them, point out their mistakes in managing their land, and make adverse comments on the fact that they do not work in the fields themselves. They suggest that land should be divided amongst those who deserve it through their labour. The latifundists hold the opposite view: they point out that only large tracts of land are economically viable and that it then becomes immaterial whether the owner works the land himself or not. What is important is for him to know how to manage it. 'The most important agricultural implement', one of them said, 'is the propelling pencil.' Any suggestion of land reform arouses their immediate opposition: in 1961 legislation designed to bring about a very mild agrarian reform was shelved by the Government following strong pressure by the latifundists.

These views of landowners and labourers reflect a basic disagreement. The present latifundists have inherited the land they own and therefore favour and support a system in which status is acquired by birth. The labourers owe nothing to their ancestors, their only capital is their work, and they therefore favour and support a system in which status would be conferred by the nobility of work itself. No one in the freguesia has risen from poverty to wealth in the last fifty years, and when some labourer or small landowner happens to spend more than usual, and appears to be better off than before, the explanations given by other peasants do not attribute these changes to the industry of the man in question. The more traditionally minded attribute his sudden affluence to 'treasure trove'; those with a more modern outlook say he must have had dealings with counterfeiters. Some existing fortunes are, in fact, said to have originated from treasure trove sometime during the last century.[5]

A static view of the order of society is also implicit in common speech. Ambition (*ambição*) is a defect, not a quality.[6] Dishonesty is equated with moving upwards in such epithets as *pulante* and *trampolineiro*, applied to people who deliberately deceive others through their actions or their words respectively. Literally, however, the terms mean 'one who jumps' and 'one who leaps off a trampoline'.

The use of such words and expressions does not necessarily imply a calm acceptance of the present order and it is not inconsistent with the labourers' wish to alter it through a redistribution of land. But this is a distant goal, a Messianic hope of justice that could only come true through the intervention of outside forces. For the time being, and in local conditions, individual endeavours are doomed to failure.

As principal beneficiaries, promoters, and supporters of the present order, the latifundists were of overwhelming importance in the life of the freguesia until very recently. Today with alternative employment taking men out of agriculture, their importance has decreased, but they retain a position as employers and patrons that no other landowner can match locally.

[5] Pitt-Rivers relates the secrecy surrounding treasure trove in Andalusia to the conflict between the community and the State: 'The hostile state wishes to get its hands upon the pristine wealth which lies buried in the pueblo." *People of the Sierra* (London, 1954), p. 206. Such an interpretation would be far-fetched in the case of Vila Velha.

[6] In American medical literature 'lack of ambition' is often listed as a general symptom of illness, together with asthenia, anorexy, fever, etc. The United States is the 'achievement society' *par excellence*.

Outside these roles, however, they are not directly involved in the day-to-day life of the freguesia. As they live in Vila Nova they are not customers of the local shops and taverns, and do not provide themes for local gossip. Their wives are not suspected of casting the evil eye. They are, in a sense, omnipresent, but they are also, for most purposes, outsiders.

PROPRIETÁRIOS

The proprietários form the group of resident landowners who earn their living exclusively from the land they own. In 1965 there were twenty-six. The two wealthiest among them are called *lavradores*, a designation reserved generally for the latifundists. There are considerable variations in wealth, from the wealthiest local *lavrador* to the poorest of the other proprietários. In a good year their net incomes range from about £400 to about £2,000.

All the agricultural machinery in the freguesia which is not owned by the latifundists is owned by the three wealthiest proprietários. The two *lavradores* have a tractor and a threshing machine, and one has a binder and reaper. Another proprietário has a tractor. These machines have been bought second-hand. The differences in the equipment possessed by the group of proprietários and the group of latifundists are related not only to the smaller areas owned by the former and their weaker financial position, but also to the fact that these areas are in many cases made up of non-contiguous small plots.

Most of the proprietários live in the villages and none lives in Vila Velha. Their houses are conspicuous in size and often built in two stories with the kitchens facing away from the streets. Four live on their farms. Only two keep resident domestic female servants now, although the others often employ a daily help. None owns a car. When they have to go to Vila Nova they take the bus or use a horse and cart. Their appearance is rural: their complexions are weather-beaten, they very rarely wear ties with their buttoned-up collared shirts, they wear boots instead of shoes, and in the winter some of them wear the traditional cloaks of the province. They are, however, distinguishable from labourers and sharecroppers: their clothes are of better quality and they do not wear the *pelico* (a sleeveless sheepskin coat cut short in front and long at the back) which is the working outer garment worn by labourers and sharecroppers. They usually wear jackets or, in the summer, go about in shirt-sleeves and waistcoat. Heavy silver or gold watch-chains are often suspended from the pockets of their waistcoats.

Although they very rarely work in the fields after they reach maturity, all of them have done so in their youth as employees of their fathers, and their sons follow in their footsteps. Even those who are away at school or university lend a hand with the farm work when they are at home on holiday. All members of this group can read and write and have been to primary school. A few went on to high school but none completed the course. The older proprietários learned a trade or craft in their youth as a form of security against agricultural mishaps. This was common until the 1920s, but nowadays the sons of proprietários are given greater educational opportunities: three of the young men from this group have recently graduated—one from university and two from technical colleges—and taken posts outside the freguesia. Their brothers, who remained at home because they preferred farm work to the intellectual efforts of high school and university, often regret their decision.

The proprietários marry into their own group, marriage partners being found among proprietário families in adjoining freguesias and concelhos and, in a few cases, among the better-off families of sharecroppers. The few from outside this circle are not university graduates as in the case of the latifundists but agricultural technicians or school teachers.

The different families of proprietários are therefore almost all related to each other: four of the wealthiest are brothers and a fifth is their brother-in-law. There are other interrelated groups of siblings. There is only one close family link between the group of the proprietários and the group of the latifundists. A first cousin of the four brothers mentioned above is married to a latifundist. She lives in Vila Nova and sees her relatives only on very formal occasions.

Since the proprietários live in the freguesia they have a constant day-to-day contact with the rest of the population. In education, *train de vie*, or dress, there is not the same distance between them and the rest of the population as in the case of the latifundists. This makes it possible for sentimental situations to arise; but only in two cases (one of the *lavradores* and the son of one of the proprietários), did these lead to marriages with girls from the labourer group. The proprietários form a relatively self-contained group, the sons or daughters of the most prosperous sharecroppers having access to the lower categories of the proprietário group. As in the case of the latifundists, the relative rank of the different families within the group is altered at each generation level by the inheritance system. However, no one has yet been found to revert to wage labour or sharecropping. When there is not enough land to provide a living for all the heirs, some seek an urban occupation and their share is rented or sold to the heirs remaining in the freguesia.

The proprietários employ men from outside the family on their farms. In 1965 the number of labourers they employed permanently throughout the year was very small. The three wealthiest proprietários employed five, four and three field-hands respectively, the others two or only one, and, in three cases, this single employee was a member of the family. For weeding and harvesting olives and cereals, additional workers have to be recruited. Workers from outside the family reinforce the family working unit or at least work under close supervision.

Proprietários are thus in a very different position from the latifundists. They are much closer to the rest of the population and are able to exercise some patronage in local employment and administration; but in Vila Nova they can only be effective with the minor clerks at a low level of the concelho bureaucracy. They do not have much power either, on their own or through their kinship networks outside the concelho. Matters that have to be solved at the civil government level of the province or in Lisbon are outside their direct scope of action. As a result, they have no say in general agricultural policies. Even in terms of local policies they have to follow the lead of the latifundists. In the days when the latifundists employed a far larger labour force throughout the year than they do at present, the proprietários had to pay higher wages if they wanted to secure labourers, particularly at peak periods. This continued even after the big estates had cut down on the number of people employed as a result of mechanization and the reduction of wheat cultivation. Their relationship with their employees is closer—there are no managers to come between them—and their practical knowledge of agricultural problems is favourably compared by labourers with the alleged ignorance of the latifundists. Most of them are known to be in a difficult financial situation and this too brings them nearer to the rest of the population.[7]

Land came into the proprietário families in two different ways: part of it was already owned before 1834 by the forbears of the present owners, respectable landowners whose estates were smaller than those of the Church, the Crown, or the noblemen from whom they rented some land. They formed the upper group of the local residents, as can be inferred from their presence on the Câmara, the Junta, and the Misericórdia. They eventually added to their land by buying plots when the commons were partitioned. The other way in which today's proprietário families acquired land was through the hard work of forebears who were sharecroppers and managers on the large estates in the last twenty-five years of the nineteenth century and the first decades of the twentieth. Most of the present proprietários have inherited land acquired in both ways. Their local ancestry, together with their present residence, gives them deeper roots in the freguesia than the latifundists, and the wealthier among them are more respected by the local population than are the latifundists. In referring to them, labourers often prefix their names by the word *senhor* (a sign of respect) which they do not do when referring to the latifundists. They are the most important men in the villages, and yet they frequent the taverns, are present at the community feasts, speak with the local accent, and send their children to the local primary schools.

Their attitude towards the social order in which they live is different from that of the latifundists. They did not cut themselves off from the land, it is only very recently that their sons have sought a way out of farming through education—mainly as a result of present difficulties—and they do not feel the need to justify their ownership of land. They make no claims to aristocracy and, since they know the labourers much better than the latifundists do, they do not live in fear of social revolution. They have supported the present Government in elections but more

[7] The financial difficulties of the latifundists are not taken seriously by the labourers. It is very difficult for a labourer to realise that a latifundist is as much a victim of a given economic situation as he is himself, when he knows that the latifundist may spend more money on an evening's drinking or gambling than he earns in a month.

as a matter of course than from enthusiam. They are, in a sense, caught between the rich and the poor. Compared with the rest of the freguesia (and regardless of their present financial troubles) they are rich but they cannot be considered really wealthy in comparison with the latifundists. If told that they have been described as rich by labourers, they say that there are no rich men in the freguesia. 'The rich', they point out, 'live in Vila Nova.'

The fact that they regard themselves as second in rank in the social order makes for some ambiguity in their views. They agree that the big estates are often mismanaged, but they do not suggest partition of land. They are critical of the behaviour of the latifundists, not of the fact that there are latifundists. They are an integral part of an arch of prestige in which the latifundists form the keystone. They approve of the existing order of society from which they too benefit. As one of them said, 'I am not rich myself. But if it were not for the rich, how could there be women costing a thousand escudos a night? How could a man go to a café, get drunk, break everything, and avoid arrest by leaving his wallet with the owner?' His lack of money barred him from these things but he found them desirable and necessary. The rich were therefore needed to guarantee their existence, even though he was unable to enjoy them himself. This enjoyment by proxy of the privileges of the rich is hardly found among labourers or sharecroppers who feel that they contribute to the existence of the wealthy through the work they perform. Their envy is not mixed with admiration but with resentment.

SEAREIROS

Seareiro is a rather difficult word to translate.[8] 'Sharecropper' is perhaps the best equivalent, but the seareiro often has some land of his own and may rent a plot instead of taking it on a sharecropping basis, although this is a less frequent arrangement.

The clearing of land which took place in the Alentejo from the middle of the last century up to the early 1930s was undertaken mainly by seareiros. They figure predominantly in local

[8] The word comes from *seara*, a grain or corn field, which is what the seareiro owns since the land does not belong to him.

lore, and are frequently mentioned in official documents and newspapers. In 1898, when explaining the advantages of government-sponsored technical assistance to local farmers, the syndicato stated that it would help the seareiros in '*clearing the land*, sowing, and harvesting'.[9] Local newspapers often called them the 'heroic class' of seareiros, leading articles described their difficult working conditions, hypothetical accounts were given of their losses or limited gains, and even poems about the hard life of the seareiro appeared in print.

The large estates (and parts of the land belonging to the proprietários) have been farmed under a mixed system of direct cultivation and sharecropping from as far back as people can remember. The areas allocated to sharecropping have varied according to the convenience of landowners and to the availability of sharecroppers. Fertilizers, the use of which became widespread at the beginning of this century, required a higher capital investment for wheat cultivation and forced many seareiros to return to wage labour.[10] After the 1929 wheat campaign some of the landowners decided to work all the land themselves in order to take advantage of the subsidies available for wheat cultivation. Those who did not, made conditions more difficult for the sharecroppers by reducing the fallow periods of the rotation system and demanding an increased share of the crop. In the traditional sharecropping contracts for cereal cultivation, one-fourth or one-fifth of the crop, according to the quality of the soil, was paid to the owner of the land. In areas where the soils were poor, agreements entitling the landowner to as little as one-tenth were sometimes found, but this was very rare. *Terras ao quarto* (to have lands on a quarter-share basis) is a traditional expression which indicates the prevalence of this type of contract. After the Wheat Campaign of 1929, contracts entitling landowners to one-third of the crop came into use at the behest of the landowners. At the end of a few years of low yields, many seareiros were forced to abandon their enterprises. The most common sharecropping agreements found nowadays provide for one-third, one-quarter, or one-fifth share for the landowner.

[9] S.c. 29 Oct. 1898. (my italics)

[10] Lands in the commons before partition were of course farmed on a sharecropping basis.

In the late 1950s, when the large estates substantially reduced the areas devoted to wheat and increased those allocated to sharecropping, some latifundists imposed a fifty-fifty sharecropping agreement but included the supply of fertilizers in the agreements. They found men in the freguesia willing to accept these conditions, but when yields in the following year proved extremely low, they had to revert to a basis of a third share of the crop for the better lands and a quarter or a fifth share for the remaining lands, with a proviso that they would no longer supply fertilizers. They also tried to impose one-year contracts, thus depriving the sharecroppers of the oat harvest—reaped a year after the wheat crop—which requires less work and less investment and could therefore compensate them for any losses on wheat. This arrangement had to be dropped after a year's experiment because willing sharecroppers could not be found.

On the large estates the share given to the owner is traditionally taken from the grain, and since the threshing is carried out with the landowners' threshing machine, he gets an additional 8 per cent of the crop as fee. In the case of the small landowners, the crop is shared out before threshing. In recent years large landowners, who now grow almost no wheat but need hay for their cattle, have begun taking the agreed share, not only from the grain, but also from the chaff. (*Agora até esquartejam a palha*—'now they even split straws' is the wry comment made on this practice.)

Although sharecropping and wage labour can be regarded as alternative forms of employment used at will according to the landowners' convenience, the seareiros were in a better position than the rural labourers. In a good year a sharecropper's net income in the early 1960s was between £250 and £350. His position was also much more stable and conveyed more social prestige than that of a *trabalhador* ('rural labourer'), and, if he moved from one form of work to the other, his prestige would be affected. On the whole, seareiros own more land than wage labourers, although there are landless seareiros and landed rural workers, and even some mixed cases: a man may take a plot on a share basis, work a small plot of his own, earn some money cutting trees for someone else, and employ one or two field hands at harvest time. In general, however, seareiros were more prosperous than rural workers and owned draught-animals which enabled them to embark on sharecropping ventures. There was a further division between those who owned only one animal—generally a mule—and those who owned *parelhas* (a pair of draught-animals), since the big houses would only admit owners of *parelhas* as sharecroppers on their land.

In the old heroic days of the seareiros there were traditional seareiro families, and rural labourers seem to have been seldom admitted to them. Even today the sons and daughters of seareiros tend to marry into seareiro families, although rural labourers are more freely admitted than before. They rarely marry outside the freguesia; when they do, it is mainly into families from the rural neighbourhood.

The admission of persons from the labourer group as marriage partners is a token of the seareiros' present decline. Conditions are changing and sharecroppers may now lead a more difficult life than wage labourers. The difficulties that led the large landowners to extend sharecropping on their estates have now hit the sharecroppers. Since 1962 their numbers have been dwindling, and, to secure enough seareiros, landowners have dropped the stipulation that sharecroppers must own a couple of animals. Anyone owning a mule or donkey may now take land as a sharecropper on the big estates. There are still people who do so, but the number has rapidly diminished over the last five years (1960–5).[11]

What is really surprising about the seareiros is not that they should be disappearing but that some of them still manage to survive as sharecroppers. In 1959, when the wealthiest latifundist decided to increase sharecropping and reduce the area farmed directly, he did so on the basis of very detailed estate accounts established by experts (in fact, these are the only accurate estate accounts to be found in the freguesia). For 1958–9 his net losses per hectare under direct cultivation were 255·88 escudos (for wheat), 978.69 escudos (for barley), 681.46 escudos (for oats) and 1,258.20 escudos (for rye). From the land allocated to sharecropping (400 hectares, with contracts generally on the basis of a quarter share for wheat), he made a net

[11] An important sideline in the economy of the seareiro families was the *fretes* or transport of goods for other people which they were able to undertake because they owned animals and carts. The greater use of railways, buses, and lorries put an end to this activity.

profit of 1,105.32 escudos per hectare. It should be remembered that the best land was always reserved for direct farming.

The seareiros' costs are less than those of landowners with big concerns and they usually operate on a family basis, resorting to hired field hands only during the harvest season. Moreover, they live very parsimonious lives. The fact that, as a group, they are now on the decline, at a time when they can get better land on better terms than ever before in living memory, is due to the problem facing all local wheat growers: the increasing gap between production costs and state-fixed wheat prices. This is particularly hard on the seareiros, who own little or no land and have therefore to concentrate on cereal growing.[12]

The basis of the seareiro economy has always been the family concern. Sons, daughters, and in-laws gain their livelihood from the common enterprise, they work harder and cost less than hired labour. This basis has been undermined in recent years. Between 1960 and 1965 many sons of seareiros have taken jobs outside farming. A few have emigrated, others are in Lisbon. Since most of them completed primary schooling, they are in a better position than labourers to take non-agricultural jobs. They may become skilled labourers, or porters, or doormen, etc. in the lower echelons of society. Some of them had enough money to take driving lessons and have now become lorry or bus drivers.

The seareiros who remain have so far managed to survive from year to year by reducing the areas sown. They are mostly men over fifty and the very few below that age are sons of some of the more elderly men who, because they did not attend school, were unable to find jobs in the factory or to migrate to the cities with reasonable hopes of finding a job. They are almost all illiterate and proud of it. In fact they attribute to technical progress (of which the expansion of literacy is an obvious characteristic) much of the débâcle they see around them. The following are some of the views they hold: motor cars have stopped the latifundists from riding around their estates on horseback and *quem o seu não vê, o Diabo o leva* ('the Devil takes what you do not look after'). Managers now rule more than owners; some of the latter do not even know the boundaries of

[12] A notion of their difficulties may be gathered from the decrease in the number of *parelhas* owned. In 1965 there were only eleven in the freguesia. In 1955 the figure was around one hundred.

their *herdades*. Television makes people go to bed much later nowadays, thus leading them to work less; together with illustrated magazines it helps to create a demand for consumer goods that strains family budgets. Mass information introduces confusion and highlights the appeal of the outside world. 'In my youth', one of them said, 'one man in a hundred could read and write. But because I cannot read or write, it does not follow that I am less able to manage my property.' They have less objection to landless labourers leaving to try their luck elsewhere, because they do not need them as much as the latifundists and proprietários do. But those who 'have something of their own' should not leave and should *tratar da vida* (freely translated—'look after their own property') *sem ter que sofrer ninguem* (literally 'without having to suffer anyone', i.e. to be employed).

Their view of the world and of themselves is more coherent and more articulate, as a rule, than that of their more literate fellow villagers. But they are obviously riding a dead horse and are probably the last generation of traditional seareiros.

LABOURERS

The groups described so far share the following characteristic: whether working on their own land or not, they employ other men or are self-employed. Most of those who depend directly on the land for their livelihood are, however, working for others. Among these the largest group is that of the labourer. There were 286 rural workers in the freguesia in 1965, of whom 206 were heads of families. They may be employed by the year (very rarely nowadays), for a season, by the week, or by the day. Their conditions of employment are worse than those of any other group. They are not paid for Sundays off, nor for rainy days when work is impossible. When the weather is bad, half days are sometimes subtracted from a labourer's wage. Traditionally wage labourers were paid by the week and, when they were no longer needed at the end of a season, they were kept on until the end of a week. Since 1963, however, men have been dismissed in the middle of a week. Wages are very low in comparison with industrial wages or even farm wages in other regions. They also vary from season to season. In recent years these seasonal variations in wage have tended to settle into two rates, one for winter and one for summer, with special rates for harvesting olives and cereals. During the time of my field-work, wages began to go up at an unprecedented rate, but in 1965 a wage labourer's average earnings were still about £97 a year.

Labourers are known as *trabalhadores* ('workers') and describe themselves as such. Fifty years ago, however, they were often described as *jornaleiros* ('journeymen' or 'workers by the day') and although this expression is sometimes still used, *trabalhador* is by far the most frequently used designation. To understand its full meaning we must understand the meaning attributed to the word *trabalho* ('work'). *Trabalho* is the blanket term for all the agricultural tasks they perform for wages and the conditions in which they have to perform them, and excludes other forms of earning a living. Craftsmen are *artistas* ('artists'); their work is an *arte*, not a *trabalho*. Shopkeepers, salesmen, and hawkers do not 'work' either. Labourers' wives, who have to manage a meagre budget and are faced with the weekly task of haggling over prices with hawkers selling goods they do not produce and obviously trying to strike a bargain with the customer,[13] will often say that pedlars are very clever because they manage to make a living without actually working. Landowners, of course, don't work: on the contrary, they have people who work for them. Their freedom from work is provided by the income from the land they own. The attitude of labourers towards this situation is ambivalent: the landowners are often called parasites, but their parasitism is envied. Because of the position to which they were born, the wealthiest of the landowners seem, in the eyes of labourers, to have reached the ideal egoistical goal of a man's life: to be able to live without having to work and still to have prestige, a selfish and immoral goal perhaps but nonetheless advantageous and desirable.

It is in border-line cases that the distinction between the *trabalho* of labourers and the work of others is of more significance. A proprietários' son who works for his father is not a *trabalhador*. A landowner who has worked on the land in his youth will not say that he did *trabalho*, but that he *knows* all there is to know about it, since he had to perform the different tasks himself. An old shepherd may say that during some years of his life he

[13] The name by which hawkers are known is *regatão* from the Portuguese verb *regatear*, 'to haggle'.

did not earn his living as a shepherd but was 'in the *trabalho*'. Proprietários' sons perform the same tasks as labourers but have different conditions of pay. Shepherds have similar pay conditions but different tasks.[14] In both cases their work is not considered *trabalho*. However, because shepherds often have experienced periods of true *trabalho*, mostly occupy a financial situation not much better than that of labourers, and perform their activities in the countryside, they are closer than anyone else to the *trabalhadores*.

The establishment of the factory created a new occupational group. There were forty-two industrial workers living in the freguesia in 1965. Industrial workers are paid wages for the performance of physical tasks which are sometimes as hard as those of labourers. But their wages are higher, their work cleaner, and they are more secure in their jobs than anyone working in agriculture. They are better off than all labourers and many seareiros, but they are aware that, at the same time, they are at the bottom of another system of stratification, created by industry. Their position inside this new system is comparable to that of the labourers inside the old. Most of them had been labourers, and, although they say that an industrial worker *has to have* better standards of living than a labourer, they know that they are all members of a working class. But what they do is not *trabalho*, although it binds them in very much the same way.

Mechanized work in agriculture seems also to be excluded from the notion of *trabalho*. Tractor drivers are not considered to be doing *trabalho*, and they themselves share this view. They are very reluctant when managers order them to perform some of the traditional tasks at times when the tractors lie idle. This annoys their latifundist employers, who can see no difference between one type of work and another, since the drivers continue

[14] When they are not paid wages in money, shepherds are entitled to a share of wool and to the lambs born to an agreed number of ewes. Shepherds in charge of big flocks could make as much as £240 a year in 1965. Although this is considerably more than what a labourer can earn, a shepherd's life is too hard and lonely and lacking in prestige to offset the advantages of better pay. Shepherds are assumed to be ignorant and to have very unsophisticated manners. They spend most of the year away from their wives and, in most stories of cuckoldry, shepherds figure as the unfortunate victims. Shepherds who look after the small flocks of proprietários and seareiros do not earn more than a rural labourer, and often less. These posts are frequently filled by old men, too weak for the efforts of farming or road work.

to receive the same pay,[15] and will point out that these tractor drivers were ordinary labourers not long ago. The attitude of the tractor drivers is an expression of the basic ambivalence towards *trabalho* in labourers' minds.

The gap between what most non-labourers actually do for a living and what labourers regard as *trabalho* is considered morally unfair by the labourers. Underlying this moral attitude on the part of the labourers is the assumption that, although they are badly paid and receive an unfair share of the available wealth, they are a vital element in the production of basic food-stuffs. The notion that Alentejo is the granary of Portugal, however inaccurate this may be, is deeply ingrained in the Alentejo mind. Everyone, from latifundist to wage labourer, feels that the rest of the country is being fed as the result of his own ill-rewarded efforts. But in none is this feeling so strong as in the labourer,[16] who will point out in moments of despair that, without them, nothing could ever be produced, and that, without their work, land and landowners would be useless. They boast about having *maõs de trabalho* ('working hand' or 'hands fit for work') and about their technical skills as labourers, and compare these qualities to the soft hands and ignorance of farming of some latifundists: 'I am a labourer, and proud of it.'

Praise for *trabalho* should not, however, lead one to think that it is valued as an activity to be preferred above others. The pride of the old labourer is like the pride of the prostitute: it makes a virtue of what is in fact a necessity. Having a reputation for honesty and hard work was probably a labourer's greatest asset in this particular society since his employment for most of the year depended on the will of the landowners. And no matter how vital the role of those who produce basic and indispensable food-stuffs, theirs is still the dirtiest and worst-paid of all jobs.

Common speech abundantly betrays this: all agricultural tasks are called *serviços* ('services') and the implication

[15] Tractor drivers receive wages in money and in kind, which in 1965 amounted to about £180 a year.

[16] There is a tradition of oral poetry in the province. 'The Poor Labourer,' a poem composed when people who are now old were young, is a complaint against working conditions, of which two lines are relevant here:

Pois sendo ele o protector	('For he is the protector
De tudo o que a terra cria.	Of all the land brings forth').

is that, while performing them, you are *serving* other people.[17]

The word used to convey the completion of work is *encimar* (literally 'to get to the top, to overcome a height') and this is used both for individual tasks (*encimar a ceifa*—'getting on top of the harvest') and for intervals of time (*encimar o dia* ('the day'), *encimar o ano* ('the year')). Years and days are cycles that repeat themselves and you *get on top* of them when you complete a yearly contract with your employer or finish your day's work. Agricultural work is, most of the time, performed with the body bent forward; most of the time too, the eyes have to be fixed on the ground. This may be regarded both as indicative of the nature of the work and as symbolic of a man's subjection in performing it. When in 1911, strikers went through the fields asking (or forcing) other labourers to stop work and join the strike, their rallying call was, '*levantar os homens do trabalho*', 'to *raise* men from work'. It could perhaps be said that agricultural work is opposed to at least one important value of this society: the very general moral value of 'uprightness'. *Andar direito* ('to walk upright'), *endireitar-se* ('to straighten up'), *levantar a cabeça* ('to raise one's head'), *um homem às direitas* ('a straight, i.e. righteous man') are all expressions relating bodily posture to moral fortitude, in which verticality becomes an image for moral integrity. A man's independence is vertical, a man's serfdom makes him bend. This is consistent with the fact that in many matters labourers are not expected to meet the same standards of moral behaviour as landowners.

The result is that a labourer, whether he is resigned to his conditions or not, feels that he is morally wronged. This helps us to understand a fact that puzzles and irritates landowners, namely that in recent years, although real wages are going up (as a consequence of emigration), productivity, already considered by landowners to be very low, apparently is not. 'The more we pay', landowners say, 'the less they work.'

A sort of permanent, lukewarm strike is tacitly endorsed by labourers, who deliberately work less than they could. Labourers

[17] An analogy with modern public services would be out of place. The people labourers are serving are real, individual, flesh and blood *masters*, not an abstract community composed of members with equal rights who in other situations may possibly be serving you.

boast of their ability to perform certain tasks better than other labourers, but they also boast about their ability to deceive their overseers, the managers of large estates, and local proprietários. The same man may boast about both talents in the same breath. He does not see any incompatibility in the two attitudes and in fact, all other considerations apart, skill is needed to deceive employers without being dismissed. These deceptions are not sporadic: they involve using a consistent body of techniques which are well known and vary according to whether the labourers are working for the latifundists or the proprietários, since the supervision of managers differs from that of the small landowners. Labourers say that, although small landowners work with the men, or are at least in close proximity with them for most of the day, they are easier to fool, because they have not worked as wage labourers themselves and do not know all the tricks of the trade. Managers have in most cases started off as labourers and, although they are less often present, they are more difficult to fool.

These deceptions obey moral considerations: individual preferences or grievances apart, labourers feel obliged to work harder for the small landowners, with whom they have a closer personal relationship and who are not as rich as the latifundists. A labourer often regulates his output of work according to the relative wealth of his employer. In the absence of trade unions or political parties to voice labourers' grievances, low productivity is an institutionalized way of fighting against what they feel to be the unfairness of their position. It is also a way of extending the period of employment and (implicitly) of guaranteeing employment to others. But a balance has to be achieved. If an unusually hard-working labourer is regarded by other labourers as either simple-minded or subservient, an unusually inefficient one will have even more difficulty than others in finding employment.

The attitudes discussed above are not new. They have existed in the freguesia at least as far back as the men now in their seventies can remember. They are related to a life in which opportunities for non-agricultural work were beyond the reach of the local labourer. The creation of such opportunities is upsetting the balance. Young men do not regard agricultural work as their only future and they feel no need to build their lives around it. From this point of view labourers in the freguesia may be roughly divided into three age groups: those born before 1920, those born between 1920 and 1940, and those born after 1940.

Those in the first group had no alternative to rural work and this fact conditioned their entire lives. A sensible man had to safeguard his prestige as a good labourer in order to secure better chances of employment. A few of these men could hope to become *concertados* on the big estates. A *concertado*, as distinguished from a *jornaleiro*, was a labourer employed all the year round,[18] whose payment often included the wheat harvested from a few specified acres of the employer's land. He had possibilities of improving his position either within the hierarchy of the 'house' by becoming a sub-manager (*guarda de herdade*) and then a manager[19] (*feitor*), or by saving enough money to buy a couple of mules and becoming a sharecropper. In both cases, he could ultimately buy some land. To become a *concertado* was therefore the first ambition of a labourer's life.

Most of the men in this group began working at the age of

[18] The situation is different now. Proprietários still employ men all the year round, as do some of the latifundists, but in much smaller numbers. A labourer employed on a yearly basis earned about £125 p.a. in 1965, less than any but the wage labourer.

[19] Latifundists with large concerns spread over different parts of the province generally employ a general manager (*feitor geral*), several estate managers in charge of each of the groups of contiguous estates, and sub-managers living in some of the more distant farm-houses on their estates.

General managers often have land of their own and have salary arrangements with their employers which vary from case to case. They seem to have a better life than all but the latifundists and the wealthiest proprietários.

Managers receive money wages, a share of the foals born on the estate, and the right to farm some land. Sub-managers are given similar conditions, but their money wages are lower. However, better pay conditions are not accompanied by any special form of security of tenure. Managers may be dismissed at twenty-four hours' notice, like any other employee. In 1965 managers earned on average about £250 a year in cash and sub-managers about £150 a year. Managers have great practical agricultural knowledge which the latifundists often lack, and they are vital elements in the latter's concerns. They hire labourers and keep them on or dismiss them often without any intervention from the owner of the estates. With mechanization and the possibility of migration, the jobs they control have become fewer and are less in demand, and their importance has therefore diminished. They are, however, still sought as patrons for certain matters. They can approach the owners of the 'House' for which they work more easily than other people. Not only labourers but also clerks, merchants, shopkeepers, and small proprietários are willing to do them favours, since they may need the help of the 'House' at some time, and it is useful to have a friend there.

seven, as shepherds' boys. They earned a very small wage and it often happened that the shepherd kept their earnings in exchange for their board and lodging. They were then said to be *perfilhados* (literally 'adopted') and, if they did not contribute to the family income, they were at least not a burden. Moving from employer to employer, they eventually became shepherds in their own right, looking after the few animals of small landowners. They would continue in this calling until the age of fourteen or fifteen, when they began to carry out certain agricultural tasks at reduced wage rates. At eighteen (or sometimes, if they were exceptionally strong, before that age) they were given their first contract work, the *empreitada* (piece-work in the cereal harvest) at full rate of pay. From then on they became full labourers and their lives were divided between wage labour in the fields and periods of unemployment, with frequent changes of employer. Piece-work during the cereal and olive harvest alternated with stints on public works, generally road repairs. Until the early 1960s work was *de sol a sol* ('from sunrise to sunset') and, since their place of work was often some miles away from their homes this meant that they left home before dawn and returned after dusk. These conditions were already an improvement: until the early 1940s work had been *de ar a ar* ('from the first light of dawn to the last light of dusk') with frequent extensions well into the night during peak periods. During the sowing and harvest seasons a man could sleep as little as four hours a night. It was an extremely hard life: wages were lower, state social welfare measures were non-existent, and formal education was practically unthinkable for a labourer's son; but there was no alternative.

The labourers in the second age group were the first to benefit from the emergence of new types of work. Their childhood and youth were still geared to agriculture, but, before the oldest among them had reached the age of twenty, mechanization was reducing the demand for manpower in agriculture. In 1950 when the cardboard factory was built near the freguesia some found jobs on the building site and stayed on as factory workers when the building was completed, while others were taken on later. Most of them have attended adult education classes in order to obtain the necessary school diploma. In 1958 the steel-mills being erected near Lisbon increased the stream of migrants that had begun to flow out of the freguesia some years before, and the stream has been swelling steadily ever since. When state-sponsored temporary emigration to France was introduced in 1964, emigrants were chosen from this age group.

Those who have remained in rural work have done so because they have failed to find other employment. They are mostly illiterates who were unable or unwilling to pass the adult education examinations. They regard the prospect of being permanently confined to agriculture as a setback for which they need to find an excuse: lack of formal education, complicated family commitments, betrayal by inefficient patrons. They have benefited from the higher agricultural wages now paid but, since these are still lower than those for non-agricultural work, they tend to move out of farming as soon as they possibly can, thus increasing the frustrations of those who have to remain in agriculture.

Labourers of the youngest group are quite different. Most of them can read and write. This means that instead of beginning their working lives at the age of seven as their elders did, they begin working at the age of thirteen or fourteen.[20] Any labourer over twenty, who is not an invalid, finds it impossible to avoid conscription and has to do three years' military service; two are spent in Africa.[21] A few volunteer when they reach eighteen to complete it as soon as possible. Once their army service is over, if they have not found a job in the factory, they leave the freguesia as soon as they can. Those who have not yet done their military service stay until they are called up and, whereas the period of army service was regarded as an obstacle in the past, it is now welcomed, in spite of the new risks attached, because

[20] In 1965 schoolteachers in the freguesia set an essay in which pupils were asked to describe what they would like to do when they grew up. Of 27 boys, aged between nine and thirteen, the only two who mentioned agriculture were landowners' sons who wanted to become agrarian engineers. Although there was a considerable proportion of would-be bullfighters and pilots, fishermen and lorrydrivers were also mentioned. Of 31 teenagers aged between fifteen and twenty (i.e. before army service) to whom the question: 'What would you do if you won the football pools?' was separately put, only four said that they would buy some land, and all four were sons of small landowners. The others thought of establishing themselves in some commercial business enterprise elsewhere. 19 were sons of labourers.

[21] In 1961 terrorism broke out in Angola and a few years later in Guinea and Mozambique.

it opens the way for an escape from the hardships of rural work.

These young men have little respect for their fathers' lifetime commitment to agriculture. Their childhood and youth were not exclusively centred on farming and, if they were forced to work on the land, they know not only the frustrations involved but also the advantages of alternative occupations. Those who leave try to persuade the old men to join them. Devoid both of the ambition to convert any possible financial rewards from *trabalho* into land ownership and of the compulsive quality that led to the ethical rationalizations made in its defence, they have no praise for *trabalho*. Indeed they regard it as the worst possible way of life. With little experience of agricultural work—and the intermittent nature of their experience makes their work less effective technically—they do not feel the ambivalence felt by old labourers towards *trabalho*. They have retained the feeling of the humiliation it entails but have lost the veneration for its alleged virtues. And they have found better means to fight against these humiliations than the traditional ways of cheating their employers and hoping for the millennium. They simply take the bus and leave the freguesia.

VI

CRISES AND CONFLICT

1. CRISES

THE labour requirements of extensive farming increased the inequality resulting from the distribution of land by creating lengthy periods during the agricultural year in which labourers were not needed on the estates. The partition of the common lands in 1874 and the substantial growth of population since the late nineteenth century made these periods of seasonal unemployment an important social problem.[1] A name was coined for them, *crises de trabalho*—'unemployment crises'—or, more simply, *crises*. The first reference to an unemployment crisis in a local document occurs in 1879.[2] The crises became very serious soon afterwards, and for many years defied the efforts made by landowners and local authorities to cope with them. Both had tried to fight the crises from the very beginning. Their concern was not only with the possibility of social unrest but also with the fear of losing manpower, either by migration[3] or by starvation. Redundant in winter, local labourers were in short supply during the cereal harvest. As early as 1856 (i.e. before the dramatic expansion of wheat cultivation and before

[1] The existence of the commons provided an outlet for the landless labourers. It gave them a small grain field (*seara*); they could grow melons and keep honey-bees or a few animals, and thus keep themselves occupied and gurantee resources to fall back on during slack periods on the estates.

[2] C.m. 19 Oct. This was not peculiar to the freguesia. As late as 1888, when the Agricultural Conference (Congresso Agrícola) met in Lisbon, rural unemployment did not seem to be an important problem. There is one single reference to it, in the report of one of the committees, in which it is stated that 'work crises' are 'one of the preoccupations that are *beginning to impose themselves* on the landowners' (my italics). *Documentos Relativos ao Congresso Agrícola* etc., p. 60.

[3] The emigration rates of the Alentejo province have always been remarkably low and up to 1962 only one individual in the concelho had gone to live in a foreign country, and only a handful had left for Portuguese Africa. The minimum sum needed to emigrate to Brazil or Venezuela was beyond the reach of a wage labourer. Until the late 1940s migration to the Lisbon industrial belt was also unimportant: industrial development was not yet sufficient to attract manpower from this sparsely populated zone. This, together with the efforts of the landowners to keep labour on the land, probably accounts for the low emigration rate.

unemployment as such had become a social problem) the Câmara, in reply to an inquiry from the Ministry of the Interior, stated that, although it could not settle new permanent residents in the concelho, it would welcome seasonal migration between March and July when 'there are not enough hands in the concelho to cope with the work', particularly during the wheat harvest.[4]

When crises of seasonal unemployment began to affect Vila Velha, it became necessary to ensure that labourers would not leave the freguesia and would be sufficiently fit to begin working as soon as local conditions permitted. If a labourer's work falls below a certain level of productivity, agricultural production is disrupted. To work well he must be minimally healthy and therefore have a minimal level of nutrition. Concern with this latter aspect is clearly expressed in official documents for 1945 and 1946, the difficult post-war years when food was in short supply and some food-stuffs were rationed. In 1945 the landowners' Grémio, arguing against a government measure that forced producers to sell more than they wished (thereby decreasing the supply usually reserved for local consumption), specified the labourer's staple foods: 'bread, olive oil, lard, chick-peas . . . and meat when he can lay hands on it (*quando a apanha*). He feeds himself well when he can (*sempre que pode*), but since his output of work on this normal diet is already small, his productivity will be *nil* if he is badly fed'.[5] In 1946 the civil government of the province suggested an increase in the *per capita* rations of olive oil and gave its reason as 'the exhaustion of strength in the rural classes, already reflected in a remarkable way in the decreased productivity of agricultural work'.[6]

The concern of landowners for minimal standards of well-being among labourers was thus in part determined by the need to safeguard their own interests. This concern found several expressions.

Alms and Theft

Charity and stealing, the traditional forms of institutionalized behaviour that helped to alleviate the extreme poverty created by the nature of social stratification, were unable to meet the

[4] 1 June. [5] G.c. 6 Jan. 1945.
[6] G.c. circular 1486, 6 Sept. 1946.

challenge represented by the scale of the new unemployment crises. However, for many years they played an important ancillary role.

'He who gives to the poor lends to God' was a motto for the rich. The biggest funeral remembered in Vila Nova was that of the wife of a latifundist who was famous for her charity. A street was later named after her and her charity is explicity mentioned on the street sign. Stories are told of how she helped even the families of labourers whom her husband had dismissed.

The richest man ever to have lived in the concelho, who died in 1886, provided clothes for twelve poor people every year. Even today, when a proprietário dies, his clothes are often distributed among the poor. Until the beginning of this century, the wills of rich people always included bequests of alms to the poor, varying with the wealth of the deceased. Today the distribution of alms is often not stipulated in wills, but the relatives of the deceased in any but the labourers' group generally make up for this. In the case of the very few 'free thinkers' to be found nowadays in the freguesia, the money that would normally be spent on a requiem mass said thirty days after the death of a relative is also given in alms. Among the rich, alms are also given during other *rites de passage*, and festive meals are served to the poor on the occasion of some marriages and christenings. Ritual singing and begging on the eve of 2 January, a tradition which is now only perpetuated by young boys, could be practised by poor adults in times of crises, and in this case the *lavradora* ('landowners' wife') would distribute bread and pork sausages instead of the usual sweets. There are traditional songs which explicitly mention these customs. Alms and food are distributed to the poor on many other festive occasions, such as the opening of a new shop or the celebration of a particularly joyful event in someone's life. The Brotherhood of the Misericórdia used to give alms to the poor at Easter every year until the 1930s and continued to make exceptional distributions on other occasions after this period. The Junta de Freguesia sometimes did the same. The Brotherhood of the Holy Sacrament regularly distributed alms to the needy up to 1910, sometimes through the Junta.

Alms were an accepted part of the system of social relations. Whenever landowners felt that the Government was forcing them to sell more of their produce than they wished to sell they cited the giving of alms as one of the reasons for keeping substantial reserves in hand. A Câmara minute for 1905 mentioned that 'the table was always laid and ready' to feed the wandering groups of beggars who called at the farms.[7] In the very difficult days of the late 1930s one of the very rich landowners would spend more than 1,000 escudos (£14)a day on alms in kind. In many rich houses there is still a prescribed day of the week when alms are given to those who come and beg. In 1937 official bodies and individual families joined in their charitable efforts when a general campaign was organized by the Government—known as the *Campanha de Auxílio aos Pobres no Inverno* ('Campaign for Aid to the Poor in Winter'). It met with an enthusiastic reception from local authorities and the Junta de Freguesia drew up a list of local poor.[8] But such concerted effort was exceptional. Charity in the form of alms was mainly local and private: it was a loan to God, and served as an atonement for sins committed in this world while at the same time helping to ward off social unrest. It was also a way of assuring personal prestige and status. The Christian elements in charity were strong, if somewhat extreme at times. In 1936 or 1937 a wealthy landowner seriously suggested that the people of his group should make the sacrifice of depriving themselves of one course in a meal each week and give an equivalent sum to the poor. (It should be noted that at that time many landowners were alarmed by the Spanish Civil War.) The prestige element was also strong. A man who boasted of giving 1,000 escudos a day in alms was demonstrating the satisfactory nature of his financial position despite the bad times afflicting everybody else.

The popularity of alms-giving has to do with its private and person-to-person nature which leaves the occasion of the gift and the amounts given to the discretion of the donor. The economic structure which creates the need for giving alms is not questioned, and there may even be a feeling that the unsatisfactory details of the structure are being corrected by this

[7] 21 Aug.

[8] The need for outside help, even for charity, was felt to be so strong that on 2 Jan. 1937 the Mayor wrote to the Junta remonstrating that it had designated only seventeen families as 'poor'. He found this number absurdly low, and explained that the smaller the number of 'poor' they registered, the less the campaign would give to the freguesia.

practice. If, as was only too obvious, alms were not enough to mitigate the conditions of the poor, this was blamed on the imperfections of human nature: rich people were not as charitable as they should be. The remedy needed was a change of heart not a redistribution of incomes. Hearts are often slow to change, however, and the poor should be patient. The same men who systematically gave alms to the poor, fought any proposed measures that would eventually lead to a reduction of the hardships suffered by labourers if these measures meant, as most of them were bound to, any curtailment of their privileges.

Among those who received charitable relief we must distinguish between traditional beggars and labourers forced by unemployment to accept alms. It is the latter who make alms an important social institution. Professional beggars were few. Begging for them was a way of life: they usually begged singly, invoking the donor's love of God while soliciting his alms, and were looked upon as somewhat abnormal personalities who, for one reason or another, had opted out of the usual modes of life. Their wretched situation was accounted for in personal terms: there was always something specifically odd about them and they themselves accepted without shame any blame that was cast on them for failing to earn their livelihoods by working. It was their nature to beg and they were virtual outcasts.

Unemployed labourers, however, were forced into beggary by circumstances, and formed quite a distinct group. They went about in large groups, often composed of men, women, and children. Although they sometimes appealed to the donor's love of God, they more often invoked their own hunger. These large groups of able-bodied people, begging their way from farm to farm and through towns and villages, provided an objective, vociferous, and violent reminder of the unfairness of the society in which they lived. The fact that at these times the landowners' usual reaction was fear of social upheaval quite clearly indicated this.

To the labourers, begging was a hateful occupation. To beg was to give up any pretence of being able to repay a favour and therefore to sink lower than a man or woman should ever do; it was to move into the marginal social groups of those who, like the traditional beggars or gypsies, were not entitled to full membership of society, and to do so was to become worthless.

The blame for this situation was put, not on a man's nature, as in the case of the professional beggars and the gypsies, but on the circumstances which had overtaken him. It meant that a man had to do things that were not in his nature. (*Um homem tem que fazer coisas que não são da natureza dele.*) He had to beg without having the *nature* of a beggar.

In 1911 a local newspaper commented that if a proposed prohibition of begging were enforced it would lead to an enormous increase in stealing. In most cases stealing is recognized as an alternative to begging. It was widespread in times of crisis, and even today outbreaks occur in winter. Private property is protected by the Republican Guards and the special guards hired by estate owners to patrol their lands (farm guards and uniformed gamekeepers knows as Forestry Guards), but these were often unable to cope with the number of thefts. References to thieving constantly occur in the local newspapers and in official correspondence. Two such references, both taken from the Syndicato's correspondence, are particularly revealing. In 1931 the Syndicato, protesting against the introduction of a new law imposing a fine on persons who fail to muzzle their watch dogs, claims that dogs not only protect the herds from wild animals but are a discouragement to the thieving practised 'by those who, thinking that they can find a justification in the lack of work and the economic crisis, feel themselves entitled to lay hands on what other people have produced.'[9] The letter ends by stating that only those who know nothing of agricultural life (*a vida agrícola*) could suppose that unmuzzled watch dogs are not absolutely necessary. In 1936[10] it asks for the number of Republican Guards to be increased because, since there are very few Guards in the concelho, 'the right to private property is only theoretical . . . acorns, olives, livestock, and firewood are constantly being stolen'. These attempts to protect their property were regarded by landowners as perfectly justified: theft is always theft and thieves are always thieves. But the labourer's point of view is different. Stealing small quantities of firewood, acorns, fruit, etc., is regarded almost as a right when those who do so are extremely poor, particularly if they are also unemployed. When a thief is caught by the Republican Guards or by an estate keeper, the villagers always take the side of the thief,

9 31 Mar. 10 31 Jan.

and their comments against the landowner involved are extremely harsh, particularly if the latter insists on lodging a complaint. All the comments follow the same line of argument: that a rich man, who had no need of what had been taken from him by the poor, should not prosecute them; they were hungry and cold, and what they had stolen would probably have been left to rot on the fields and been of no use to anyone.

In the eyes of the poor, the local pattern of social inequality justifies this type of stealing. This does not mean that theft, as such, is not condemned in abstract terms. Nor does the above qualification apply in the very rare cases when a poor man is robbed, or in the case of gypsies. Gypsies are regarded as thieves by nature who rob rich and poor alike.[11]

The ideal norms are clear: one should not beg, and one should not steal. And whatever powerful justifications may be found for infringing them, a debasement of moral standards does take place. To account for this, the distinction is made between an honest man's true *nature* and the alien behaviour to which he is occasionally forced to resort. The impossibility of adhering to the proper norms in day-to-day living, the unbridgeable gap often found between ideal and actual behaviour, undermines any serious claims to moral strength, makes people sceptical, and saps the foundations of their self-respect.

An attitude of cynical resignation to life, often found among labourers, is associated with the material impossibility of living up to ideal standards of behaviour. And although, being poor, they are not in fact expected by others to behave any differently, they carry within themselves the burden of their failure to live up to these standards.

The moral implications of institutionalized charity seem, then, to be different for labourers and landowners—the latter derive

[11] Debts are seen in much the same light as petty theft. Labourers, and even sharecroppers and small landowners, have credit accounts with the local shops which mount up during the year and should be settled after the harvest. In every village there are two or three families (not necessarily among the poorest) who are notorious for their reluctance to pay their accounts and whose reputation suffers in consequence. They are pointed out as *gente sem vergonha* ('shameless people'). But there are many more who are unable to pay the full account, and although the outstanding debts accumulate from year to year this is no reflection on their reputation for honesty. As one debtor told me: '*Um homem tem que fazer ciganices sem ter natureza de cigano*' ('A man has to behave like a gypsy without being one by nature'). When such families are pressed for payment they are pitied, not condemned.

a moral benefit from charity, whereas the former are morally damaged by it. In theft we find an extension of this moral damage, but, for an honourable man, to steal or to beg may be alternatives equally hard to bear. Indeed stealing may be easier to accept: a man who steals and is not caught does not lose prestige, whereas begging is almost always public and therefore openly debasing. Landowners do not see it quite in the same way: they much prefer beggars to thieves.

But the two institutions are part of a traditional way of life which benefits the landowners and from which they derive prestige. They can keep theft under control with the help of the Guards and the courts, and they can decide what alms they are prepared to give away. By giving alms they show both their relative financial strength and their generosity. Only those who have something that can be stolen are victims of theft, and forgiving petty theft is again a way of displaying generosity. These institutions (together with chronic indebtedness) have helped to relieve to some extent the hardships of the poor, but they have become increasingly inadequate since the end of the last century.

Organized Relief

The main method used to prevent migration or starvation of labourers during the slack periods of the agricultural cycle was to provide alternative employment in public works, usually commissioned by the local authorities. At first this met a genuine need in the public works sector. In the last quarter of the nineteenth century the opening and rebuilding of roads was of vital importance. Roads (and railways) were needed for transporting crops to market and, after 1893, for bringing chemical fertilizers to the farms and estates. With agriculture largely non-mechanized and a population much smaller than today, public works were able to absorb most of the labourers temporarily unemployed.

In 1879[12] public works were undertaken because labourers 'would subject themselves to lower wages' since they had no work on the estates. In 1891[13] the Câmara decided to interrupt its road-works programme because the workers were now busy

[12] C.m. 19 Oct. 1879. The first minutes to mention unemployment.
[13] C.m. 28 Aug. 1891.

in the vineyards and their wages had gone up. The same situation recurred just before the 1895 harvest.[14] In 1898 public works were still being undertaken 'in order to take advantage of the low wages' (*aproveitar a ocasião dos jornais serem agora mais baratos*).[15] This wording contrasts sharply with that of a 1916 minute[16] in which an alderman states that certain sums have been allocated in the budget for the road works in progress but that he thinks it is better to postpone such works 'until such time as there is (and one has to accept there will be) a work crisis'. By 1916 the crises had become fully institutionalized, and the main purpose of undertaking public works had become to alleviate the effect of unemployment.[17] Superfluous works were undertaken with the sole purpose of mitigating the effects of the crises, a typical case being the paving of the Rocio[18] in Vila Nova which was done so often that it became known as 'the Rocio of the crises' (*O Rocio das crises*). Similar tactics were employed until the early 1960s: the contractor who worked for the Câmara of Vila Nova deliberately allowed the works to be carried out badly (thinner surfaces for the roads, poorer materials) so that repairs would be needed in one or two years' time, a situation which suited both his own interests and those of the landowners. Public works wages were deliberately kept well below agricultural wages[19] so that, as soon as the yearly cycle reached a phase of demand, men would leave the road for the fields.

Despite the cheap cost of labour, public works projects were beyond the budget of the local authorities, and government help became necessary. Assistance was first sought in 1896 when the Câmara asked the Government to pay for one-third of the road works in progress so that it would not have to dismiss any

[14] C.m. 4 Sept. 1895. [15] C.m. 28 Aug. 1898.

[16] C.m. 4 Sept. 1916.

[17] Landowners have since pressed for public works programmes to be undertaken during the seasonal periods of unemployment. This contrasts with fears expressed at the end of the nineteenth century that public works would raise labourers' wages. See *Documentos Relativos ao Primeiro Congresso Agricola* . . . (Lisboa, 1888), pp. 7, 56, 60, 67.

[18] Rocio is an open space situated just outside towns in Alentejo, where seasonal markets are held.

[19] In the winter of 1965 crisis wages averaged nineteen escudos a day (about five shillings), whereas the minimum agricultural wage was twenty-five escudos (about seven shillings).

labourers[20] Subsidies were again requested in 1905,[21] 1907,[22] and 1908,[23] and from then on the Câmara received subsidies every year. Even with these subsidies, however, public works were insufficient to absorb the surplus of labour, and major crises continued to occur.

The following extracts are relevant: '. . . a crowd of beggars now fills the fields after the end of the harvest', 1905;[24] 'whole families go through the fields begging', 1916;[25] '. . . the crisis is making itself felt in a really fearful manner. Every day large groups of men, women, and children go through villages, towns, and country houses begging', 1932;[26] 'there is a large number of unemployed men in these villages and therefore we find great misery and hunger in many homes', 1937;[27] 'there is a serious crisis, . . . there is hunger, and the fact that begging is forbidden makes things worse', 1948.[28] In February of that year more than one hundred rural workers had been forced to go out and beg.[29] In July 1949, 108 heads of families and 57 other men are reported to be unemployed.[30] In 1954 an estimate of the peak number of unemployed labourers in the crises of the previous five years is given. The relevant figures are set out in the table below:

Year	*Unemployed labourers*	*Estimated labour force*
1950	140	390
1951	180	395
1952	180	400
1953	130	411
1954	120	405

The seriousness of the crises and the manifest impossibility of coping with them either through the traditional forms of charity or through locally organized public works projects, demanded new solutions. Government and landowners were both committed to curbing unemployment. There was less agreement, however, as to who should assume financial responsibility. On several occasions the Government decided that landowners should

[20] C.m. 21 Aug. 1905.
[21] 27 Apr.
[22] 1 Aug.
[23] LN II, 352, 17 Mar. 1916.
[24] 21 Aug.
[25] 21 Sept.
[26] S.c. 21 Jan. 1932.
[27] J.c. 14 Feb. 1937.
[28] C.P.c. 18 Sept. 1948.
[29] C.P.c. 13 Feb. 1948.
[30] Since 1947 a quantitative assessment of unemployment in the freguesia is regularly attempted in the correspondence of the Casa do Povo. On 8 July of that year there were 120 unemployed men, and the figure was expected to rise.

V. Rural labourer

VI. Young factory worker and labourers

carry a greater share of the burden and imposed, or sought to impose, a system of allocating labourers to different landowners in times of crises. The system operated as follows. Landowners were allocated a number of unemployed labourers in proportion to their wealth, and were required to pay them crisis wages and keep them on their estate during working hours, even if there was no work to do. Promoted through reluctant local administrative authorities or corporative bodies, allocations were extremely unpopular with landowners, who resented this form of enforced charity as an unfair added burden to an enterprise already encumbered with very low profit margins. Allocations took place in 1910[31] and 1912[32]. In 1916 a fresh attempt to apply the system met with firm opposition from the landowners, and the authorities were unable to overcome their resistance.[33]

The system appears to have been shelved until 1941, when, acting on instructions from the National Institute of Labour, the Junta de Freguesia of Vila Nova organized the allocation of labourers to landowners on the basis of one man for each 2,000 escudos of the landowner's 'taxable income'. The authorities found it difficult to get landowners to agree to this arrangement. Proprietários raised the most difficulties, and in a letter to the National Institute of Labour the Junta specifically mentioned seven such proprietários 'who lead comfortable lives and could easily give work to a few men, but choose to play the destitute in cases like these.[34]

This partial failure silenced the central authorities for a time, but new and more eventful allocations took place in the winter of 1949. Labourers were allocated on the basis on one man for every 1,500 escudos of a landowner's 'taxable income'.[35] 165 men were allocated to landowners in the freguesia of Vila Velha: some accepted all the men they were sent, some refused outright to take any of the labourers allocated to them, while others accepted a few but not all. The Casa do Povo sent the men back to the reluctant landowners but with the same result. The manager of one of the estates told the men that he could not take

[31] C.m. 12 Dec 1910. [32] LN II, 137, 25 Feb. 1912.

[33] C.m. 20 Mar. 1916.

[34] There is no reference to this in the minutes nor is there a proper record of correspondence at that time. This information comes from a sheaf of papers kept in an envelope labelled *CRISE 1941*, kept in the Junta office.

[35] G.c. 27 Aug. 1949.

them on and was not prepared to give them 'water to drink, firewood to keep them warm, or a roof to protect them from the rain'.[36] Some men reported to the estates daily only to be turned away. When they were eventually accepted on the estate they were dismissed the following morning because thay had refused to work *de ar a ar*. Since such working hours had long since ceased to be customary in the region, this was an obvious manoeuvre to get rid of the men.[37] In other cases men were allowed to stay but were paid no wages.[38] The governing body of the landowners' Grémio eventually persuaded the higher authorities that it was impossible for the majority of landowners to comply with the conditions of the contract and denounced it.[39]

In 1950 the Grémio reluctantly agreed to an allocation on the basis of one man for every 4,000 escudos of a landowner's 'taxable income'.[40] This meant fewer places were available and a fortnight before the harvest the landowners' 'reception capacity' was exhausted and many men had to remain idle.[41] In the winter of 1951 a new allocation was organized and thirteen of the freguesia's main latifundists and proprietários refused to take the men they had been allocated.[42] No further allocations were attempted.

This was a victory for the landowners, and in 1956 their battle to make the Government provide adequate alternative employment was also finally won when a public works project, largely financed by the State, covering the whole province, was organized with the avowed aim of putting an end to seasonal unemployment.

In 1960 the Landowners' Grémio stated that unemployment had disappeared from the region. Nonetheless graph 1 shows that although unemployment had fallen, it still existed in Vila Velha between 1956 and 1965. Labourers always had to wait several days between dismissal from agricultural work and employment on public works, and those who were dismissed first often had to wait for over a fortnight. It if rained (as it did almost constantly during January and February of 1965) there would be no work at all and hence no pay. Even when men

[36] C.P.c. 19 Oct. 1949.
[37] C.P.c. 23 Oct. 1949.
[38] C.P.c. 2 Oct. 1949.
[39] G.c. 15 Nov. 1949.
[40] G.c. 6 Feb. 1950.
[41] G.c. 4 May 1950.
[42] G.c. 21 Feb. 1951.

were employed, the low wages were seldom paid in time because of bureaucratic delays, and the work was much harder than agricultural labour and often carried out on roads and quarries far from their homes. These factors made this form of alternative employment extremely unpopular among the labourers. For them public works were necessary if they were to survive, but they hated them.

These concerted efforts to keep a labour force in the freguesia eventually proved inadequate in the face of competition from outside. There are men from the freguesia now working in and around Lisbon, and in France, Switzerland, Holland, and Great Britain.[43] At the beginning of 1966 the co-ordinated system of public works for relief of unemployment was abandoned. There were still unemployed men during slack periods but the number was so drastically reduced that it was no longer considered worth the expensive and elaborate bureaucracy that co-ordination required.

2. CONFLICT

In exceptional circumstances the conflict of interests between labourers and landowners has become open.

Landowners have always expressed fears of social upheaval during the unemployment crises, but the only times when it did in fact occur coincided with the beginning of the harvest season (late May and early June). This is easily explained: it is at this period that the labourers' position is strongest since all hands are needed in the fields.[44] It is at such times that small wage increases are obtained almost every year, a proportion of

[43] The local paper-mill was not expanded after it took on the first batch of local labourers. There were long application lists for employment, but the mill did not constitute a threat to the landowners.

[44] Local labourers objected to the solution of labour shortages at harvest time by temporary migration from the north. Such migrant movements sporadically occurred until the mid 1950s when they stopped altogether. Labourers from the northern province of Beira now find it more worthwhile to go to France. But even when they came they did not always solve the problem of lack of manpower. Landowners had sometimes to resort to rather desperate pleas to the government which were not heard. In 1923 their association cabled asking for conscripts to be given leave from the army during the harvest and protesting against the migration of labourers to Spain to work on the harvest there at higher wages (19 May). Forty-two years later they repeat their first demand and ask for legal emigration to be stopped (8 Apr. 1965). To ask for leave for the conscripts in 1965 indicates a

the increases often being maintained for the rest of the year. In Vila Velha, however, and for that matter, in the Concelho as a whole, only twice in living memory (in 1911 and 1962) did labourers' demands find collective expression in strikes assuming sufficient strength to force collective concessions from the landowners.

Apart from these two occasions all attempts to improve the labourers' conditions have been made on the basis of individual bargaining between landowner and labourer or small groups of labourers, both sides taking conditions prevalent in neighbouring regions as the point of departure. These attempts have consistently followed the same pattern from as far back as people can remember.

Labourers working for a landowner would agree amongst themselves that wages were too low for the work they were doing and one or two of the more vocal among them, generally young bachelors, approached the *patrão* ('employer') or sometimes the manager if they were working on one of the big estates. As a rule their complaints were heard out, but at the end of the week wages would not be increased and those who had advanced the claim for an increase were dismissed. Although the labourers involved had agreed beforehand to work only for the new wages claimed, they failed to respect the agreement and continued to work for the old rate. Sometimes wages were increased two or three weeks later. This was such a consistent pattern that labourers generally agreed on the foolishness of such attempts to obtain higher wages, and this contributes to their sceptical attitude towards any collective effort.

Bargaining is part of the arrangements between landowners and heads of piece-work gangs that take place before the harvest when a piece-work price is eventually agreed. Labourers working for wages as reinforcements for the piece-work gangs sometimes demand increases after the harvest has begun. Although they are in a stronger bargaining position then than at other times of the year,[45] they have to proceed cautiously. As landowners

desperate need for manpower. Most landowners, including all those who direct the Grémio, are avowed supporters of the Government's African policies and would not suggest any measures that might undermine the success of these policies, if they did not feel themselves to be in an extremely difficult situation.

[45] Wages for these men always increase from the first to the third week of the harvest, and are then reduced again in the fourth week.

and managers put it: if they come 'with their hats in their hands' at the end of a week's work, an acceptable deal can be made. But if they lay down their sickles in the middle of the week and come with what are regarded as arrogant or threatening manners, they have no chance of success and will be dismissed. Because these are all isolated instances, the latifundists can even afford to lose part of their crop for lack of harvesters, rather than submit to their claims.[46] Collective action by labourers on a bigger scale was only possible when political and social agitation in the outside world made itself felt.

The first occasion on which effective collective action was taken by labourers in the freguesia was during the labour unrest following the intensive political activity that preceded and accompanied the republican revolution of October 1910. Labourers became politically conscious as a result of the active propaganda campaigns that swept the country, and once the Republic was established, organized labour groups pressed for a settlement of their grievances. Enthusiasm was high throughout the province, and in the winter of 1910, immediately after the revolution, labourers made their first attempt to gain substantial overall wage increases. The timing was bad (labour is not in demand during the winter season) and their attempts failed,[47] but as soon as conditions allowed, they renewed their demands. Labour unrest came to a head at the beginning of June

[46] The latifundists' awareness of the relative strength of their position is such that when a labourer who had been dismissed set fire to a wheat field, the only comment of the latifundist concerned was: 'the match he used cost him more than the wheat cost me.' Arson of this type sometimes occurred in the past, but I know of no case in the last fifteen years.

[47] In the first days of December 1910, a large number of local labourers met and, according to the report published in a local newspaper (LN II 70, 4 Dec. 1910) which claimed not to know whether they had been 'led to this by someone else or not' (a political innuendo), decided to ask the *lavradores* and proprietários of the concelho for a wage increase, to be progressively increased later 'according to the difficulty of the work and the length of the working day'. Their demands were not met, and in any case rain brought work to a standstill. Some of the labourers involved appeared before the Câmara in person on 5 Dec. 1910 to report that, since it was still raining, they had been forced to resort to begging. They asked for a wage increase as soon as work could be resumed, since this had been granted in other concelhos. The Câmara replied that a committee would be set up to arrange for the collection of subscriptions to tide over the period of unemployment. It pointed out that landowners would dismiss men rather than increase wages: the increase was impossible since it would paralyse agriculture, and the Câmara suggested longer working hours to make up the money.

1911 and a general strike was organized throughout the province.

Two labour leaders from the provincial capital arrived in the concelho to help organize local strike action and a meeting was held in the main square of Vila Nova on 5 June to discuss the labourers' claims. A thousand men (150 from the freguesia of Vila Velha) turned up in support of the strike and its claims.[48]

The Câmara called a meeting of landowners through the Syndicato, and a committee was appointed which came to terms with the strikers. The minutes of the Câmara session record that 'an agreement was reached at considerable cost to local agriculture [i.e. the landowners] but the circumstances of the negotiations and the fact that concessions had already been made by landowners from other concelhos, led the landowners to accept the agreement as an urgent measure to avoid possible conflicts whose seriousness it was impossible to foresee. The general lack of culture among the claimants had led them to make some claims that were more than local agriculture could sustain without accumulated damage to its economy.'[49]

The claims which the landowners agreed to meet were: a wage increase, the abolition of piece-work and night work (with some few exceptions), the retention of *ar a ar* hours of work for harvesting and threshing only and *de sol a sol* hours for all other tasks, the institution of a *praça*[50] every Sunday. Preference was to be given to local workers, no able-bodied men were to refuse work, and begging was to be strictly forbidden for healthy men and women.

Once the harvest was over, however, many landowners refused to continue to comply with the agreement, particularly with the clauses covering wages and hours of work. The directors of the Workers' Association, who had been the most prominent local organizers of the strike, decided to seek a compromise, and on the morning of 18 July went to see the *Administrador de Concelho* proposing new terms of agreement and lower wage rates.

[48] The minutes of the Câmara session held on 8 June 1911 record that the aldermen had not met on the previous Monday 'because of the danger represented by a big crowd'.

[49] C.m. 8 June 1911.

[50] *Praça* was the labour-market. Labourers gathered in one of the squares of Vila Nova and landowners collected them from there. It did not exist in the freguesia since the settlements were too small for it to be needed.

He recommended moderation, but had them arrested the following afternoon and sent to prison in Lisbon. They returned to Vila Nova some days later, provisionally at liberty, were brought to trial in November, and sentenced to short terms of imprisonment.[51]

Old men in the freguesia who still remember the strike say that the leaders were all 'good workers' and that if they had been otherwise they could not possibly have rallied so many followers. The strength of their claims was based on their awareness of what was due to them as productive workers. The leaders of the movement were certainly exceptional men: all those brought to trial could read and write. It was alleged in court that fellow workers had paid one of the leaders a daily wage of 700 *reis* to lead them. (This was the wage claimed by the strikers for that period of the year.) Another of the leaders, when questioned on his motives, said that labourers had always been exploited and that he was only helping them to defend their rights. Although some of the witnesses were threatened with imprisonment and deportation by the Administrador de Concelho at the preliminary enquiry, and may have adjusted their statements in view of this, there was no suggestion that land reform was mentioned by the accused. During the trial a local newspaper charged them with being led astray by the influence of political ideas on the 'mirage of social equality', but they were making demands from their position of labourers, not attempting to change that position. These demands made life more difficult for their employers but did not directly threaten the latter's ownership of land. The newspaper states that in the period between the signature of the agreement and repression by the authorities a number of families who usually hired men for the harvest had been obliged to bring it in themselves, that the Syndicato had cut back drastically on its advance orders for fertilizers, and that some landowners were thinking of renting or selling their land, while tenants would abandon the land if rents were not lowered.[52] In the letter to the Civil Governor which was sent to Lisbon with the arrested strike leaders, the

[51] The files of their trial are found in the Vila Nova court archives (*Polícia Correccional* 1° Oficio, Maço 7, n° 36) and except where otherwise stated all the information used here is taken from these files.

[52] LN II 99, 22 June 1911.

Adminstrador of the Concelho states that they were upsetting the 'natural order and interfering with the freedom of work', that they were making impossible demands on the landowners and spreading false ideas among the workers, and that peace would only be restored 'once they had been removed from the concelho.'

A belief in this 'natural order' was not shared by the labourers. After the strike agreement had been signed, the Workers' Association of one of the freguesias complained, in a letter to the Administrador of the Concelho, that landowners were ignoring the clause abolishing piece-work and that workers would soon 'find themselves returning to the old slavery'. Although not all of them expressed themselves so clearly, the fact is that there were a thousand men at the meeting held in Vila Nova on 5 June in support of strike action.

It is only possible to understand the outbreak and the eventual failure of the strike if it is seen within the general context of Portuguese political and social conditions at the time which cannot be discussed here. What is important, however, is the fact in itself. Local conditions were ripe for a strike, but no more so in 1911 than in 1910 or 1912 or indeed in any other year. Nonetheless it had to be sparked off from outside.[53]

The degree to which labourers were aware of what the strike involved must have varied, and political consciousness was certainly stronger in the main agricultural towns of the province than in the remoter areas. When the agreement was signed in Vila Nova, for instance, the labourers are alleged to have asked for 'the same conditions as those of the Evora[54] agreement', although it appeared that nobody seemed to know exactly what those were until someone finally managed to produce a printed copy. Events in one of the villages of Vila Velha were even more startling: elderly people still remember that when it became known that the strike was on its way (*vem aí a greve*) everyone in the village shut himself up at home because its exact nature was not understood. Once the strike has started, however, with all its potential violence, the sheer difference in numbers between

[53] Old labourers remember that the wheat was particularly hard in 1911 and hence more difficult to harvest. This may have played a part by giving more justification to the labourers' position. But it could not have been a cause of the strike.

[54] The provincial capital where the strike had started.

the two opposed groups would probably have led to very different results, had there not been outside intervention, this time in support of the landowners. The republican government sent in the army, and the strike was crushed throughout the province.

Although civil disturbances are known to have occurred on various occasions since 1911 in other parts of Alentejo, it was only in 1962 that rural unrest again came to a head in the concelho. Once more it was part of a general strike movement.[55] During the 1962 harvest, labourers throughout the province pressed a claim for an eight-hour day, which concealed, in fact a demand for the total abolition of piece-work for harvesting. Strike action in support of this claim was organized;[56] landowners' reactions varied, and the movement itself spread with differing local consequences. In some concelhos the claims were met immediately, in others the struggle was prolonged. The Grémio of Vila Nova organized a meeting of landowners who agreed not to give in to the labourers' claims. A few days later, however, some of those who had attended the meeting broke the agreement, and from then on a united front was no longer possible. Labourers pressed their claims on several estates, but the most active were those on the estates of the mayor himself. After failing to persuade the workers to accept traditional conditions, he sent for the Guards and asked the Ministry of the Interior to send soldiers to the town, but was refused. The Câmara registered the facts in its minutes and commented: 'We all know that agitators in the pay of foreigners (*a soldo do estrangeiro*) and coming from outside the concelho were responsible for such demands, damaging to the national economy and even to the labourers who unwittingly put them forward. Only those who have never done any harvesting will find it difficult to

[55] Although no mention of an abnormal situation is to be found in Câmara or Syndicato papers, the following notice was printed on the front page of a local newspaper in 1932. 'It has come to our attention that several more labourers have recently refused to work. Anyone who has witnessed such refusals is asked to send the name of the labourer concerned to this newspaper.' (LN IIa, 10, 12, and 19, 12 June 1932.) (The newspaper was edited by a man who had been the last mayor under the monarchy and was financed by one of the more zealous right-wing landowners.) I was unable to establish precisely what this item meant. Since press censorship was established in 1926, even official minutes and letters have become more discreet in their references to matters of this kind.

[56] Allegedly by the underground Communist Party. Strikes are illegal in Portugal now but, on certain conditions, they were not in 1911.

grasp that an eight-hour day, with two unbroken periods of four hours each, will wear out even the strongest worker. The old system is more practical and is also better financially.'[57] The minutes go on to state, untruthfully, that all the landowners in the concelho are firmly opposed to the eight-hour day and end by thanking the mayor for having taken action over the incident. In Vila Velha, although there were no open conflicts, the eight-hour day was gradually introduced, beginning with state-sponsored public works in 1963.

As in 1911, the movement came from outside. There was one main difference, however: Government and landowners did not feel as threatened as in 1911 by the demands of the labourers, and these were eventually met. The Republican Guard and the political police kept a firm hand on the more troubled regions to prevent agitation from continuing once the limited goals of the strikers were achieved.

At the risk of some repetition, it is worth emphasizing the main points that emerge from analysis of the 1911 and 1962 strikes.

First, although local conditions are such that any year would have offered equally good opportunities for pressing collective and organized claims, in fact they were only put forward on two occasions, in both cases as part of a general movement affecting the freguesia from outside. Once the claims were put forward, however, the landowners were obliged to resort to outside help to safeguard their position. The strikes offer particularly illustrative instances of the region's dependence on the outside world.

The second point is that, as suddenly as they appeared, the strikes were over, without leaving, in either case, any trace of an organization that could support any further claims by the labourers. This was also to be expected. In 1911 there were freely elected associations which provided the local basis for organization of labourers, but they were dissolved by the authorities over the strikes and were not revived afterwards. Nothing similar existed in 1962. There are no legal political parties in Portugal today, nor are there representative trade unions whose local branches could take action over labour problems. *Ad hoc* local organizations tend to collapse after a very short time, particularly if they are regarded by the authorities as

[57] 23 May 1962.

liable to take an anti-government line. Once external pressure ceased and the strikes were over, the labourers had no organization on which to fall back in order to seek vindication of any further claims.

Thirdly, neither in 1911 nor in 1962 was there any collectively expressed hope for a change in the property structure. Labourers fought *qua* labourers within a given order; they did not query that order. This contrasts sharply with the situation in Andalucia described by Diaz del Moral[58] and must be attributed to less effective political instruction. Even in present-day conditions labourers express, in private, the conviction that land should be redistributed. But, in the absence of outside stimulus and support, individual aspirations are not organized in any significant and operative way.

Fourthly, although the presence of the outside world may act as a factor for strengthening community feelings in exceptional circumstances, the strikes illustrate another result of the impact of the outside world on the community. The policies of the State have helped so far to perpetuate latent conflicts, while not allowing them to be openly expressed and solved. Civil peace and public order are thus maintained, but do not result from an historical evolution of mutual concessions made between landowners and labourers. They are not part of an accepted social contract from which violence would have been implicitly ruled out. On the contrary, violent outcomes are implicitly accepted and feared, and the 1911 and 1962 strikes show that they can take place. On such occasions local patterns of social life are upset. The two conflicting groups move from latent to overt hostility, and their relative positions may be better understood if they are considered not only in local terms, but also as elements in a much wider, potential class struggle. Law and order tend to prevail, partly because working-class consciousness and loyalties are ill-defined and difficult to express for lack of political organization and for fear of repression, and partly because local loyalties and compromises cut across the class structure and function as mechanisms of social and political control.[59]

[58] cf. Diaz del Moral, *op. cit.*

[59] A fuller discussion of this problem is carried out in the Epilogue, after other institutions of the society have been analyzed.

There is a final important point. Until a few years ago the minority group that owned land hoped to retain it, while the majority group that worked the land hoped, one day to be able to obtain a share. As long as general economic conditions made land profitable and alternative forms of employment and investment were, in practice, beyond the reach of the local people, the system continued to operate. Labourers did not go away, landowners went to some expense to make their land more profitable. Millennarian hopes (and fears) of agrarian reform were at the same time an expression of local tensions and a proof that such tensions arose from a shared belief in the value of land.

This is no longer so. The land is still there, but there is less eagerness to keep or acquire it. The problem has not been solved: it has been diluted in a wider measure. As migrants and emigrants, labourers are beginning to move into a wider world where they still find themselves at the bottom rung of the social ladder, but their struggle to move upwards, either at an individual or at a collective level, is no longer confined within the narrow boundaries of Vila Velha.

PART TWO
FAMILY, KINSHIP, AND NEIGHBOURHOOD

VII

NAMORO

FAMILY begins with marriage, and social stratification conditions the choice of marriage partners in Vila Velha. Latifundists marry among themselves or marry outsiders whose wealth and prestige are comparable to their own. The same applies to the proprietários. Seareiro families marry into other seareiro families, and people from labouring stock marry into the same group. In recent years, however, the financial decline of the seareiros, the increase in labourers' wages and the establishment of the mill, have tended to blur the distinctions between the two groups and have led to the emergence of a single marriage market. This marriage market does not, as a rule, extend beyond the freguesia, except in the west, where, for at least four generations, seareiros from one of the villages have married seareiros from an adjoining freguesia. Conversely, there is a tendency among the labourers to marry not only within the freguesia but within their own villages. The marriage market of the proprietários, on the other hand, extends to nearby freguesias and concelhos. That of the latifundists covers the whole of the latifundia areas of the south and, in recent years, has extended to include wealthy people from all over the country.

In Vila Velha, in the last thirty years or so, this order has been infringed only twice. Two sons of proprietários married below their rank, one marrying the daughter of seareiro and the other the daughter of a labourer. Both men were slightly defective intellectually, however, and would have found it difficult to marry within their own group. At first their families opposed the marriages, but later came to accept them.[1] This almost

[1] Where the positions are reversed (as when a wealthy heiress wishes to marry a man of socially inferior rank) the outcome is generally quite different. I did not come across any such marriages during my field-work, but I learned that there had been two or three cases in the province of heiresses who had been declared insane by their families because they had wanted to marry below their own class. Although these cases occurred some sixty years ago they are still remembered.

total absence of inter-group marriage is a result of the widely extended segregation of the different groups. Young people are confined mainly to their own social groups. Schooling, dances, parties, and reciprocal visiting among the respective families obey the limitations imposed by social position and help to prevent the development of sentimental attachments which would conflict with social position.

The recreational societies in Vila Nova where young people often meet reflect this social stratification: the 'Club' is for the latifundists, professional men, high ranking civil servants, and, recently, one or two wealthy shopkeepers; the '*Artística*' is frequented by better-off artisans, shopkeepers, clerks, and proprietários, and the '*Atlético*' is mainly for labourers. Industrial workers are among the members of the *Atlético*, but a few have been accepted by the *Artística*. The societies have facilities for games, drinking, and television and are used each evening as meeting-places for men. On festive occasions dances are organized for members and their families. Many courtships begin at these dances and the stratified nature of the choice of spouse is formalized in them. To belong to one of the societies is to be a member of one of the three marriage markets, or to make them available to one's sons and daughters.

In the freguesia itself there are no recreational societies. Dances are held privately, and those who attend strictly follow the pattern of social stratification. In the local public feasts these patterns determine the way in which people cluster in different groups.

Property is therefore usually matched in marriage, since spouses are chosen from each of the social and economic groups and not from the population as a whole. Within each group, however, marriage is very much the result of the free option of those who enter into it.

People establish the courtship relationships that necessarily precede marriage of their own free will. These courtship relationships are institutionalized under the general name of *namoro*. The parents of those concerned in a namoro may show various degrees of approval or disapproval, but only very rarely will they offer any efficient opposition. In landless and landed families alike, the matter is left very much to the discretion and judgement of the young man and woman

VII. The dangers of womanhood

VIII. Mother and daughter

involved,[2] and sentiment determines the overwhelming majority of the marriages that take place.

An indication of the personal nature of matrimonial arrangements is the absence of a dowry. Brides do not bring to marriage more than their trousseaux, which vary according to the financial position of their families but do not represent any considerable part of the wealth to which they may eventually be entitled by inheritance, if they belong to landed families. The transfer of substantial amounts of money and property from one generation to the next takes place at death and not on the marriage of a son or daughter. Bride and groom do not gain the detailed knowledge of the financial situation of their families which is necessarily imparted in societies where the transfer of property takes place at marriage. Moreover, the wealth of a family may increase or diminish between the marriage of a child and the death of the parents. All this tends to reinforce the sentimental side of marriage and to weaken the influence of the family in the choice of a spouse. Namoro is best understood when seen in this light. The purpose of the relationship is the creation of a new, independent, and self-sufficient individual family unit, not the establishment of an alliance between two kinship groups.

A namoro seldom lasts less than three years. A few decades ago it would normally be of much longer duration, though namoros lasting seven or eight years are found even today. There are several reasons for this. An obvious one in the labourer group is that the bride's trousseau and the furnishings for the couple's future home have to be bought, mainly with money saved from the meagre wages of the two *namorados*. This also applies—although less rigidly—to the sons and daughters of small landowners. Among the wealthier families the young man is expected to have taken his university degree or finished his technical training (and generally he does not do so before the age of twenty-four) or to have definitely given up his studies and settled down to working with his father, before he contemplates marriage. He ought to be able to support his household without

[2] Until the end of the last century, there were cases in which landed families made matches in order to secure a convenient property arrangement, the Church being asked sometimes to give special permission for the marriages of first cousins or uncles and nieces. But these are things that belong to the past.

the need of family allowances. In all groups, a young man is generally considered fit for marriage only after he has completed his three or four years of military service.

A namoro relationship generally begins when the girl is fourteen or fifteen and the young man three or four years older. It is formalized about a year after when the young man sees the girl's father and asks his official permission to court her. From then on a namoro should continue until marriage, and marriage in its turn should last until death. Ideally people should not have more than one namoro.

The behaviour of the *namorados* is assumed to foreshadow the future behaviour of the spouses. The girl's modesty and the young man's capacity to save and look after the money he earns will show that they are both gearing their lives to marriage. The girl's duties in the relationship are stricter than those of her *namorado*. When she goes to dances she should dance only with him; if he is absent, she should stay away altogether. Talking to unrelated men is reduced to a bare minimum and even her way of walking becomes stiff and self-conscious. The eyes and ears of her village will be only too willing to detect the slightest evidence of any behaviour improper to her status. And if this happens, her life may become difficult. Even if the rumours or gossip are false, her reputation suffers nonetheless. Ideally *namorados* are not supposed to have sexual intercourse, and among proprietário and latifundist families the supposition is mostly correct. Their meeting always take place in the presence of some members of the girl's family. It is therefore easier for girls of these groups to begin a new namoro if the first one fails. In the poor groups, however, this is not so. Many girls have sexual relations with their *namorados* and even those who do not, have considerable physical intimacy with them. Poor *namorados* are left alone on their doorsteps during the evenings and on their way to and from the fields they often manage to escape and be alone together. If the namoro ends, the chances for the girl to start another are remote. A woman who has been *cevada* (literally 'used by a pig'), i.e. who is known to have had amorous physical contact with a man, is defiled and will not be acceptable to another man if he is to keep his ideal self-respect. Defloration of the woman one marries—either before or after marriage—is a basic assumption and all departures from this norm have to be accounted for by exceptional circumstances.[3]

There are, of course, cases in which a girl ends a namoro and afterwards starts a new one with an eligible young man whom she eventually marries. This is likely to happen if the first namoro was of short duration, but, whatever its duration, there must be no suggestion that she ever had sexual intercourse with her first *namorado*.

Young women known to have had intercourse with *namorados* who have broken off the namoro or to have had affairs with other men are precluded from contracting a proper marriage. Some have tried to commit suicide: Luíza, whose second *namorado* was told by a drunken friend that she had had intercourse with the first, threw herself into a well when he broke off their namoro. This action gave credit to the man's suspicions. Many others remain spinsters, some becoming the occasional lovers of wealthier men. A few do marry, but in far from ideal circumstances: Ana, who had been seduced by a landowner when she was very young and had given birth to a stillborn child, married a labourer who had poor health and little wit, and then only when both of them were in their late thirties. Amelia, daughter of a proprietário, was supposed to have had a love affair with a priest and, although attractive and prosperous, could not marry, and eventually went to live with Jorge, a proprietário with a reputation for cuckoldry and weakness, whose wife had left him. She enjoys the material comforts of married life but is barred from the moral prominence associated with it.

The wisest course for a girl to follow is not to allow her first *namorado* any extreme physical intimacies and to try to keep him, even when circumstances seem adverse. If she fails to marry him she will face a regrettable but respectable spinsterhood. If she eventually marries him, she enters marriage with the added prestige arising from the consistency and modesty displayed during her years of namoro.

[3] Young men who go off to do their military service sometimes leave *namoradas* behind. Since 1961, they usually serve two years in Africa. To guarantee that their *namoradas* will wait for them, some of these men deflower them before leaving (if they have not already done so). In this way they eliminate the possibility that some other man will try to take advantage of their absence and begin a namoro with their *namoradas*.

A paradigmatic case is that of Penelope, the daughter of a rural worker. She had a namoro with a young man from a nearby village which had lasted for five years when he joined the Navy. After two years abroad, he wrote to her saying that an early marriage was not possible, that she would probably not want to wait, and that it would, therefore, be better for both of them if they went their separate ways. Four years elapsed with no further news from him, and then his family received a letter informing them that he had settled in Lisbon and started a namoro with a Lisbon girl. His mother immediately wrote back saying that he ought to marry 'the girl he left behind', who had always been faithful to him. Her fidelity had involved six years of not attending dances, a modest demeanour at all times, and the refusal of a job as a maid in Vila Nova because there were young men in the house. The sailor came back to the village some weeks later and spent a week gathering information about the girl's behaviour during his absence. They were married two months later—she being twenty-eight and he thirty-one. 'I could have married a girl in Lisbon earning 2,000 escudos a month in her job', he said, 'but this one knew how to wait for me and how to respect me before marriage—and this augurs well for the future.'

In recent years, increasing contact with a wider and more complex society has led to some changes in the traditional patterns of namoro. An interplay takes place between the traditional set of values that imposes a rigid and prolonged faithfulness on the girl and obliges her *namorado* to marry her if she maintains this, and a more tolerant attitude towards lapses in the behaviour of both. This allows for a wider range of morally accepted options—more second namoros for girls, more breaking off of namoros for men, shorter namoros—but the basic assumptions underlying the institution of namoro have remained the same. It is a preparation for marriage and a trial of the characteristics of the prospective spouses which would be likely to ensure, eventually, a stable family life. The most important of these characteristics is an ability to earn or manage money on the part of the man; and sexual modesty on the part of the woman. A woman enters marriage with the hope that she will not have to work outside her household or, if she belongs to the poor groups, that at least she will not have to beg. The material support of the family is the responsibility of the husband.

A man enters marriage hoping that he will not become a cuckold. The bride's virginity and the wife's fidelity are the basic moral assumptions on which the family is built. The ideal state for a woman is a state of purity, but purity is only one part of her nature: her *vício* ('vice'), the predisposition responsible for the potential social dangers attached to her active sexual life[4], is also part of it. Between puberty and climacteric[5] the moral integrity of a woman is threatened by her *vício*. Before she marries, her virginity should be protected from it, and during the years of namoro she has to show the disposition that will make her a modest and faithful wife, able to control her *vício* against the temptations of adultery, thus securing an honourable reputation for her family and her husband.

[4] The whitewashing of houses, carried out several times a year, is a feminine task. Even when new houses are built, whitewashing is generally done by women, unless men are out of work as a result of a serious unemployment crisis. White is for purity, the houses are white, and the house is the realm of the woman. When women are menstruating, however, they are not allowed to perform this task.

[5] Girls before puberty and women who have passed their climacteric are not supposed to carry *vício*. The word *vício*, when applied to men, generally refers to drinking or gambling—traditional ways for men to endanger the stability of their families. But their libido is not a *vício*, since it cannot disrupt their family life or threaten their reputation, except in the rare cases of homosexuality or incest.

VIII

HUSBAND AND WIFE

THE HUSBAND

A man reaches full manhood only when he marries. Until then he is still a *rapaz* ('boy'). In the taverns, when games between married and unmarried men are organized, the rival groups are not described as bachelors and married men but as boys (*rapazes*) and men (*homens*). Old bachelors are looked upon with some pity and are even slightly despised and scorned. Most of them have to do some of the domestic chores usually performed by women when they live by themselves, but this in itself does not entirely account for the attitude towards them[1] since rich bachelors have female servants to do their domestic work. The slight contempt or the feeling that there is something odd about a middle-aged bachelor is found at all levels of society and springs from the feeling that for one reason or another he has not been entrusted with the full responsibility of manhood, i.e. marriage.

After marriage a man becomes a head of family, an elector to the Junta, and the owner and/or guardian of the family property. Even if an ante-nuptial contract has been signed—and this is frequent nowadays among the wealthy—a wife cannot dispose of any part of her property without her husband's consent. Conversely, as long as the marriage lasts, he will be responsible for any debts contracted by her and, if they decide to live separately, all children she may eventually bear are still legally his. His financial responsibilities will be increased and his freedom of movement curtailed. He knows, from observation, that after the first years of marriage his wife's attentions will be more and more devoted to their children

[1] Some indulge in sexual practices with animals. At least two elderly bachelors had sporadic relations with a local homosexual, and although this was viewed as odd, they were not considered homosexual themselves. The luckier ones manage to come to some sort of arrangement with some widow or spinster in her forties from the lower social groups. Rich, elderly bachelors solve their sexual problems with urban prostitutes or with women of the poor groups whom they pay.

and less and less to him. Indeed his sons will be so favoured by their mother that there will be little room left for him in her affections in a few years' time. And if he has only daughters, or more daughters than sons, he will have to cope with further moral and financial responsibilities in the future.

His responsibilities towards the women of his new household contribute most both to the strength and to the vulnerability of his new position. A young bachelor is by definition a potential philanderer. His status, conferred on him by his age and his sex, gives him great freedom in sexual matters. The risks he incurs are slight, even if he does get involved with several girls, and the possibility of philandering (which is in theory not completely excluded for married men) is not tempered by the sense of responsibility he must assume after he marries. Moreover, the women of his household do not represent the same potential liability to his honour as does a wife. He may of course have been born out of wedlock which, theoretically is a dishonourable beginning, affecting his honour from the outset. There are some such men in the freguesia but the circumstances of their birth do not in practice prevent them from building as honourable a life as any other man of the same social group. Among the poor, the few who have eventually managed to be recognized as the illegitimate sons of landowners have even benefited from their irregular birth. It may also happen that their mothers were caught in adultery and had to leave home and village. But in most cases the sons were mere children at the time and are hence immune from direct blame.

Sisters do not create great problems of honour either. Ideally, a young man should protect his sisters from the less honourable intentions of other men. But the need for such action seldom arises. The villages are small and there are few outsiders. Local men will not, as a rule, attempt any violence against local women. I know of no case of rape. There are married men who have, or try to have, affairs with single women, but these are very secretive moves which often involve men of the wealthy landowning group against whom the girl's brothers would be unable to react openly anyway. Situations that could indeed require the intervention of the girl's brother, if he performed his theoretical duties with respect to honour, arise out of broken namoros. Here again, however, nothing of consequence really happens.

If the blame for the break is put entirely on the man, a certain estrangement or even a severance of the relationship may take place between the *namorado* and the brother. In other cases they continue on the same friendly terms as before.[2]

When a man becomes a husband, however, matters are quite different. He becomes for the first time the full trustee of a woman's honour, and her behaviour is intimately tied up with his reputation and the fate of their family. The risk of his wife's adultery (and even the most carefully chosen wife may err in this respect) is the risk of perpetual dishonour: if it happens he will be forever a *cabrão* or *corno* ('cuckold').

Because he has now become a full member of the community, he is also a trustee of the reputation of the community itself. A frequent expression of localism is the assertion that women of a nearby village have a strong propensity for adultery and therefore that men are cuckolds there more than elsewhere. The historical decay of Vila Velha was explained by a proprietário living in one of the villages as a consequence of the past debauchery of its women.

Marriage is, therefore, a dangerous proposition, but the courage and ability to face it are the marks of a true man. Attitudes towards bachelors (and homosexuals) can now be better understood. Homosexuals are biologically, so to say, outside the male sex and their fate is considered below that of a criminal. Elderly heterosexual bachelors are still regarded as men, but because they have failed to marry after a certain age, they have evaded (albeit unwillingly) their share of the risks involved in protecting the good name of the community against the dangers implicit in the sexuality of its women, thus increasing the burden of those who took the step of marrying. And they cannot, therefore, enjoy a reputation comparable to that arising from the harassed but honourable status of a married man.

Given the division of roles in marriage, a man knows little about the affairs of the household: this is the wife's province and he leaves it entirely to her.

If, however, he learns through a relative, generally an

[2] If the girl has been seduced by her former *namorado*, a court action may be brought against him by her family. The stain on the family honour is not wiped out by any direct action from her father or brothers.

elderly woman, that his wife is secretly protecting a namoro of their daughter's or that she spends too much time outside the home on errands to the shops and in small talk with neighbours or that she is otherwise becoming an object of public disapproval and gossip, he gives her a thorough beating to remind her who is master in the home. In many cases these beatings have little effect, but when they are made public by the neighbours who heard the wife's screams, there is general approval. This illusion of marital authority is well expressed in the saying painted on decorated plates or pottery to be found in some kitchens: *Cá em casa manda ela/Quem manda nela sou eu* ('she rules the home but I rule her'). The wishful thinking behind this saying is the public assumption on which the whole fabric of family life is based. In private, however, a man will recognize the boundaries of the wife's realm and consider it improper to trespass.

Ostensibly and publicly the wife's position should be one of subordination. When a woman dies the bells toll twice only, whereas for a man they toll three times. If a man praises his wife in conversation, he will first make some qualification, making it clear that because she is a woman she cannot be expected to attain moral perfection. When a couple go out together, the wife often walks a little behind. On the rare occasions when a man invites friends home for a meal, the wife eats at a separate table after the men have finished. But this apparent subordination is contradicted by the fact that, although the husband does not trespass upon the wife's territory, she often enters his. He may even accept this with resignation. Domingos Silva, a tavern owner in Vila Velha, decided to hire out his tavern on the day of the September feast. He was tired of missing the feast every year as the result of being confined behind the counter day and night. His wife opposed the idea, since she thought it would be a pity to lose the brisk trade of the feast days. They discussed the matter and she seemed to be convinced by his arguments. He then asked Raimundo, the man who is in charge of delivering the mail in the freguesia, to distribute advertisements stating that the tavern was for hire during the feast. There were no replies and Domingos Silva had to spend yet another feast day behind the counter. He commented afterwards: 'One of two things has happened. Either Raimundo really forgot to distribute the advertisements—as he confessed the other day—or my wife told him not to do so. I think the latter is the more likely explanation.' This was said, not as a protest, but rather as an admission of his wife's right to intervene, even in the management of his affairs.

The legal dispositions which make the husband the head of the family, the elector, the evident source of power and authority, conceal the fact that, among all but the latifundists and wealthiest proprietários, the wife has extensive power and authority herself. This is so widely recognized, however, that one of the minutes of the local Misericórdia records that subsidies above a certain number of escudos will be given to poor families 'only in the rare event that *both heads* of the family [i.e. the husband and the wife] are unable to earn a living'.[3]

THE WIFE

A woman is supposed to surrender her virginity to her husband on the first night of their marriage. In many cases this does not happen, since the couple may have had sexual relations during their namoro, but the fiction is maintained. The bride's friends will help her to prepare the bed with brand-new linen of the best quality she can afford, and it is shown off to relatives and neighbours, particularly the women who are very eager to see the *cama do primeiro dia* ('first-day bed'). The bed-linen should be put away and not used again except for the marriage of the eldest daughter, although this rule is often broken in times of financial hardship. The ceremonial bed is a symbol of the bride's successful struggle against her *vício*—a struggle which has lasted since puberty—and the attendant publicity represents the account rendered to the community of this intimate and fundamental fact. Even very poor brides have a 'first-day bed': it marks their proper accession to the enviable status conferred by marriage, 'the nicest of states' (*o mais bonito estado*) as the traditional song puts it. Legally, the change in the woman's status is not radical: she passes from one legal tutelage (that of her father) to another (that of her husband), and it is only if she becomes a widow that she acquires the legal status of a head of family. In practice, however, matters

[3] Mm. 10 June 1928. This minute was written by a local man, not by a Civil Servant.

stand very differently. From a rather subdued position in her parents' home she comes to a prominent one in her own.

The traditional division of roles between the couple leaves the household duties to the wife. The preparation of food is entirely her province. Some years ago, a poor wife would also make all her husband's clothes, and even nowadays the appearance of her husband and children, outward manifestations of the honour and pride of her family, is held to be the wife's responsibility. If she is fussy over such matters, the argument she uses runs: 'What sort of wife (or mother) will people say you have if you go out looking like this?'

Except among latifundists or wealthy proprietários, she is also the family treasurer. And if her husband is a wage labourer or a poor salaried worker, her control over the family budget is complete. The husband gives her his wages every Saturday evening, taking small amounts in the course of the week for buying cigarettes, for drinking wine in the tavern, and for having himself shaved by the barber once a week. To be able to manage the family budget properly, she must not allow herself any form of extravagance. An extremely mean woman may be scorned, but she is not subject to the harsh criticism that would be made if she were extravagant. Meanness may affect the external community, the outsiders, but extravagance hurts her family, and her first duties are towards husband and children. She haggles, cent by cent, over every item she buys. Indeed the hawker expects this to happen, since bargaining is usual in these transactions, and he may express his contempt for a woman who does not beat him down with the usual efficiency and pays him more for the goods than others do. Besides the role of treasurer, poor women generally also have that of wage earner during the short periods in which feminine labour is needed in agriculture. Girls are, however, becoming increasingly reluctant to work in the fields, and even when this was not so, the wife's wages contributed only a small proportion of the family's total earnings.

An executive role, which finds various expressions, is also attributed to the poor wife. In the past, husbands often spent long periods on the estates when they worked away from home, coming back only at week-ends or once a fortnight. More recently, unemployment has led men to seek work in state-sponsored public works being carried out in other concelhos. During these absences, wives were even more responsible for the household, and this rendered them much more capable than their husbands of dealing with problems involving money and of handling relations with local authorities.

In recent years when migration and emigration became new factors for change in this society, women were of paramount importance in the decisions taken by those who eventually emigrated or decided to stay. On hearing of successful migrants from other concelhos, wives often insisted that their husbands should go, although they themselves stayed behind, at least during their husbands' first few seasons as field hands for the French sugar-beet harvest. To have a husband in France became a matter of some prestige, and the suffering entailed in separation was eventually rewarded by the golden dividends brought back by the husband.[4] Conversely, some men who had thought of emigrating decided otherwise on their wives' advice.

Poor wives play other important roles in the relationship of the family with the outside world. They often maintain client-patron relations with former wealthy mistresses whose service they have left on marrying. They supply them with details about prospective new servants, keep them informed of village gossip, and may perform occasional specific services such as looking out for antiques in poor village houses. They benefit in return from a protection which may express itself in many ways: gifts of money, intercession with hospitals, the authorities, or the prospective employers of their husbands or sons. Even when there has not been a prior mistress-servant relationship, relations between two women of different social groups are generally much closer than those between their respective husbands. Labourers' wives may obtain favours from the wives of proprietários or managers in matters of employment concerning the men of their families.

Finally, women are more pious than men, and often pray or make vows to the saints on behalf of the male members of their families, thus assuring spiritual protection for the household.

The extensive nature of a poor wife's role implies frequent

[4] Little children, hardly able to speak, were trained by their mothers to make the Portuguese gesture for money when asked: 'What has your father gone away for?'

contacts with men and this is in contradiction with the need to protect her virtue. She is not as secluded as wealthier wives are and is exposed, both at work and while buying from hawkers or out shopping, to the looks and conversations of unrelated men. Deprived of protective surroundings, the fight for her virtue becomes more difficult, and this day-to-day struggle does not allow for prudish language and restrained manners. She is, therefore, very far removed from the ideal model of a wife.

A mulher em casa, o homem na praça ('the woman at home, the man in the square'), a traditional saying runs. The square immediately evokes cafés, taverns, administrative offices, business transactions, working agreements—the whole outside world with which a man must come into contact in order to guarantee the family's material survival and which should ideally be only the husband's province. The wife should remain secluded at home. This is only possible amongst the wealthy, however. Wealthy wives are much more restricted to their houses, and the layout of these houses makes their seclusion even greater. In the houses of the proprietários, the kitchen faces the back yard, and in most cases it is necessary to go through the whole house in order to get to it from the street. The room nearest the street door is often the husband's office.[5] In most labourers' houses the outside door opens into the kitchen and thus exposes the women of the house to a close contact with the outside world.

Wives of latifundists and wealthy proprietários have servants, either living in the house or coming in to work for the day, who do all the basic shopping and the laundry. This excludes the wives from the gossip that takes place in the shops and washing places where the women pool their information about local affairs. They seldom leave their houses, and if they do so after sunset, they are accompanied by a female servant. The servants may sometimes return home alone, which well illustrates the difference in their status.

The existence of servants exempts these women from many of the household tasks. The wealthiest retain only a supervisory function and devote the rest of their time to needlework, church-going, charity work, visiting, and, last but not least, sheer idleness.

[5] The houses of the latifundists are big mansions similar to other big mansions found elsewhere in Portugal.

They do not contribute to the family income through any form of work. They may have inherited wealth, but even when they have signed ante-nuptial contracts, husbands are by law the trustees of their wives' property. In some cases this trusteeship is carried to extremes. A wife, wealthy in her own right, may complain that she has not enough pocket-money, or ask for a few escudos from her husband to make some payment. Even when she retains some financial autonomy in the management of the household, the household expenses represent a much smaller proportion of the family budget than among poor families. Wealthy wives are not the family treasurers.

The restricted roles of the wealthy wives are, however, envied by the poor ones. The life of a wealthy wife is an embodiment of the ideal life for a wife. Her wealth spares her the unpleasantness of work, and, as she is cut off from the world, she is also cut off from many opportunities for temptation. The wealthy wives are not women (*mulheres*), but ladies (*senhoras*)—the form of address *Dona* is used for them and not for the wives of labourers, sharecroppers, factory workers, small shopkeepers, or small proprietários.[6] When they reach their fifties without any lapse in their sexual morality, they are considered paradigms of the feminine virtues.

The girls and young married women of the poor groups, who now refuse to work in the fields or as household servants and confine themselves as much as they can to their homes, hold these rich women as models of behaviour. They make efforts to approximate to them as much as possible in dress, manners, speech, and general way of life. For financial reasons, however, the model is obviously unattainable for most women in the freguesia.

[6] In the freguesia the only other women who are addressed as *Dona* are the doctor's wife, the chemist's wife, and the schoolteachers. The latter often come from middle-class families and enjoy also the prestige conveyed by formal education.

IX

PARENTS AND CHILDREN

UP to some thirty years ago many families were rather prolific and many children died very young. People still say that children are *gado muito ruim de criar* ('very difficult cattle to raise') and a general term applied to very young children is *anjinhos* ('little angels'), the implication being that they may die while still in the age of innocence and join the ranks of the heavenly angels.[1] Mourning is not worn for any child who dies before the age of seven. This is in sharp contrast with the norm, which requires that a mother wear perpetual mourning when an older son or daughter dies. It is perhaps significant that seven was the traditional age at which a boy began contributing to the household earnings.

Nowadays, couples tend to have fewer children. Contraception (mainly by *coitus interruptus*) is widespread, and most couples now in their thirties do not have more than two or three children, and sometimes only one. To have an only child is, however, considered a very risky proposition: *Um filho só é um susto* ('an only child is constant fear'), and a barren couple is pitied.

Infant mortality, still very high by European standards, has decreased in recent years. Medical factors (vaccination, improved drugs, modern notions of child-care) have helped to reduce the vulnerability of children, and the resigned attitude towards their fate that this once created has tended to disappear.

Children are privileged centres of attention and during their

[1] Doubt about their survival made expenditure on very young children somewhat unwarranted. In 1867 (19 Dec.) the Misericórdia ruled that poor sick children between the ages of two and seven who were in its care should be entitled to only half the bread and mutton ration and a quarter of the chicken ration given to sick adults. In 1870 (17 Aug.), after considering whether it should provide assistance to children or only to heads of families, it decided by majority vote that children up to seven years of age should be entitled to free medical attention and medicines but not to any food allowance.

first years of life they are in constant contact with their mothers.[2] They are breast-fed, sometimes until they are three years old, for the prohibition against sexual relations with women who have given birth applies only to the first forty days after childbirth and women may bear children year after year, the youngest sometimes being nursed on the milk of the oldest. A woman will not work in the fields while she is nursing an infant. If she absolutely has to work, however, she takes the baby with her. Mothers beat their children from infancy since this is considered a fundamental part of education.[3] These beatings, besides being in themselves a form of attention and care, alternate with frequent displays of affection, in which a great deal of gratifying physical contact takes place between mother and child. Mothers are extraordinarily tolerant of the moods and wishes of children, giving in to many of their whims. All this builds up a unique relationship. No one, in later life, will provide the same warmth and devotion which children have from their mothers.

The relationship with the father is different. He does not co-operate in the routines of feeding, washing, and dressing children as these are women's activities. Albeit more distant, he is very affectionate and openly demonstrative to his young children, particularly to the boys, and is proud if they are found to resemble him. On Sundays he will walk along the street with his three- or four-year-old son by the hand and take great pride in showing him off. He will sometimes supervise his sons' games in the street. Football matches and sometimes other group games are arranged between teams of little boys of five or six and the adults stand around to watch, the fathers tensely following the game in a sort of agonistic exercise by proxy. A father rarely beats his children. He spends much less time with

[2] A description of child rearing and of the general ways of dealing with children in any society always reveals features that find parallels in the social life of adults. This is hardly surprising and of doubtful explanatory usefulness. In any society, children are trained to become members of the society. An analysis of this training will enable the analyst to make plausible predictions on some of the characteristics of adult society. But an analysis of the adult society will equally lead to plausible predictions on the nature of child training. The present case is no exception. The microcosm of family life and the macrocosm of society reflect to some extent the main characteristics of each.

[3] As an old widow said, complaining about the lack of help from her six grown up children, '*E eduquei-os bem . . . era cada carga de porrada*' ('And I brought them up properly . . . I spanked them a lot)'.

them than does the mother, and, in matters of discipline, is regarded as a kind of supreme court: 'If you do that again I will tell your father', is a frequent threat heard from mothers. From very early childhood the authority of the father is emphasized and the mother plays the role of an intermediary between father and children in matters that need his sanction; she seldom fails to obtain a favourable response.

The tenderness of parents towards their children is echoed in the kindness of grandparents, other relatives, and even non-relatives. Whenever weather permits, the streets are an extension of the house for poor village families, and children very quickly come to know and make friends with other children, women, old men who cannot work any more, and adult unemployed men. Children from wealthier families, whose mothers do not sit on the doorsteps of their houses sewing, do not play so often in the streets. They lead a more secluded life until they reach school age, and, as in later life, mix only with their own group.

The different fates of the sexes are stressed from birth.[4] When a couple has only daughters, this is considered a misfortune, and even more so if the family is poor, since daughters earn less money. Moreover, the parents will have to pay for the wedding festivities when the girls grow up and marry. Daughters also increase the family's liability in matters of honour, and if they never marry, they will be an added financial burden on their fathers. Boys, on the other hand, will contribute towards the family budget as long as they remain single, will not involve their parents in expenditure when they marry (weddings are paid for by the bride's parents), and are much less liable to bring shame on the family.

Young children are regarded as miniature adults in many respects and the expressions *está uma mulher* ('she's quite the little woman') or *está um homem* ('he's quite the little man') are frequently uttered in admiring tones about very small children. A clear distinction in dress is usual from the first months of a baby's life. A girl of about two is taught to 'behave like a young woman' (*faz-te lá moça*) and little boys are jokingly offered cigarettes, or wine, or beer. Very young boys and girls

[4] A midwife once made a very telling remark about the baby she had just delivered '*Que linda criança. Mal empregada ser rapariga.*' ('It is a beautiful child. What a pity she is a girl.')

are often asked whether they already have a namoro. Although primary schooling is co-educational, boys and girls generally play in different groups, and often play quite different games.

These differences, however, do not lead to a complete segregation of sex roles until early adolescence. In poor families brothers and sisters sleep together in the same room—sometimes with their parents—and often share the same bed. Young boys go shopping on their mothers' behalf, although shopping is a feminine chore. At about the age of twelve, however, they cease to do so. At that age also they cease to sleep in the same bed as their sisters and sleep on a mattress on the floor or in another room if there is one. When they do their first piece-work during the harvest, at about the age of fourteen, they are still paid at women's rates. Later they earn 'three-quarters' rates, and at eighteen they finally earn the full rate for a man. Occupationally, their adulthood is reached through these stages.[5]

At about fourteen or fifteen most girls begin a namoro and from then on spend part of their time preparing their trousseaux. They have become young women.

The relationship of the mother with her growing sons and daughters retains the warmth it had during their childhood. The characteristics of this relationship are, however, different for sons and daughters. Whereas the mother–son relationship appears to have higher moments of emotional expression, the mother–daughter relationship is of more practical significance in the fabric of social life.

The mother–son bond is thought to be the strongest possible bond between two human beings. At a spiritual level this is well marked in the cult of the Virgin. The Virgin is asked to intercede with Her son, the assumption being that a son will not refuse his mother anything. At another level, the traditional songs of the province emphasize the strength of the relationship time and again: 'He who has a mother has all/He who has none has nought.' 'Earth, open up, I want to see/the bones of my little mother.' In the several cases of 'irregular' families found in the freguesia, a woman's children by different fathers

[5] There are other moments that mark the transition from childhood to adulthood. The first time a boy goes to a prostitute, for instance, and the medical inspection that precedes conscription at nineteen.

remain more united throughout life than the children of a common father and different mothers. Young men serving in the army address their letters to their mothers, not to their fathers, when they write home. During the adolescence and youth of their sons, mothers spend more time looking after them than they do looking after their husbands. If a man protests that his son's clothes are better cared for than his own, he will often hear the retort: '*Deixa lá que não perdes casamento.*' ('Don't worry, your chances of marriage won't be ruined.') In fact, the great care mothers generally lavish on their sons begins to be directed at the time of the latter's adolescence towards helping them make the best possible marriage. The mother knows that marriage will cut her son off from her and that it is important for him to find the right kind of wife. If the boy begins courting a girl whom his mother finds unsuitable, there is little she can do about it since he will not heed her advice, but she nonetheless insists, either directly or by innuendo, on the foolishness of his attachment. If the attachment persists she says that the boy seems to have been 'given something to drink', thus putting the blame on magic potions to account for her failure to convince him of his mistake. By saying this she will, in a way, retain a position of strength, since only supernatural means could have prevented her from having her way.

Some mothers say that they already feel jealous of the future wives of their little boys of five or six. This jealousy is related to the fact that a son's marriage takes him away from the authority and care of his mother. When it does not, friction between a man's wife and his mother is certain to arise, and there is an entire body of local lore concerning mothers-in-law and their evils. In the rare cases in which mothers and sons had broken off personal relations, the son was always married and the break was the result of problems between the two women.[6]

The mother–daughter relationship is also very affectionate and much more intimate than that of mother–son, albeit not so expressive. Girls remain at home much longer than boys and

[6] The perennial feeling of dissatisfaction with the world in general and women in particular, the conviction that whatever life gives is much less than one deserves, so often found in Portuguese men, may perhaps be partly ascribed to the over-indulgent way their mothers treat them in childhood and adolescence. Mothers tend to put it the other way round: 'The poor thing is going to suffer so much in later life that I give all I can to him now.'

help their mothers about the house. If they work in the fields when they are very young, they generally accompany their mothers.

The girl learns from direct contact with her mother all the techniques she will need in her future life, ranging from cooking, sewing, and taking part in the preparation of innumerable pork delicacies that always follows the slaughtering of pigs, to the more subtle art of dealing with a husband. Their constant, day-to-day, matter-of-fact relationship works steadily and slowly and is not marked by the explosive episodes that punctuate relations between mother and son. Daughters do not go away to work and are not conscripted for the army. This protracted contact leads a daughter to take after her mother in many ways, regardless of temperamental differences. It is known that the daughter of a jealous wife will also be jealous, a mean mother will have a mean daughter, a quarrelsome one a quarrelsome daughter, and so forth. This repetitive pattern of behaviour is generally attributed to 'the blood'—i.e. hereditary transmission—but is most probably due to the years of intimate contact between mother and daughter. This intimacy is often of a secretive and conspiratorial nature. Mother and daughter sometimes help and protect each other against the men of the house. Seareiros and proprietários keep stores of cereals and olives at home for household use or for sale. Wives and daughters sometimes raid these stores without the knowledge of their menfolk in order to buy things for themselves which they would be unable to afford out of the housekeeping money.

The relationship may become strained during the girl's namoro. The daughter is then at the most critical stage of her struggle against her inborn *vício*. Her potentially dangerous tendencies have to be watched very carefully. After she is safely married, however, her sexual behaviour ceases to be the responsibility of her family of origin and the mother–daughter relationship is restored and sometimes even enhanced.

The relationship between fathers and sons is marked from the beginning of the boy's adolescence by a distant respect and authority for the father which balances the more intimate and affectionate mother–son relationship. A boy may already smoke in front of his mother and yet not dare to do so in his father's presence, while the father pretends that he does not know his son smokes. This mark of deference is so strongly respected that on one occasion, when a boy of fifteen inadvertently set fire to his father's threshing floor by dropping a lighted cigarette while working, the insurance company agent sent to investigate the case respected the boy's plea not to tell his father that he had been smoking. The boy was not afraid that his father would be angry about the fire but that he would find out that he smoked.

Young men often address their fathers as *Senhor*. They very rarely sit with them in the same groups in taverns or cafés, and they often avoid them even at home. They are shy of discussing personal problems with them and, when the father's intervention is needed, it is sought through the mother.

The father–daughter relationship is of an even more distant nature than that of father and son. Daughters are mostly confined to the household tasks in which their fathers do not intervene. Their other main concerns centre around problems of courtship and a man should not involve himself in the details of his daughters' namoros. The potential harm that daughters can do to their fathers' reputations makes them a constant threat, but it is up to the mothers to keep a watchful eye on their behaviour. A man prefers to keep aloof from his daughters' day-to-day life and reserve his intervention for any untoward critical situation that may arise.

X

FATHERS, SONS, LAND, AND WORK

As sons grow older their relationship with their fathers is marked by their relative positions towards work in the case of labourers and seareiros, and by the problems arising from the ownership and management of land in the case of latifundists and proprietários.

LABOURERS AND SEAREIROS

Among labourers, fathers and sons are fairly independent of each other in their working relations. They may work together in the same gangs and the son may work under his father at harvest time but this is by no means the rule after a young man has gone through his first three or four harvests. Even then, however, they are both working on other people's land, and no particular grounds exist for friction between them or for the son to feel that his father is a threat to his own interests. Sons admire their fathers' greater experience and learn from it, and the devoted respect for the father on the part of the son, which is an ideal value at all levels of society, finds its closest realization among rural workers.

When sons marry, their relationship with their families of origin undergoes a basic change. They cease to contribute to the economy of their parents' household, set up in their own homes, and decide their own affairs independently of their parents' advice or authority. Their responsibilities and duties, as well as their rights, are thenceforth vested in their new families, and their respectful and affectionate attitude towards their fathers is not challenged by any ambiguous situations. Ideally this attitude should remain the same for life and, if the lives of labourers do not provide many opportunities for its practical expression, they also do not contribute to the creation of tension and friction.

Seareiros employ field hands only for the grain harvest. During the rest of the year they work only with their families and rely on their grown-up sons to help them meet their share-cropping commitments. When a grown-up married son has to work under his father, an underlying tension permeates the whole relationship. A married man's first duties are towards his wife and children and not towards his family of origin; furthermore, in marrying, he has, in principle, become independent of paternal authority, but both obligations and independence are compromised if he works under his father. He is not his father's partner, but a peculiar type of employee who sometimes has to carry out instructions which he considers harmful to what he regards as his own interest. Fathers in their turn do not trust their sons completely. When the Grémio, as an agent of the National Federation of Wheat Growers, became the sole buyer of wheat after 1933, wheat had to be taken to Vila Nova, and new bureaucratic regulations were introduced governing the 'declaration' and selling of the crop which required accurate statements of its weight, quality, etc. This meant the end of the traditional middle men who had exploited the small producer but with whom it had been much easier to deal, since the whole transaction was carried out verbally. With the new regulations most of the older and illiterate seareiros handed over the actual details of selling to their sons. This led to some difficult situations, particularly in the first years. The son would take a certain number of kilos of wheat to be sold which, at the official price, should represent a certain amount. But he would often come back with less money than expected due to discounts made because of the poor quality of the wheat. Fathers to whom this had happened raised the matter privately with the local administrative clerk, obviously suspecting that their sons were cheating them. In a few cases, this may have been true, but it is significant that the suspicion should have arisen consistently.

These tense relationships between fathers and sons in seareiro families did not, however, find an opportunity for more open expression. The survival of the seareiro family group is based on the economic co-operation of its members. Owning comparatively small areas of land or no land at all, their main wealth is their work, and this work is most profitable while the family team remains united. The age, authority and experience of the fathers make them the natural leaders of the group: the sharecropping agreements with landowners are made by them. The sons contribute their greater capacity for physical work.

This traditional picture is changing. Many young men have become industrial workers or tractor drivers or, after completing their military service, have decided to leave the freguesia. Tractor drivers, even when single, may live away from home: being employed by the year or by the month, they often stay on the farms where they work. But young unmarried industrial workers who live at home may earn twice as much as their middle-aged fathers, and their relationship is marked by this discrepancy in earning power. The father feels more and more ill at ease, and the son tends to contribute only part of his earnings to the household and to spend more on himself. The father is still respected, but the conflict between money and the values of age and fatherhood deprives the relationship of the near-sacred character it had before. Even if the son remains a rural worker, however, among the younger generation of youths between the ages of fifteen and twenty (that is, before they have been called up by the army), criticism of their fathers' traditional conformist attitude is often heard, and the outlook of fathers and sons does not coincide. This is not a ground for open friction but a parting of ways, with the approval of the fathers themselves, despite their inability to share their sons' prospects. As a rule, sons know how to read and write whereas their fathers do not, and this is a further difference in their respective situations offering new opportunities for the son. After completing their army service, sons have had an experience of town life and money which makes life in the freguesia seem all the more unbearable.

In the case of seareiros, these problems have practical consequences. In recent years, a growing number of sons of seareiros are giving up work with their fathers. A few have found jobs in the mill, but most have gone away. As a result, their elderly fathers have had to reduce the areas of land they once farmed, since their financial situation does not permit them to hire labourers on a permanent basis at the normal agricultural wages now obtaining.

In these cases the situation of both father and son is felt to be ambivalent. On the one hand, traditional loyalty to the family acts as a strong pull on the sons; on the other, the attempt to improve the place ascribed by birth by taking advantage of better opportunities has an even stronger pull. When the sons eventually leave, they do not sever relations with their fathers, and their relationship is not soured beyond remedy. The fathers regret the situation in which they are left but they understand and accept that a life devoted to farming is no longer a viable proposition. They may even regret that they are too old to follow in their sons' footsteps.

In the days when the society was more self-contained—before alternative opportunities to agriculture were offered, either locally as in the cases of the mill or in the industrialized areas near Lisbon and the more industrialized countries of Europe—men generally lived all their lives within the groups to which they had been born, both in geographical terms and in terms of social stratification. Among the landless and near-landless families there were few opportunities for any discrepancy to arise between the father's position of moral authority and a comparatively weak financial position. This could change when old age rendered him unfit for work, but while he was active the moral and material positions of the father were intertwined.

The material elements of cohesion in the domestic family unit of the labourer and the family working group of the seareiro are being destroyed by the opportunities for better alternative employment available to the men of the younger generation. The prestige and authority of the father is consequently being undermined. In this respect the traditional structure of the family seems to be unable to sustain the impact of economic changes.

LATIFUNDISTS AND PROPRIETÁRIOS

Among the latifundists and proprietários, conflicts are bound to arise between fathers and sons over problems of work or management. To the reasons for the existence of tensions found in the seareiro families are added those arising from the ownership of substantial tracts of land. The adult married sons of these landowners know that they will eventually inherit the land now owned by their fathers. But even when they co-operate in management and take over many responsibilities from an elderly father, the father's authority is always present, even if not fully accepted.

Since all latifundists and proprietários employ other men, conflicts of authority are bound to arise. Their subordinates are affected by them, and in some cases try to take advantage. In 1964 one of the latifundists made a sharecropping agreement with his general manager as part of his policy to diversify production from wheat cultivation alone. The landowner's son, then in his forties, came to an understanding with the manager, whereby he would use his credit to finance the latter's sharecropping activities without the father's knowledge. The father eventually learned about the deal, fired the manager, and gave his son a beating. Their relationship went on very much as before, however, since there was no obvious way out.

Some latifundists' sons are known for their extravagance, and managers are afraid to give them the proceeds from sales of estate products because they are never sure whether the father has agreed. Difficult situations have arisen on this account in the past. When such cases do occur, however, the manager's position is safe for a time, because it would be improper of him to suspect his employer's son, and the father does not want his son's misconduct to be known to an employee. At the first opportunity, however, the manager will be fired.

Sons may also have reasons for complaint. João Caeiro, an important proprietário in a very difficult financial situation, concealed his circumstances from his sons until he was finally sued by his creditors. The sons resented this bitterly and complained to friends that their father had behaved badly. Problems become more acute when the father reaches old age with all its temperamental implications. At this stage his authority is bitterly resented by the adult sons who work under him and feel that they could do better if they managed the land themselves.[1]

The existence of inheritable land is an underlying factor in all these situations. When there is more than one heir, the matter is further aggravated, for in this case not only is the

[1] In recent years some sons of proprietários have gone to the university and technical colleges, and a few of them have urban jobs now. This represents a different but equally important, type of difficulty. Proprietários are often willing to give their sons the best type of education they can afford. If they succeed, however, the continuity of their agricultural concerns is forfeited.

father's management difficult to accept, but each of the sons tries to compete for the father's favour. Elderly landowners are unwilling to divide their land among their sons and live at their expense afterwards. Experience shows that they would find themselves in a degrading position, sent from one son's house to another's, badly treated, and a constant pretext for friction over the cost of their keep. The years of tension and concealed conflict are therefore prolonged until the death of the father brings it all out into the open amongst heirs.

XI

SIBLINGS, AFFINES, AND INHERITANCE

CONFLICTS over inheritance may involve the surviving parent and his or her adult sons and daughters and their respective spouses, if they are married, or may be restricted to brothers and sisters when both parents are dead. Such conflicts do not take place only among the wealthy: they may arise over small plots owned by poor peasants. In every case, however, conflicts of this nature unmistakably contradict the ideal norms of obedience to parents and of harmonious relations among siblings.

Affines, particularly sisters' husbands who are the legal guardians of their wives' property, play an important role in inheritance conflicts. They do not share the cohesive feelings that may have remained among the members of the family, and their intervention emphasizes the grounds for divergence and hostility among the former.

Joaquim Dias, a widowed proprietário, lived with his favourite married daughter, preferring her to either his other married daughter or his son. To ensure that his property would pass into the hands of this favourite, he faked its sale to a friend, who then 'sold' it to the husband of the preferred daughter. When this ruse was discovered, the other daughter and son severed relations with the favoured sister and her husband.

Bento Rosado, a small proprietário, had two sons and a daughter who were all married at the time of his wife's death. The wife had had a marked preference for one of her sons, and had not wholly approved of her daughter's marriage, She had made a will leaving the best plot of land in her share of the property to her favourite son. Anticipating this, the other son had already made an alliance with his brother-in-law, and they tried to persuade Bento Rosado to ignore this clause in the will. But the old man insisted on respecting his wife's will and the favourite took possession of his plot. Shortly afterwards, he found that all his olive trees had been severely mutilated during the night. He lodged a complaint with the *Guarda* who made short work of discovering the culprits, since a few days before this episode the guilty brother had been heard saying in the tavern that his brother would soon regret his windfall.

In these stories affines played important roles by allying themselves with one of the conflicting parties inside their wives' families. This is not infrequent in cases where one of the conflicting parties is a woman. The brother who allies himself with his brother-in-law says that the latter has behaved more like a brother than a brother-in-law. The brother on the other side of the fence has, of course, a different opinion: he says that his brother has behaved more like a brother-in-law than a brother. Vested interests determine in each case how alliances are formed. Between the ideal values of brotherhood and the ideal values of commitment to one's family of marriage, a man can choose whichever suits him best as the avowed explanation for his action. He is able, therefore, to protect both his interests and his moral integrity in each particular case.

Problems between one surviving parent and sons and daughters become problems among the siblings after the parent's death. There are very few cases of joint ownership by brothers and/or in-laws of undivided estates, small holdings or commercial enterprises, since it is generally agreed that this only postpones the final conflict between the partners, with the added complication that, through years of management difficulties, the original inheritance may have diminished. Joint ownership is incompatible with an adult man's independence, and is made more difficult by the absence of any principle which would clearly establish priority of rights for the eldest and render his position similar to that of the deceased father. He may invoke his primogeniture, but such a claim for authority is ignored by the others when problems arise. Indeed, when the 'house' is eventually divided, those concerned express their regret that *partilhas*[1] were not made much earlier.

Except in such rare cases, the *partilhas*, usually made immediately after the death of the legal owner of the wealth, are

[1] *Partilhas* is the general name given to the formal partition of the estate of a deceased person among his or her heirs.

the last important occasion for open friction in the life of siblings. If they survive the *partilhas* on good terms, further problems seldom arise. This, however, is rare. Even when no temporary or permanent estrangement occurs, there is always some bitterness among those involved (*sempre se criam más impressões*) which persists throughout their lives.

Partilhas are always difficult. In the first place, rural and urban property ('urban' in this case meaning houses in the villages) is often not yet registered in the names of the last owners but is still in the name of some forefather. Furthermore, up to 1951, there were no precise official measurements or maps of rural holdings and their limits were often open to discussion. Heirs often bribed clerks in the Land Record Office and Tax Bureau and people still complain nowadays of how they were deprived of this or that plot through the machinations of their brothers or uncles. Secondly, property is often scattered among several plots. Land is of very variable quality and it may be difficult to arrive at a fair division or even to establish acceptable compensation to those who end up with the poorer plots in a necessarily unequal division. Thirdly, the *partilhas* are the critical moment when the heirs' relationship to the family wealth is reassessed. This is so particularly among the less wealthy. If, for instance, one of the sons had married when the parents were better off and had, therefore, received a larger contribution to his household, this is brought up by his less fortunate brothers and sisters when the *partilhas* are being made and they demand suitable compensation.

It is not surprising, then, that disagreements should arise. There is not necessarily any relation between the amount to be divided and the extent of the disagreement. A group of five brothers acquired their wealth in two successive stages: at their father's death, their mother made very evenly balanced gifts to her sons out of her own share, keeping about 10 per cent of the 'house' for herself. This first partition proved uneventful. But when their mother died, arguments broke out among the brothers over the division of her 10 per cent share, leading to a temporary severance of relations among three of the five.

Partilhas are sometimes made, cancelled, and remade several times before a settlement is finally reached. This may take years. When the heirs find themselves unable to establish shares acceptable to all, they may summon the help of other landowners and ask two of them to act as assessors. The verdict of these experts, who should not be related to any of the heirs, is, in principle, final and if the heirs ask for their help they show a basic willingness to come to an understanding.

There are a few cases, however, in which agreement cannot be reached and the matter is taken to the courts. This happens more frequently in the case of small landowners than among the wealthier ones, and they will spend sometimes almost as much as they eventually inherit on lawyers' fees and court dues.[2] The wealthier landowners are more aware of the expenses involved in such proceedings, and there is generally enough wealth in their case to assure that even an unfair division will leave them with a generous share.

Matters are taken to court because those involved are unable to settle them otherwise, each party claiming to be completely right. If they reached a private agreement this would mean that one or both of them had made a concession, implying the acknowledgement of his own lack of judgement and his subordination to the authority of the other, which would be contrary to a man's ideal of independence. Whatever the court's decision, this independence is not affected. The winning party will have his claim vindicated while the losing party can always say that the verdict was the result of the corruption of lawyers and judges, or, at a more general level, that official justice has nothing to do with true justice and that the laws of the state do not conform to the true notions of right and wrong.[3] A man may have lost his lawsuit, but he has not lost face.

The sharply conflicting nature of the interests of siblings overcomes the ideal values of brotherhood. Even in cases that do not reach the courts, these values are far from being fully embraced. Ownership of property itself is blamed for this general

[2] In eight cases brought to the court of Vila Nova between 1956 and 1965 the value of the properties concerned did not exceed £250.

[3] A fully documented case took place in 1907 over a former communal plot of which the Câmara had the lease. C.m. 19 Aug. 1907 and 28 Oct. 1907. This is clearly demonstrated in cases where prior arrangements for the eventual decision of family land have been made among parents and sons and daughters. These arrangements are often recorded privately (*escritos particulares*) and should be respected by the signatories. When disagreements arise, one of the parties may produce the *escrito* in court. But it has no force in law and the matter is judged independently of the recorded arrangement.

situation among landed families. It is sometimes said that 'it would be better to have nothing at all' (*'Às vezes era melhor não ter nada*).

The sibling group in landless families has a different fate which affects brothers and sisters in different ways. As brothers marry, they drift away from their family of origin. The commitments undertaken towards their families of marriage determine their main moral obligations and absorb their meagre financial resources. These commitments do not make them more eager for their share of the family wealth because there is none to share. *Partilhas* do not therefore provide grounds for friction between them and their parents or siblings. The progressive estrangement from the family of origin that takes place among married brothers is not tainted by the ill feelings or open rifts that mark the process in the case of landed families. At marriages and funerals, the formal importance of the relationship is reasserted. But these are exceptional ritual moments. Outside them the duties and rights of married brothers do not appear, from an observation of their behaviour, to be very different from those of unrelated men; indeed a man may often rely more on his friends than on his brothers for help or advice.

The situation is different with sisters. The advantages of poverty for harmonious relations between siblings, implicit in the statement, 'There are times when it would be better to have nothing', are inferred from the persistence of friendly relationships among married sisters and their mothers in the poor groups. A daughter's marriage brings the mother–daughter relationship to full blossom and married sisters generally remain on close terms and maintain a relationship of mutual help.

A newly married couple generally remains in close contact with the wife's family, mainly the wife's mother or sisters, and these contacts increase after children are born. The influence of the husband's family, on the other hand, is progressively less felt. When bride and groom are from different villages they try to find a house in the bride's village.[4] If this is not possible, the mother often visits her married daughter and vice-versa. If an old couple living on a distant farm have to stay for a while in a

[4] In landed families the choice of residence by a newly married couple is governed by the needs of the land.

village where they have married sons and daughters, they always stay with one of the daughters, not with one of the sons. In warm weather, groups of women sit and sew on their doorsteps while the children play in the streets. These groups are often centred around a maternal grandmother, not a paternal one. In 1965 when a few houses in Vila Velha were bought by rich outsiders,[5] the couples who had sold them and who consequently had to find temporary accommodation, stayed with relatives of the wife: in three cases with the wife's parents and in the other with the wife's married sisters. If a child reaches school age while his parents are living on an isolated farm, he will stay with his maternal grandparents in the village. When lonely old widows or widowers, too ill or disabled to live alone, have to stay with their children, it is generally said that their lot is worse if they have to stay with a son (and therefore with a daughter-in-law) than with a daughter. If a young couple living on a farm comes to Vila Velha or one of the villages for the christening of a child, they will as a rule stay with the wife's parents rather than with the husband's.

The exchanges of services and favours between poor married sisters or married daughters and their mother includes gifts of food, small loans of money, baby-sitting, and protection and complicity, should one of them be guilty of irregular behaviour. Family life is conditioned by the operations of these feminine networks in which men have little say. They are determined by feminine links, persist through the women's determination and needs, and are manipulated by them. Restricted as they are to mothers, daughters, and sisters, these networks form the only operative groupings based on kinship found in this society.

[5] The charm of Vila Velha has attracted many tourists, and wealthy city dwellers have bought houses in the town for week-ends and holidays.

XII

KINSHIP

In the freguesia we do not find a formal kindred with reciprocal and exclusive rights and duties. Outside the nuclear family, kinship obligations soon fade: among the landless, in the absence of material support that would help to give concrete expression to these obligations, and among the landed, because although this material support exists it is more a cause for friction and conflict than for agreement and mutual help. The solidarity of mothers and married daughters and of married sisters in the poor groups of the population is not extended, as a rule, to more distant relatives.

In principle everyone agrees that kin deserve more consideration than non-kin but, except in the case of mourning, there is not a well defined charter that would make explicit the forms that this consideration should take in different contexts of life. The stipulated periods of mourning emphasize the comparatively unimportant position of relations outside the nuclear family. While people mourn their parents for two and a half years, and their brothers and sisters for two years, grandparents deserve only six months of mourning and great-grandparents, first uncles, first aunts, and first cousins only two weeks. The difference between the mourning period stipulated for first cousins and for siblings is particularly striking. It points to the fact that cousinhood is not institutionalized in any important way even at this formal level. People sometimes emphasize in conversation the difference between a first cousin and more distant cousins, describing the former as 'brother-cousin' (*primo-irmão*) or 'right-cousin' (*primo direito*). But in many other instances they just refer to them as *primo*. The fact that the word *primo* also means 'prime' is, therefore, devoid of significance. Ideally a man should always help a brother in distress, but for a cousin no such ideal obligation exists, and each case is judged on its merits. In day-to-day life the practice does not depart from this outline. The playmates of schoolboys and girls include cousins and non-cousins alike. Sometimes a particularly friendly relationship develops between adolescent cousins of different sexes. The girl is often an intermediary between the young man and her female friends. But after adolescence the relationship loses part of its purpose and is allowed to lapse.

In the landed groups, cousins may be reminders of a partition of property already made or still to be effected, and their relationship in such cases inherits the tensions created between their parents over such matters. Among the poor, the new family commitments created by marriage which lead to the estrangement of brothers, further emphasize the unimportance of the cousin relationship.

First uncles and first aunts are, together with cousins, an individual's nearest relatives. In the less prosperous groups, and more generally amongst those families which have not been split by inheritance problems, a man's paternal uncles and aunts are accorded part of the respect he owes to his father, while his maternal uncles and aunts generally develop a closer and warmer relationship with him. This is facilitated by the fact that residence among the poor is generally in the maternal locality. Uncles and aunts may have their own children to whom they have many more obligations than to their nephews or nieces. If they are childless, however, the relationship may be prolonged and affectionate: childless couples sometimes bring up a niece or a nephew as their own child. The word *tio* ('uncle') has passed into wider usage and is sometimes affectionately applied to old men by young peasants unrelated to them.[1]

In landed families the relationship of nephews or nieces and uncles or aunts may become particularly important. Wealthy and childless uncles and aunts generally leave their estates to nephews and nieces who compete to become the favourite heir. This competition is even more likely to end in open conflict than the similar situation that arises between a surviving parent and his grown up children. On the one hand, not all the potential heirs are siblings, and cousins feel freer to compete over these matters than brothers and sisters. Between cousins, the infringement of an ideal code of behaviour is minimal, since the ideal obligations of cousinhood are, as we have seen, few and

[1] This usage also occurs in the Portuguese upper classes. Children address their parents' friends as 'aunt' or 'uncle'.

ill-defined. On the other hand, childless couples are by law allowed to dispose of the whole of their estate as they wish, whereas parents must legally divide half their property equally among their sons and daughters.

Competition for the goodwill of these childless relations is therefore fierce. Nephews and nieces visit them frequently, sometimes try to persuade them to come and live in their own houses, and intrigue against each other. The reasons given for such behaviour by those who practise it are, of course, of a noble nature: ideal kinship obligations and personal affection. But the true purpose of their conduct is obvious to everybody and may become quite open. When one of these old uncles or aunts dies leaving a surviving spouse, the will of the deceased is read and the choice of his or her favourite heirs becomes known.[2] The other potential heirs frequently cease to pay any attention to the surviving spouse, since it is assumed that his or her intentions will correspond to those of the deceased.

Cousins and siblings, competing for the wealth of an uncle or aunt, sometimes manage to keep on apparently good terms while the latter are alive so as to avoid displeasing them. After the death of the uncle or aunt, however, those who feel wronged will show it without restraint. In 1965, when, somewhat surprisingly, only one of five cousins inherited property from an aunt, the others accused him of having intrigued against them. Another case, running through three generations, will show how the obligations of kinship and the greed for land are intertwined. In 1889 the daughter of the wealthiest latifundist in Vila Nova fell in love with a poor Civil Servant who had been appointed to a position in the civil registry of the town. To prevent the marriage, her father managed to have her declared insane by the court and she was duly confined to a mental institution. After the father's death some decades later, one of her brothers undertook the lengthy task of having her case reviewed. He died before the proceedings were completed and his eldest son took the matter over. Eventually the first sentence was reversed and the old lady, reinstated in her rights, came to live with her nephew. Her brother and her nephew always justified their behaviour on humanitarian grounds. They pointed out that

[2] Among proprietários the will is read in the presence of the corpse, before the funeral. Such is the importance of individual ownership.

she had been ruthlessly victimized by her father to avoid a *mésalliance* that would damage the family's prestige; that the two psychiatrists on whose report the first court had based its verdict had been bribed; and that the old lady was as fit as anyone else. They held that they had simply obtained for her the justice she deserved. This was not, however, the opinion of some of her other relatives, who unsuccessfully tried to oppose her rehabilitation. These included her other brothers and sisters, their spouses, and their children. They maintained that the first court decision was the right one and that the true motive for its reversal was to reinstate the old lady in her rights so as to gain from her will, since she was bound to favour (as she eventually did) the nephew who had taken her from the asylum. They held that she had always been mad, and mad she should remain. Nor was this stand taken for the sake of correct psychiatric diagnosis. Had she died while still legally insane, her property would have been divided in equal shares amongst all her nephews and nieces. After her rehabilitation only the favourite nephew would benefit. As might be expected all the others severed relations with him when her will was finally read.

This case, involving siblings in one generation and cousins in the next, was particularly striking, but the principles underlying the events are not exceptional. In landed families the relations between uncles/cousins, nephews/nieces, and between cousins are always strained.

There are many circumstances when, in the interest of preventing tensions and conflicts from arising, it is preferable to deal with non-kinsmen. When a piece of property is rented out, the owner generally prefers to be unrelated to the tenant. Agricultural years are often bad and rents may be difficult to exact. A kinsman would evoke his kinship to try to obtain rebates or deferments of payment. When seareiros engage men and women from outside the family for the harvest season they also prefer non-kinsmen. '*Está a gente mais à vontade para mandar.* ('One feels freer to order them about.')

These attitudes result from the fact that, however tenuous and ill-defined kinship obligations are, they may nonetheless be invoked for personal convenience. Those against whom such obligations are invoked have to take the more or less embarrassing step of having to disclaim them, if their personal interests are at stake. In doing so, they expose themselves to blame, and create ill feelings that it would be wiser to prevent.

To side-step the possibility of such situations arising, deals or working relations with kinsmen are often avoided. Personal interests may lead a man to manipulate for his own benefit the ascribed relationship established by kinship. They may be emphasized or underplayed according to convenience. In practice, kinship in itself does not enforce a specific set of rights and duties among either landed or landless families. In difficult moments of life people rely more often on their friends than on their kinsmen. Friends rather than kinsmen build up the operative networks of patronage.

So far this discussion has emphasized the lack of institutionalized forms of mutual help based on kinship.

However, seen from another angle, kinship is a means of identification. The 'family' (i.e. the lines of descent traced through both mother and father) to which a man belongs is not irrelevant in terms of his prestige and self-respect. In describing the main groups of social stratification we have seen that people in each group tend to marry within the same group, and that there is little inter-group marriage, particularly in the case of latifundists and proprietários. Some families are exclusively restricted in their near relations and affines to these wealthiest groups. At the other end of the social scale there are families of labourers with no relations in any of the other groups. No family names are exclusive to any of the groups, although some occur more often among the rich than among the poor, and vice versa. Names in themselves, therefore, do not often provide a means of identification. But a man's origins are obviously always known, and part of the esteem to which he may be entitled derives from his family background.

This use of kinship as a framework for identification is, as could be expected, related to wealth and subject to personal manipulation. We have seen how some latifundists unjustifiably claim aristocratic descent. A similar form of status insecurity is found in the freguesia itself. Some of the proprietários who are now less well off and a few seareiros whose parents or grandparents were proprietários, like to emphasize explicitly the number of their close relatives who are members of wealthier social groups. Unlike the latifundists, however, the boasting of these men is based on fact. The society is too small and the span of time involved too short to allow them to lie in such matters without being immediately exposed. Less glamorous connexions are, of course, conveniently forgotten.

Some decades ago the daughter of a proprietário married a labourer and their sons subsequently took the name of their mother and not that of their father. This desire to claim membership of a wealthy family is not so marked among those who do not need to remind others of their family connexions. But whatever the case may be, the relationship of wealth and kinship is institutionalized far beyond these personal options. Until the beginning of this century, landowners were sometimes described by their Christian names followed by the name of their farm. Since the main agricultural 'houses' have sometimes been inherited through the mothers of the present owners, they may be known by their maternal rather than their paternal surnames. Whether there is a correspondence between the names of holdings and family names or not, however, there is, among landed families, a keen awareness of kinship which is absent among labourers. The latter are often ignorant of the ages of their fathers' or mothers' siblings or of the exact number and sex of their grandparents' siblings, and do not know with absolute certainty who are their second cousins. Beyond this, their ignorance of the family tree is almost total.

This is not surprising. Their grandfathers and great-grandfathers were labourers like themselves. They were landless, they did not achieve any particular eminence, and there is therefore no advantage, either in terms of wealth or prestige, in claiming them as ancestors. This is reflected in the use of family names. In Portuguese usage, the name of the father is the surname that follows that of the mother. In many poor families of the freguesia the order is inverted, in others one or both of the names are suppressed and replaced by other family names, chosen at will from among the eight possibilities provided by the combination of the names of grandfathers and grandmothers. It does not really matter for a labourer to signify exactly to which family he belongs since all labourers' families share the same basic incapacity for providing themselves with either wealth or prestige.

Outside the circle of their nearest relatives, kinship is of no consequence for labourers. They are not even designated—nor do they describe themselves—by their family names, whatever these might be, but by their nicknames which are in most cases specifically individual. Family names relate a man to a given kinship group spread in time and space: nicknames relate him only to the neighbourhood where he lives.

XIII

NEIGHBOURHOOD

I

THE widespread use of nicknames among the labourer and seareiro groups helps to provide identification when family names fail. This is only possible in the context of small face-to-face communities. Only in a fairly limited group is it possible to have such a system of classification, where everyone remembers the nicknames of people, without the help of the co-ordinates that family names provide.[1] Because people live in different settlements, some repetition occurs. *O Quadrado* of Vila Velha is not to be confused with *O Quadrado* of one of the villages. Two different people are nicknamed 'Guitar', in two different villages, and there are a few more such cases. But owing to the frequency of intercourse between people from different villages and the fact that many nicknames are coined when young men from different villages work together in the fields, in most cases a person's nickname is enough for him to be identified throughout the freguesia.

This identification is often—although by no means always—the expression of a social sanction of some kind. Aspects of behaviour or character which deviate from what is considered normal are expressed in nicknames: a very wicked man has been called 'the Jesuit', a very stubborn one, 'the spirit of contradiction'. The possibility of conveying social sanctions in this way is again related to the size and relative isolation of the community.

Each village is a neighbourhood. There are native families in each of them whose main branches have been there for generations. After a few months of residence one is able to distinguish the accent of Vila Velha and the two nearest villages, from the accents of the two most distant ones. People from Vila

[1] There are a few family nicknames but they are not of great help since individual members of the family will nevertheless be given their own nicknames. Joaquim do Couto Ferreira is a member of the *Paixão* family. But he is known by his own nickname, *o Souza*, and not by theirs.

Velha see a hierarchy of civilization and civility in these differences. Because they live in the town they feel superior, although they may often be poorer. The town has an 'urban space' that reflects its past importance: the square, with its civic and religious buildings, and the well planned streets that lead harmoniously to the centre, have no parallel in the disorganized 'urban space' of the villages, with their very irregular networks of streets which do not seem to have obeyed any over-all plan and are not organized around the main buildings that stand for faith and authority. The castle and the wall are reminders of the town's past military strength and of the protection it provided for those who sought its shelter in times of war. Besides, the town is on top of a hill and stands well above the rest of the freguesia.

These are obvious facts, but villagers explicitly deny that the town derives any form of superiority from them. Whereas townsmen say 'Vila Velha' to describe the freguesia as a whole, villagers say 'the freguesia'. They point out the town's present comparative poverty: none of the proprietários lives there. But that the town has some form of superiority is implicitly acknowledged in the fact that village women don their Sunday best to go there. This is also true of women who live in that part of the town lying outside the wall. This distinction between the part of the town lying within the wall and the outlying parts finds parallels in the villages. Although each settlement is a neighbourhood, there are smaller neighbourhoods within each of them.

The people who may be acknowledged as one's neighbours are partly determined by the social group to which one belongs. A latifundist from Vila Nova may say that an unrelated latifundist from Evora is his neighbour because their estates are contiguous, although their houses are half an hour's drive from each other. Unrelated proprietários from nearby villages also address each other as neighbours. Such forms of address are used in these cases to emphasize an equality of status existing between two individuals. Poorer people who actually live much closer are not addressed in the same manner.

In these cases neighbourhood does not imply the proximity of residence and the constant intercourse found among poor neighbours (labourers and seareiros). Even among the latter, however, the range of neighbourhood is associated with material wealth. One feature of their marriage rituals is illustrative of this fact. After the church ceremony and wedding luncheon served in the house of the bride's parents, the bride and groom call on neighbours who were not invited and offer them cakes and liqueurs from the marriage feast. This is known as 'paying compliments'. By 'paying compliments', the newly formed family asserts its position and establishes a bond with the already established families whose favours and goodwill may become necessary in the course of their neighbourly relations. Very poor couples only 'pay compliments' to people in the street where they will be living; those who are better off do so throughout the village.

Since women remain in the villages most of the time, whereas men go to work outside, neighbourly relations are basically feminine relations. These relationships sometimes express themselves in forms of mutual help, but are never as developed as the mother–daughter relation or that between sisters. Supervising children's play, borrowing cooking utensils or provisions (eggs, sugar, etc.) are some of the favours exchanged among poor neighbours, but the exchange of favours does not exhaust the features of the neighbourhood relationship. Neighbours are basically watchers of their neighbours' behaviour.

II

Houses in the villages are tightly packed and separated by narrow streets. Village life is very public since much of it is led outdoors. From her doorstep a woman can hear what is said at five or six other doorsteps and see what goes on in front of an even larger number of houses. This range of immediate observation provides her with the original information that she exchanges with other women when she goes shopping, or visiting a close relative, or when she goes to do the washing. The speed with which any event becomes known throughout the village is remarkable. The news takes longer to reach other villages not only because of the distance involved but also because there is less eagerness to spread it among a public that is not so interested in the latest village events. The choicer items of news break this rule: when someone dies, when a wife leaves her husband, or a young man returns from Africa, or when a donkey is stolen by gypsies, the news travels quickly throughout the whole freguesia. But most village events, although they may inspire hours of vivid comment locally, are of restricted interest elsewhere. Even in the village concerned, there is a hierarchy of interest: the first short skirt worn by a local girl was of interest to the whole village; women's quarrels over their children, or the killing of a cat only arouse the interest of a single street.

Some zones in a village are better than others for gathering information: the houses bordering the road that leads to Vila Nova are thought to be the best placed. The country bus stops in this road, and the people who come and go can therefore be observed by its residents. Outsiders who arrive by car are spotted here first. These circumstances contribute to a feeling that the road offers certain advantages as a place to live, which is expressed in the phrase *tem mais movimento* ('it is more lively'). The streets in the outskirts of the villages, and the part of Vila Velha lying outside the wall are correspondingly considered less suitable residential areas and are inhabited by the poorer people.

To know as much as possible about other people's lives is a general preoccupation often disguised by open affirmations of the opposite intent: '*Que me importa a mim a vida dos outros?*' ('What do I care about other people's lives?') When public telephones were installed, shopkeepers in the villages vied with each other to have one. Not only does the telephone bring more customers to the shop where it is installed, but the person in charge learns much more about the lives of those who use it. Letters are collected and posted in these same shops: postcards are always carefully read and the external details of all other correspondence are scrutinized by the man or woman in charge.

The freguesia receives copies of only two national newspapers daily (one of them is received by the Casa do Povo); and once a week three proprietários receive copies of one of the national daily papers. Television is regarded as a form of entertainment: people do not gather to see the news. The lack of information and lack of curiosity about what is happening in the outside world is striking and contrasts sharply with the close scrutiny to which the local world is submitted.[2]

[2] This is changing now because of migration and emigration. But people prefer the first-hand accounts of those who come back to the more general information that could be gathered from newspapers, television, or listening to the radio.

Everybody pays attention to what everybody else does, but women play a more important role than men in the establishment of information networks. These exchanges of information and comment, which may generally be called gossip, make up the bulk of conversations held in the villages. Inter-linked groups of mothers, daughters, sisters, and neighbours secure the gossip coverage of the village, and washing places and shops are local 'exchange markets' for dealing in such currency. There are two specific groups of women which play a particularly important role: the first is the group of old women, generally widows, who are called to bless the sick, to assist women in childbirth, and, less often, to help with household chores. Since they have access to the homes of unrelated families, they are able to observe things that are generally concealed from outsiders. The second group is that of the female domestic servants of wealthy families generally living in Vila Nova. They provide their mistresses with information about the villages which the latter would be unable to obtain directly in view of their secluded lives. They also keep the village informed about affairs in their mistresses' houses. But their main role as links in gossip-chains results from the fact that through their conversations with other servants they pass information from one wealthy house to another. This is particularly feared by their mistresses. Wealthy *namorados*, who are sometimes left alone together when staying with relatives or friends in Lisbon, have to have a permanent chaperon when they are at home in Vila Nova 'because of the servants'. And even small details of home life have to be carefully watched since they may, at any time, be reported.

The information provided by gossip is meant to evoke in the listener reprobation or envy. With suitable subject-matter, an experienced gossip achieves both effects in a single stroke. 'What a beautiful dress Maria's daughter is wearing today. I don't know how they can afford it.' No aspect of living escapes gossip.

Sometimes the gossip is defiantly courted: if a factory worker buys his child an expensive toy or a young unmarried woman flaunts her long nails (an overt indication that she will no longer work in the fields), they are bound to provoke unfavourable comment. In such cases the aspersions of gossips will be a direct result of envy, since people only envy what is enviable, and those who incur this type of gossip are really adding to their prestige.

Gossips are careful to avoid the possibility of a direct confrontation with their victims. If the victim of gossip tries to trace its source, the attempt is generally frustrated; suspicion may be strong but guilt cannot be proved. Gossip is voiced by identifiable people but the origin of the information on which it is based remains anonymous. The third person plural is the most concrete person blamed: '*Dizem* . . .' ('They say . . .')

Gossip is therefore the expression of judgements by everyone and no one. This makes it a particularly effective form of social control. The most minute details of appearance and behaviour have to be carefully watched, since comments will always be made and unfavourable comment will spread through the whole village.

Latifundists and proprietários have their own gossip. They are not included in the gossip of others. To be effective as a form of social control, gossip must be a threat to the reputation of its victims, and reputations are assessed among equals. Judgements formed by labourers on the behaviour of individual latifundists or proprietários would be of no consequence to the latter and cannot act, therefore, as a form of social control. And when latifundists and proprietários are displeased with labourers their position enables them to express their displeasure in a more direct and effective way.

In cases in which a person's behaviour clearly infringes major ideal norms, however, gossip is no longer adequate as an institutionalized means of dealing with reprehensible behaviour and more violent sanctions are called for. The most serious situations of this kind are those that threaten the reputation of the family.

III

The prestige of any family is related to its material position and to the moral behaviour of its members. Ideally, the family's material position is the responsibility of its men, particularly the husband; and nothing threatens its moral reputation more than sexual misbehaviour by its women, particularly the wife.[3]

[3] This is well illustrated by what happens in cases of alcoholism amongst poor peasants. When a man begins drinking, not only is his working capacity diminished but he begins to withhold money from his wife, thus upsetting the always precarious

The second is of greater consequence. There is no reprieve for an adulterous wife, and the stain on her own reputation and that of her family is indelible. The complex nature of the wife's roles identifies her more fully and exclusively with her family, and judgements passed on her actions tend to consider her person as a totality.

A man who is unable to provide for his family, has failed in one of his roles but may still fulfil others, in relation both to his family and other people. This relative independence of roles does not take place in the case of women. The story of Helena, a mill worker's wife, is illustrative of this. The rumour was spread in her village that one of her cousins, himself a married man, had been seen leaving her house at three in the morning when her husband was on night-shift duty in the mill. Both she and her cousin strongly denied the rumour, and the matter was eventually reported to the Guards, who were unable to find out who had originated the story. Opinion on the matter was divided: to many people in the village her adultery became an accepted fact. Her marriage was not broken, but from then on her husband began doing the weekly shopping himself. His suspicion was extended from sexual to financial matters.

Some years ago, when it was discovered that Ema, the wife of a wealthy professional man of Vila Nova, had committed adultery, the women who knew her were not surprised: they had noticed that she spent too much money on herself and her household, and that was a bad omen. A woman's behaviour is measured against a yardstick of moral and sexual significance and any lapse in her sexual morality renders her unreliable in other fields.

The seriousness of adultery[4] is more fully understood when the foregoing aspects are kept in mind. A woman's intimacy with

balance of the family budget. The stability of his household thus threatened, he himself becomes insecure and jealous. Indeed, when a man begins drinking too much and too often, female neighbours and relations will immediately ask his wife if he has begun to show signs of jealousy, and, if he has, it augurs ill for his recovery. Since a typical reason for the break-up of a family is the wife's adultery, the alcoholic husband tries to find symptoms of infidelity and to persuade himself that adultery exists so that his own behaviour, which is the true destructive factor, may become of secondary importance and seem justified.

[4] Adultery as a disruptive form of behaviour is the privilege of wives. The extra-marital affairs of husbands are taken for granted and do not have the same implications. The adulterous husband is not a figure of oral or written literature.

a man other than her husband introduces a cataclysmic change in her life and the life of her family in every conceivable field. The first step of the outraged husband is to take his adulterous wife back to her parents or, if they are dead, to her closest relative, thus trying to disclaim part of his responsibility for what has happened. If her family lives in the region, however, she stays only a short period, before going away (generally to Lisbon). Although a man is ideally justified if he kills his adulterous wife,[5] this has happened only once in the last fifty years.[6] Except in this unique case, physical removal of the woman from the local scene has been substituted for her death. Her name ceases to be mentioned in the presence of her husband and a moral vacuum is created. In one case, after learning from a servant about his wife's adultery, the husband took her back to the town and the street where they had first met, thus symbolically undoing the whole of their relationship.

Neither husband nor lover leaves the place where he lives and I know of no case in which either of the men involved felt the need to go away. Although the husband is for ever stigmatized as a cuckold (*cabrão*) and the lover is not praised for his deed, both continue to be accepted as full members of the community. The truly defiling person is the adulterous wife who has destroyed the viability of her family by destroying the main moral assumption on which it was based and must therefore disappear.

There is a parallel situation for men which, as might be expected, is not related to sexual behaviour but to financial problems. If a woman can wreck the moral basis of her family's prestige through adultery, a man can destroy his family's material basis by becoming, through carelessness, unable to provide for it financially. In most of these cases the man, like the adulterous woman, has to leave.

Landowners and shopkeepers who have lost their money cannot bear to live in the same place with lower standards of

[5] The Portuguese Criminal Law Code lays down a very mild punishment for the husband if the lovers are caught *in flagrante delicto*.

[6] In 1922, a man released from prison learned of his wife's adultery during his absence. He went to live with her nonetheless, but a month later he axed her to death. Significantly, the local paper published the news under the headline 'A Case of Adultery', and the article ended by regretting that the foolish behaviour of a woman should have brought four children to the miseries of orphanhood.

living and their plight witnessed by those who had known them in more opulent days. They also leave to avoid some of the consequences of the discovery of the more or less dishonest dealings they may have made in the years preceding their final crash. But these reasons do not fully account for their departure. There are indeed some men who fail to pay even their small debts, who break agreements, and who generally do not respect their commitments. But as long as they are not definitely endangering their families' material position, they do not come within the same category as those who have done so by becoming bankrupt. A bankrupt man has endangered the future of his children and proved himself unfit to act as trustee of the family's wealth. Although in recent years people take a more lenient view of his situation—since conditions in agriculture are generally bad—to fail the family is morally more reprehensible than to create difficulties for those outside the family. In some cases he may be pitied, but, whatever the extenuating circumstances, he becomes something of an outcast, a man who, by losing his property, has placed himself in an impossible situation and has to leave. In some cases he tries to find employment elsewhere, but even bankrupt landowners who are unable or unwilling to find a job and manage to make ends meet with the help of relatives often move to another town.

The fact that both the adulterous wife and the bankrupt husband have to leave the community is significant. No other moral situations have this institutionalized outcome. This points to the central position of the family in the system of moral values of the community. The practical implementation of ideal abstract values is mostly enforced for the protection of the family as such. For the sake of their families, men and women are allowed to behave in ways ordinarily regarded as reprehensible (deception, theft, fraud) and their behaviour may even be condoned in some cases. An unemployed labourer who steals to feed his family has the approval of his fellow labourers. Clerks who expedite the affairs of those who have bribed them are often forgiven the trouble this may cause those whose affairs are delayed as a result, because it is known that they have to keep their families on very low salaries. When a local draughtsman, whose delay in presenting plans for a building commissioned by the Câmara had surpassed all reasonable limits, was reprimanded by the mayor, he justified himself by saying that he had nine children and had to provide for them by accepting extra work, even if this meant disregarding some previous commitment. The exacting loyalties to the family which govern such behaviour are designed to maintain and reinforce its material and moral position.

The ideal behaviour towards the wife's unfaithfulness and the husband's inability to provide for his family is often enforced in practice, but there are deviations from the norm. As is often the case in the freguesia, these deviations are related to social stratification.

Labourers have no property and the financial blows they may inflict on their families are due mostly to drinking, which leads them to work less and less. Since they have little possibility of going away, they lead miserable lives and are often openly reproached for their behaviour.

Correspondingly, the poorer a family is, the more its women will be allowed to deviate from the ideal chaste behaviour expected of them. A family of tinkers which moved into a semi-ruined house near one of the villages a few years ago, is perhaps the poorest in the freguesia. The family lives in extraordinary squalor, and its male members have to take on small odd jobs in addition to their tinkering to keep themselves above mere subsistence level. The female members of this family are not expected to have any moral integrity. Two of the daughters have become itinerant prostitutes travelling with a group of hucksters and come home only sporadically. The matter is regretted but hardly commented upon. The family is well below the minimal standards of honourable behaviour.

Wives of labourers, particularly of those permanently employed on the big estates, may commit adultery of a type which does not generally imply the disruption of their families and has become institutionalized as a means of securing patronage benefits. In these cases, the husbands pretend that they are ignorant of their wives' affairs, although this is often not so. Such affairs are less frequent nowadays but were very common up to some ten or fifteen years ago. Latifundists, proprietários, managers of the big estates, a few of the wealthier shopkeepers, and professional men always found mistresses among their female employees and the wives of their male employees or poorer customers, some of these relationships having begun when the women were still unmarried and employed as their domestic servants. It is generally believed that there is no man in the above groups who has not had one such affair or in most cases several. The husbands benefit materially from these situations, gaining greater security of tenure in their jobs or the financial rewards brought home by their wives. In a few cases they even prompted the relationship. When their applications for work were turned down by an estate manager, some men would send their wives to present their case to the latifundist.

Affairs of this nature were not promiscuously random. A rich man from Vila Nova who had been kept waiting longer than usual by one of his mistresses, the wife of a village labourer, accused her of having been with a shopkeeper whom he suspected of also being her lover. The woman was outraged: 'What do you think I am? Only my husband and you lay their trousers on me.' The relationship must be fairly stable if it is to fulfil its role as a patronage bond, which in most cases was clearly the *raison d'être* for the wife's acceptance of the propositions made to her and for the husband's connivance. Indeed, if a landowner dismisses or otherwise harms the interests of the husband of one of his mistresses, he may be sure that her favours will cease. These situations are disappearing for the same reasons that make it more difficult nowadays for landowners to find labourers, sharecroppers, and domestic servants. While they exist, however, they are not, in practice, dealt with according to the rules ideally applicable in cases of adultery. Labourers cannot afford, in these cases, to behave in accordance with the ideal procedure that should be dictated by their personal honour and the shame of their families. In the first place, the social distance between the husband and the wife's lover prevents him from retaliating; secondly, the material benefits to be gained from his wife's adultery are important for the precarious economy of the household. Furthermore, should he decide to repudiate his wife, he would stand to lose much more in practical terms, than would a landowner or a professional man in a comparable situation, in view of the roles she performs.

It could be argued that the differing roles of the wife according to her family's financial situation determine both the frequency of adulterous situations and their acceptance by the community.

A poor wife contributes to the material stability of her family when she accepts a wealthy lover as much as a rich wife contributes to the moral stability of hers if she refuses to take a lover. Since moral integrity seems to require a material basis, a priority of family needs could be established, according to which adultery might be justified.

Matters are not so simple, however. Tinkers' daughters who turn prostitute, or someone like Madalena, an old woman who had nine illegitimate sons from different men and had been a local prostitute for over forty years, have crossed the frontiers of shame and, since nothing is expected from them, they are accepted for what they are without reproach. But the case of poor adulterous wives is different. They are certainly not expected to live up to the same moral standards as the wives of latifundists and proprietários, but this is in itself a moral hardship of which they are painfully aware. Their position does not make them insensitive to shame (*vergonha*).

It is *vergonha* that drives the bankrupt landowner and the adulterous wife out of the community. The shame they inflict on the community is reflected in them and obliges them to leave. By going away they lighten their burden of shame, since the witnesses of their shameful acts are left behind. Poor people who are unable to take this step—the destitute labourer or the poor wife who is involved in an adulterous relationship with a landowner—have to bear their shame and inflict it on the community. Because of this, although some of these affairs are publicly known while others are strongly suspected, and although people in the village disapprove of them and express a certain contempt for the husband, they are never the subject of elaborate gossip, and one becomes aware of a general underlying agreement not to mention them. They are illustrations of the moral handicaps of poverty. Most families in the freguesia belong to the labourer or sharecropper groups and could therefore in principle be affected by similar situations.

To the degree that a community shows tolerance towards the ideally unforgivable behaviour of a poor adulterous wife, the shame resulting from her irregular behaviour is in some way shared by all. The community is obviously not, nor is it regarded by those who live in it as being, a unified entity expressing its will or having feelings that are imposed on its individual members. Villages are networks of social relations which are competitive rather than co-operative. Judgements on individual actions are seldom unanimous, and the local assessment of prestige varies according to who makes it and the occasion on which it is made.

Towards the outside world, however, the attitude is different. The views found in localistic expressions ignore the inner tensions and conflicts and present communities as homogeneous wholes. An association is often made between the behaviour of women and the places where they live. People of Vila Velha sometimes refer to one of the villages in depreciating terms because its women are considered very promiscuous and its men very dishonest. Throughout the freguesia similar feelings are expressed about the people of St. James, the next freguesia to the north.

Those who form these judgements are not taken in by them. They know that the attitude is reciprocal and that their own reputation in nearby places is low. But they also know that, however biased such judgements may be, there is some truth in them. This is certainly attributable, in part, to the wickedness of men in general: saints are in Heaven and all living men are sinners. It is partly, however, specifically related to local conditions, of which the adulterous relations mentioned above are an expression. The poverty of the villages is seen not only in low purchasing power and the general lack of what are considered the 'good things' of this world. Poverty also means that men and women find it more difficult to lead an honourable life.

PART THREE

POLITICAL STRUCTURE

XIV

CORPORATIVE BODIES

THE main official bodies which integrate the freguesia into the Portuguese State can be divided into those concerned with economic life (*organismos corporativos*) and those responsible for civil government. The political structure of the Portuguese State reinforces the social order of Vila Velha, with its disparity between the powerlessness of the many poor and the power of the few rich. This political structure is rooted in the reshaping of the administration carried out in the first half of the nineteenth century by the Liberal governments that succeeded the *ancien régime*, but it underwent many modifications and additions, the most important of which were introduced by the 'New State', created in 1926. On the May in that year, a bloodless military coup ended sixteen troubled years of democratic republican rule. Soon afterwards important changes and innovations in the political structure of the country were introduced, and by 1933, with the promulgation of a new constitution, the basic framework of the New State had been constructed.

The main innovation of the present regime was not, however, in the sphere of civil administration but in the social and economic sectors. The regime is based on the concept of *corporativismo*, which assumes that capital and labour, or owners of the means of production and workers, do not have conflicting interests to be expressed in syndical or political strife but complementary interests to be dealt with harmoniously. Thus disagreements between employers and employees are to be solved through the machinery of the Corporative State and not through freely elected trade unions and employers' associations. *Corporativismo* envisages a moderate degree of state intervention as a means of correcting the evils of capitalist society and protecting the interests of the workers and of the country as a whole against the dangers of free enterprise. The former Prime Minister,

Dr. António de Oliveira Salazar, expressed this quite clearly more than thirty years ago:

The State believes that it should exercise its action on national economy as guide and protector; that it should encourage certain trends and discourage others; and that it should co-ordinate scattered efforts for the general good of the commonwealth.

Though we have repudiated the individualism and liberalism of the nineteenth century and their attendant disorders, we are unwilling to attribute to the State a universal competence to administer the economic life of the country as it pleases.

The lack of technical ability or of financial resources on the part of private concerns will compel us to go much too far (according to my way of thinking and my own individual tastes) along the road of state control. But though resolved to go as far as may be absolutely necessary, we should go no further.[1]

The ultimate results of this intervention have, however, been limited by the fact that the machinery of the State is often manipulated precisely by those whom it is supposed to control.

Corporativism has had its apologists and denigrators and their positions have often been passionately defended: in 1938 a sympathetic English observer expressed his view of the prospects for success of the corporative system:

The most important feature of Portuguese economic development is the adoption of the corporative state, which does not bear so close a relationship to any similar system as is commonly supposed. The ideology of the New State is necessarily somewhat fixed in character, for its principles possess the immutability of virtues. But the execution of the idea is tentative and exploratory in character, and the guiding principle is to adapt it to the Portuguese attitude of mind so that the spirit of independence which is strong in the national character shall not be outraged to the detriment of the community as a whole. The test of the system will lie in the acquisition of a proper balance between corporative endeavour and the innate independence of the individual, but, whatever happens, a programme of social amelioration and economic development has been embarked upon which is bearing fruit, if slowly, and will continue to do so irrespective of the statutory form which may be given to the machinery for its execution.[2]

[1] Cited in A. H. W. King, Commercial Secretary, Her Majesty's Embassy, Lisbon, *Report on Economic and Commercial Conditions in Portugal* (London, H.M.S.O., 1938). Other expressions of the same doctrine are to be found in A. O. Salazar, *Doctrine and Action* (London, 1939), especially pp. 18–19, 165–9, 192.

[2] A. H. W. King, op. cit., p. 2.

Thirty years later the virtues of *Corporativismo* are being questioned even by officials of the regime. State intervention has stifled the organized labour and protected vested interests in agriculture and industry. *Corporativismo* has been accused of having failed to promote either economic development or social amelioration. Some of the reasons for this failure in the agricultural sector are implicit in the analysis that follows.

THE CASA DO POVO

The most typical of all corporative bodies are the Casas do Povo ('Houses of the People') which are to be found in almost all rural freguesias. Casas do Povo were designed to promote the welfare of rural labourers through the provision of unemployment and sickness benefit schemes. In the characteristic spirit of *Corporativismo*, membership is not restricted to labourers and is compulsory for landowners with taxable incomes from land above 150 escudos.

The Casa do Povo of Vila Velha was founded in 1945. It was imposed from the outside as part of a measure based on general policies and did not result from any local attempt at organization by labourers and landowners. In 1965 the membership consisted of 313 landowners and 365 labourers.[3] Landowners pay a fee of 0.4 per cent of their taxable income per month if this is above 1,250 escudos; 5 escudos if it is between 150 and 1,250 escudos, which means that those with higher incomes pay less in proportion to the others. They have no right to the social benefits available to labourers. The latter pay a fee of 3 escudos a month and are entitled to the free services of the doctor employed by the Casa do Povo, to a discount on medicines, and to allowances for sickness, old age, etc. As members of the Casa do Povo, they are also covered by schemes of alternative employment in public works. Membership is not compulsory for labourers, but in Vila Velha, after showing some reluctance in the early years, all the labourers eventually became members to take advantage of unemployment and sickness benefits.

This reluctance, a mixture of distrust and scepticism, was shared by landowners, particularly by the small landowners

[3] The number of labourer members is higher than the number of labourers living in the freguesia because labourers who have gone away did not bother to cancel their membership. Landowners, in this context, means 'owners of land' not independent farmers. Most of them are seareiros.

who could not see any general political and social advantage in the Casa do Povo as a deterrent against social unrest and were rightly unable to see any personal advantage for themselves either. But a true test case occurred in 1947 when two somewhat feeble-minded landowners resisted all attempts to make them pay their fees and had their property seized and sold by auction. Quite typically, the original number of voluntary defaulters was much larger (13), but the other landowners involved, who were more cautious and certainly craftier, discreetly paid their fees while instigating the two to go ahead 'and see what happens.' What happened conclusively settled the issue.

It was also in 1947 that another basic misunderstanding was solved. About 200 of the less prosperous landowning members thought that they should also be entitled to free medical assistance and it had to be made clear to them by the authorities that this was out of the question. The majority of its landowning members regard the Casa do Povo as a government agency to which they pay a kind of tax and from which they fail to derive any benefit. The wealthier landowners were quicker to understand the general advantages of the Casa do Povo and they even put some pressure on labourers to join in the first years by not accepting workers who were not members.

Landowner members are represented on the governing body of the Casa do Povo. Since 1947 a latifundist and an important local proprietário have sat on this body. The other posts on the governing body, including that of executive chairman, are filled by labourer members. In the freguesia, the chairman has always been a permanent employee of the latifundist member of the governing body. By statute, the governing body should be elected every three years; each type of member voting for representatives from his group. But since the very first election, held in 1947, although they are always advertised, nobody turns out on polling day and there have therefore been no votes for the directors, who are, in fact, appointed by high officials at the provincial headquarters of the corporative organization (National Institute of Labour).

Minutes of the meetings of the governing body are dutifully written out by the clerk every month but in fact it meets only once or twice a year. As a rule, it is the clerk who runs matters in direct subordination to the provincial delegation of the

National Institute of Labour (I.N.T.), which is responsible for supervising the Casas do Povo. Whenever the governing body intervenes, however, it is to back landowners' interests, whether general or private. In 1953, for instance, it asked for a reduction of the membership fees payable by landowners (but not by labourers); in 1962 it informed the Landowners' Grémio that local labourers were not interested in the eight-hour day; in 1965 it dismissed the doctor over an alleged disagreement as to payment, the true reason being the personal conflict between the latifundist director (who lives in Vila Nova) and the doctor. Since it is at present difficult to recruit doctors this meant that the freguesia was without a resident doctor for more than a year.

Although labourers are often told that the Casa do Povo is theirs, they are suspicious about it and stand off even from possible benefits. No one took advantage of a scheme providing long-term credit facilities at cheap interest rates for building new homes; children entitled to free holidays at the sea-side are never sent, and membership fees are paid reluctantly and late. Indeed it is not infrequent for a man to borrow money to pay overdue fees because he has become ill or unemployed and needs the help of the Casa do Povo. Labourers are perhaps right when they regard the Casa do Povo as simply another instrument for serving the interests of landowners. In 1949 a labourer had a disagreement over a piece-work agreement with his employer and felt that the latter had deceived him. He reported the matter to the Casa do Povo and the clerk referred it to the provincial delegation of the I.N.T. The answer came back that if the labourer felt aggrieved he would have to take the case to the labour courts himself: the Casa do Povo was unable to assist him in any way over such a matter.[4]

This is clearly in the corporativistic spirit that informs the Casa do Povo and shows that, deprived of any syndical capacity, it can never attract labourers and give them a feeling of membership that would differ from their present attitude: the feeling that the Casa do Povo is, like every other organized body, alien to their interests, and is, in fact, a cross between a tax collecting office and a charity organization.

The most important functions of the Casa do Povo are the provision of medical aid and the handling of unemployment.

[4] C.P.c. 28 June 1949; reply 6 July 1949.

Both functions are directed from the provincial capital. In this sense, as an extension of the National Institute of Labour, it may sometimes act against the interests of individual landowners in a way that a more local body could not, but on important matters, it is ultimately subject to indirect pressures exerted by the landowners at a higher level. Such was the case in 1952 when landowners managed to put an end to the allocation of labourers. This is not surprising. The structure and functioning of the Casa do Povo reflects the social *status quo* which the landowners support.

THE GRÉMIO DA LAVOURA

Landowners are not only members of the Casa do Povo but also of an *organismo corporativo* designed solely for them. This is the Grémio da Lavoura (Landowners' Guild) of which membership is compulsory. Of the 2,500 members in the concelho, 313 are from the freguesia. Only members with a 'taxable income' of over 500 escudos are entitled to be electors and to be elected to the governing body. Although Grémios were created by the present regime and exist in most concelhos, by historical accident the Grémio of Vila Nova was developed from a previous voluntary body, the Syndicato Agrícola founded in 1895. Employing several clerks and occupying a large building in Vila Nova, the Grémio is a more conspicuous institution than the Casa do Povo. One of its main functions is to administer government credits for wheat cultivation. This is done both by the Grémio and by the Caixa de Crédito Agrícola, created as a local mutual credit association in 1911 and absorbed by the Syndicato and afterwards by the Grémio before becoming an independent body in 1941.[5]

[5] Between 1911 and 1933 the only official credit facilities available were dependent on membership of the Caixa; from 1933 onwards a state-controlled credit agency offered cheap credit facilities, but these were not used to their full extent until 1941. For the first thirty years of its existence, the Caixa's role as a source of credit was minimal and if, up to 1933, sheer lack of funds could be seen to account for this, from then on this reason can no longer be considered sufficient. What in fact happened, I was told, is that the secretary of the Syndicato was, in his private capacity, an important moneylender, both as broker and from his own capital. As broker he managed to divert into his own business money that could have gone to the Caixa at a much lower rate of interest. And as secretary he explained to members that the Caixa lacked sufficient capital and that it was difficult to obtain funds from the State, offering to find the money they needed privately.

It is generally thought and said that, should the Grémio and the Caixa call in their loans, almost all the freguesia's landowners would go bankrupt. It is difficult to assess whether this is true or not, since the detailed information is of a strictly confidential nature, but it is clear that, without official credit agencies, the existing agricultural situation would be impossible. Whether this is good or bad is an open question: the credit facilities available since 1933 are often indicated as one of the main causes of the progressive financial decline of most landowners.[6] In recent years legislation has been passed extending the facilities for repayments of Grémio and Caixa loans. Some landowners have seriously suggested that the State—which, by keeping agricultural prices low, is in their eyes chiefly responsible for their difficulties—should simply 'forget about previous loans', stop all further loans other than for exceptional cases, and increase prices.

Besides this one important function, the Grémio, as an agent of the National Federation of Wheat Producers, buys the wheat crop on behalf of the Government, supplies improved seed, organizes the public auction of wool produced by its members. collects statistical data on local agriculture, and seeks to co-ordinate local agricultural problems and general state policies both at the legislative level and in a number of specific matters such as technical guidance, new market opportunities, etc. This liaison function is often reduced to the voicing of local protest against general measures. The Grémio also lends or hires machinery to members and sells tools and fertilizers.

As could be expected, the president of the Grémio and the other two members of the governing body, elected by the general council of electors every three years, are latifundists or professional men related to latifundist families. The general council

The Caixa's untapped resources under the management of the Grémio are clear from the following figures: in its last year under the Grémio, the Caixa had about 114,000 escudos on loan, of which only about 10,000 escudos belonged to depositors, the rest having been provided by the State. In 1965 the respective figures were 23,000,000 escudos and 1,650 escudos. Full use of the Caixa's credit facilities has greatly decreased the local importance of private money-lenders, but they still exist because, with the progressive decline of agriculture, many people have exhausted their credit with the official credit agencies.

[6] There are two reasons for this. Since credits are allowed mostly for wheat cultivation, there has been undue emphasis on this crop, which in present economic conditions is of doubtful viability. The second reason is that a considerable proportion of the loans is diverted into consumption.

has forty members, half of whom are 'born members' (the richest landowners of the concelho, i.e. the biggest taxpayers), while the other half is elected in accordance with the representation quota established for each freguesia. Hardly anyone bothers to vote in these elections: in fact, some locally important proprietários are simply appointed by the existing members. The general council meets twice a year by statute but may have extraordinary meetings, and every three years it elects the governing body from among its own members. Attendance at council meetings is low, and with the exception of matters such as the allocation of labourers in 1950, all important business is dealt with by the governing body. Between 1945 and 1965 the council met forty-three times. At only three of these meetings did 50 per cent or more of the members attend (24 Mar. 1957—24; 26 Mar. 1962—20; 25 Mar. 1964—21), while nineteen meetings were attended by only ten members or fewer. At the meeting held on 24 Mar. 1957 those present unanimously passed a motion recommending that, according to the law, all those who failed to attend the general council meetings without justifiable cause should be fined. However, to my knowledge, no one has ever been fined for being absent from meetings—either before or after the motion. In 1963 the chairman of the council made the same suggestion. A proprietário of Vila Velha objected that it was not worth coming to the meetings since the gentlemen on the governing body dealt with all the business themselves and did exactly as they liked. He claims that he was heartily congratulated after the meeting by many members who felt he had voiced their own feelings.

This lack of direct participation by members is not a recent phenomenon, and seems not to be related only to the mandatory nature of membership. The turn-out for Syndicato elections (a wholly voluntary association, which never managed to have more than some 800 members) was very low, at least for the years in which the number of votes was recorded[7] and this seemed to reflect a genuine lack of interest in its affairs. In 1912 a local newspaper stated that the only reasons landowners had joined the Syndicato were to acquire cheaper fertilizers, to borrow machinery, and to obtain marketing facilities for their products.

[7] 1932—63; 1933—34; 1934—40; 1937—17; 1938—8; 1939—14; Books of the Elections of the Syndicato.

When it was necessary to protest against a law which would be harmful to farming interests, the Syndicato convened meetings which landowners failed to attend. When there were demonstrations of new machines or new techniques, they were not present. 'Our landowner', the article concluded, 'prefers, above all, his independence in the narrow but comfortable confinement of his estates.'[8] In 1934, in reply to a government survey of agricultural conditions, the Syndicato stated that members' concern for the progress of their association 'leaves much to be desired'.[9] And according to directors and clerks of the Grémio the situation had not improved in 1965. The following are recent illustrations of this indifference, all dating from 1965. Small cattle farmers who lack the resources to transport stock to the central market in Lisbon are constantly victimized by dealers who force them to accept lower prices locally. The Grémio has tried to promote the co-operative hiring of a cattle truck to transport the animals to the Lisbon market, but all efforts have failed. A number of difficulties were raised such as that of identifying individual animals, the problem posed by animals which might fall sick on the journey, etc. This reluctance to agree to co-operative measures, which is always found when projects of this type are suggested, tends to perpetuate the exploitation of small producers by dealers. The Grémio managed to obtain a baling machine and arranged to lend it out to associates in accordance with the order of their names on a list drawn up for the purpose. When their turn came to use the machine, some of these men began to hire it out to neighbours who had not bothered to add their names to the list, or whose names were at the bottom of the list. Moreover, Grémio directors and clerks were suspected of having changed the order of names to suit their own interests and that of their friends. The Grémio had acquired large quantities of packing wire and was able to put it up for sale to its members at a lower price than that obtaining in the free market. Landowners placed their orders with the Grémio, but when the free market reacted by lowering prices to slightly below those of the Grémio, they immediately suspended their orders and began buying from other suppliers, only to find that prices were rising again, so that in the end they spent more money than if they had bought the wire from the Grémio.

[8] LN II 160, 12 July 1912.

[9] S.c. 26 Feb. 1934.

This difficulty of association is both a result of, and a condition for, the control of the Grémio by latifundists. In a wider sphere, however, their control is qualified. Both Syndicato and Grémio have protested against government measures, but the political allegiance of the governing members of the Grémio is a condition for holding office, and however powerful they may be locally or however good their connexions in government circles, there is always the risk that, since agriculture is a hazardous activity, their discontent will grow beyond the point that the Government finds tolerable or that it might be used by them or by others for political purposes. Some control must be maintained. In 1945, during the most significant anti-government movement since the establishment of the present regime in 1926, two Grémio directors together with thousands of other people all over Portugal signed a petition for the holding of free national elections. There were no free elections, however, and the two directors had to resign. Since then, only persons regarded as politically reliable have become directors. But even with this guarantee further measures were taken. Although Grémio publications do not have to be submitted to the national censors before release, they are censored by a special body of the National Federation of Grémios. Provided it remains politically reliable, however, the Grémio is accepted by the Government as being the mouthpiece of the landowners.

In matters such as crop prices, subsidies, and so forth, the Grémio's interests and those of the small producer frequently coincide but, given the structure of the Grémio's governing bodies, the opinion of the small producer is never sought. The view expressed by the proprietário mentioned above that 'the gentlemen of the council dealt with it all themselves' holds true. Moreover, it is taken for granted that directors will take advantage of their position, even if they in fact do not do so. I was often told by small proprietários that the reason they did not send their wool to the Grémio was that 'only the wool of rich people is given a proper deal'. The fact is that the wool of these small proprietários does not meet the standards of the Grémio buyers.

In important matters, however, the Grémio's wealthiest members may make their own arrangements. In 1965 none of the four main latifundists in the concelho was on the board of the Grémio when the new Minister of the Economy, who had promised to pursue more favourable agricultural policies, visited Vila Nova to enquire into local conditions. Instead of visiting the Grémio, he stayed in the house of one of the latifundists and all discussions took place privately.

Control over the Grémio by the latifundists does not preclude them from using their personal network of relationships in matters that should be handled within the official framework of the corporate state. Marriage alliances of the latifundists extend far beyond the concelho or even the province, and through these alliances relationships are established with other influential groups, which are also organized on the basis of kinship and friendship ties. As a result, the politicians or top Civil Servants responsible for formal decisions on matters concerning the latifundists are involved in this network. If they entered the higher circles of Portuguese life, through a career in the administration, they are easily brought into the latifundists' social circle.

The relevant exchanges preceding government measures relating to agriculture may not take place in Parliament or in the appropriate government departments, but over dining tables or in the course of the shooting parties given by the latifundists. These shooting parties hold such charms for ministers and other high officials that the contradiction between the financial difficulties of which the latifundists are constantly complaining and their lavish way of life are apparently overlooked.

In recent years with the development of industry and the poor performance of the agricultural sector, particularly of cereal farming, the relative importance of the landowners' contribution to the country's economy has decreased and their political leverage has been correspondingly affected. For instance, they have been unable to press for any substantial increase in wheat prices for many years now. Nonetheless, in matters that do not clash with fundamental tenets of government economic policy the position of the wealthiest landowners is still very strong. They exercise considerable control not only over the Grémio and the Casa do Povo to which they belong *qua* landowners, but also over other bodies of the political structure. When we move into the sphere of the civil administration they become the most prominent citizens whose whims and wishes have to be taken into account.

XV

ADMINISTRATIVE BODIES

THE effect of 'New State' legislation on the traditional bodies of local government was to increase their subordination to central authority. This, together with the discouragement of open political activities, the banning of political parties, the establishment of permanent censorship of the press, gave the broad mass of the population even less access to political life and led to progressive political apathy. The rules and institutions of the body politic became increasingly the instrument of government rather than the safeguards of the citizen.

THE JUNTA DE FREGUESIA

Vila Velha, the five villages, and the land around them constitute the smallest division of the Portuguese administration, the freguesia. Several freguesias make a concelho.[1] The concelho of Vila Nova has four freguesias, the smallest of them being Vila Velha. The freguesia is administered by the Junta de Freguesia which is composed of three elected members. Its powers are small and it is unable to influence any decisions on the area's basic agricultural and economic problems. Although it can initiate public works with assistance from the State (and has sometimes done so in the past), for many years this has been a function of the Câmara ('Town Council) in the concelho town of Vila Nova. The Junta does not even contribute to the relief of unemployment that public works are designed to provide. In fact the Câmara has far more power than the Junta de Freguesia and many matters are only brought up and settled at concelho level.

The Junta draws its income (which is between 20,000 and 30,000 escudos a year—approximately £285 and £428 respectively) from the annual rents on some 60 hectares of land (the

[1] Concelhos are grouped in distritos, each of them headed by a Civil Governor responsible to the Minister of the Interior.

remnants of the ancient common lands), from taxes on the water-supply, and from a yearly subsidy of about 2,000 escudos (about £28) provided by the Câmara. It also earns some money from the cemetery and from fees for certificates. Although in the last twenty years many more people have applied for certificates (required for receiving free medical assistance in the provincial medical centres or in Lisbon), in most cases these certificates are issued free of charge, and not much money comes from this source. The Junta could also charge for the earth and stones, used for building purposes, removed from some of its properties but has never done so, 'so as not to be too heavy on the people'. In principle, it is also entitled to the proceeds from the sale of olives picked from the olive-trees lining some of the paths in the freguesia. But for many years the owners of plots adjoining the roadside have picked the olives themselves. Since Junta members are local landowners who have to attend to their own affairs, they usually do not bother about the Junta's olives, and from 1930 to 1944 they were left to rot on the trees.[2] The Junta is responsible for the upkeep of the cemetery and pays the grave-digger. It also keeps up some of the roads and paths in the freguesia. Apart from a salaried clerk (the secretary) and a man responsible for cleaning and repairing the clock in Vila Velha, who is paid gratuities, the Junta has no permanent employees. The local doctor, when there is one, is paid by the Casa do Povo, the schoolteachers are paid directly by the Ministry of Education, the Customs Guards—stationed in one of the villages since the days when smuggling was widespread, and now permanently idle—are paid by the Ministry of Finance, and the Republican Guards, who patrol the freguesia but are not stationed there, are on the pay-roll of the Ministry of the Interior.

Since its functions are in practice so limited, it is natural that the Junta's members should meet very seldom, although by statute meetings should be held twice a month. In fact, they meet only once or twice a year, but minutes are written out every fortnight by the clerk as if the meetings had been held. This man (who also holds the post of clerk of the Casa do Povo) handles all the Junta's routine work. References to the fact that the members did not meet because it was harvest time or for

[2] LN II 591, 14 Mar. 1944.

some other reason related to farming are found in earlier Junta minutes, but nowadays not even this is recorded.

The members of the Junta should be elected every three years by all heads of households in the freguesia. In practice, the nominations are made by the chairman of the Câmara (the mayor) who chooses from amongst the local landowners or important shopkeepers the names of three he thinks competent to fill the post and has the list of names printed. In the last thirty years there has never been an alternative list, nor do I know of any in the past. Elections are held in October, and literally no one bothers to attend. The newly 'elected' members, who receive no payment, take up their duties at the beginning of the year. The Junta's members are usually chosen from different villages. Since Vila Velha has a historical tradition and is the head of the freguesia, some six years ago an attempt was made to have a Junta composed only of Vila Velha members. This was decided by the Câmara and the Junta clerk, but the experiment did not work. Of the three members chosen, two became involved in questions of prestige over trivial matters such as which of them should keep the keys of the committee room and of the old castle. They eventually broke off personal relations after a brawl, and when their term of office ended it was decided to pick men from different villages again. They certainly met less frequently, but because they were from different villages, competition between them was less likely to arise.

Although by statute juntas de freguesia may take a number of initiatives and may play a political role, lack of funds and dependence on the Câmara on the one hand, and the general characteristics of political life in the country on the other, prevent the local Junta from doing anything of the kind. The difficult financial position of the Junta is not new, and the minutes (from 1836 onwards) frequently record complaints of lack of funds.[3] But some of the Junta's difficulties, as indeed those of any other institution of its type, stem from the lack of understanding in

[3] There are thirty-one explicit complaints in the minutes, but given the fact that many problems dealt with in correspondence are not recorded in the minutes, we may assume that more were made. There are no records of correspondence prior to 1947, only a few odd letters having survived. The first complaint recorded in the minutes is dated 23 Feb. 1836: the chairman had to pay for the oil for the church from his own pocket; the last is dated 18 Feb. 1950 when the Junta declared itself unable to finance the installation of telephones.

people's minds of any notion of public good. The Junta, in caring for the interests of the residents as a whole, sometimes has to take, or try to take, steps that are difficult for individuals and sometimes even for members of the Junta itself to accept. As long as the chairman of the Junta was also usually the parish priest (up to 1910) he could, in certain cases, behave more like an outsider. In 1903 the cemetery was in such a bad state that the chairman decided to impose a special tax in order to restore it. The tax had to be agreed to by all members and the chairman warned them that he knew the measure was unpopular but would not accept excuses to postpone the necessary meeting.[4] Six months later he had to insist once more on a meeting and threaten them with the higher authorities if they continued to avoid the issue.[5] This does not mean that when the chairman was the parish priest, he was always eager to uphold the public interest. Indeed, in both 1836 and 1882, the newly arrived priests complained that certain of the Church's belongings had remained unlawfully in the hands of their predecessors.[6] But when the Junta is entirely constituted by local men, things are even more difficult. The case that follows illustrates the kind of problem involved and shows also that when private interests conflict with the public good, private interests tend to triumph. The Junta had generally neglected its olive-trees,[7] but in 1937 it was decided to establish its ownership of the trees by marking them. This was never carried out, and in 1949 we learn from a letter sent by the Junta to the Câmara that landowners ,whose land adjoined the public pathways bordered by the Junta's olive-trees, were placing their boundary marks in such a way as to include the olive-trees in their land.[8] Eventually, in 1951, the Junta marked the trees with paint, but this was of no avail, and it was obliged to complain to the guards that landowners were still picking Junta olives.[9] The situation worsened and late in the same year the chairman of the Junta resigned;[10] as a shopkeeper he was much more dependent on local sanctions than a landowner would have been. The Câmara intervened at this stage, appointed a trusted landowner as chairman, and brought in a

[4] J.m. 29 Nov. 1903.
[5] J.m. 2 May 1904.
[6] J.m. 1 Feb. 1836; 19 Mar. 1882.
[7] There are 1,060 olive-trees belonging to the Junta; J.c. 27 Aug. 1952.
[8] J.c. 4 Mar.
[9] J.c. 23 May 1951.
[10] J.m. 16 Sept. 1951.

lawyer to look after the interests of the Junta. But the lawyer did nothing. The Junta clerk (in 1965 the post was still occupied by the same man as in 1951) is convinced that some of the landowners paid the lawyer to ensure his inefficiency. Finally, the Câmara convened a meeting of the seventy-eight landowners involved and most of them attended. When the meeting ended the matter was settled—they were to continue harvesting the olives as before. It should be noted that it was not only small landowners who were involved: one of the richest latifundists wrote to the Junta protesting against the fact that the trees had been marked with red paint. Being a polemical right-winger, he even mentioned in his letter 'the international symbolism of that colour'.

There are many more instances in which private interest has triumphed over public good, but this is the best documented illustration of the situation.

These private interests may be the private interests of the members of the Junta. The Junta's budget is small but the need for cash among some of its members has led them to use Junta funds for private purposes on several occasions. These 'loans' were sometimes repaid, but the incoming Junta would often find discrepancies between accounts and funds. This happened, for instance, in 1893, 1896, 1910, 1914, and 1922[11]. In 1955 the new Junta complained that the former chairman had not returned some tools borrowed from the Junta's warehouse.[12] In 1965 he still had them. They were not very valuable and the Juntas in office during these ten years had not thought it worth forcing a direct confrontation over the matter. It should be noted that what was condemned in the former chairman's action was that he had kept the tools after his term of office expired and not that he had used them as his own and kept them at home while still in office.

THE CÂMARA MUNICIPAL

The Junta plays an unimportant role in the administrative framework and for some vital matters, such as the electricity supply, the undertaking of public works during periods of unemployment, payment of rates, licences, etc, the freguesia

[11] J.m. 4 June 1893; 22 Mar. 1896; 31 July 1904; 24 Nov. 1910; 18 Jan. 1914; 15 Jan. 1922.

[12] J.c. 24 Mar. 1955.

depends on the Câmara of Vila Nova. The latter, covering the whole concelho, is a much more complex institution, with a mayor, a deputy-mayor, four aldermen, a secretary and several clerks. The mayor, deputy mayor, aldermen, and most of the clerks are local men, while the secretary is an outsider, a civil servant. The secretary is the man who is familiar with the intricacies of bureaucracy—what can or cannot be done—but he does not run the Câmara as the freguesia clerk runs the Junta because the mayor and aldermen play a much more important role than do the members of the Junta.

The mayor is an important landowner or a professional man related to some landowning family. This has been so with a few brief exceptions at least since 1834. He is now appointed by the Government and is responsible to the Civil Governor of the province. This is comparatively new and should be emphasized. Between 1834 and 1928 there were two top authorities in the concelho: the president of the Câmara (the mayor) and the administrator of the concelho. The president, like the aldermen (*vereadores*), was elected locally and was always a local man, while the administrator was appointed by the Government and in some cases, although not very often, was an outsider. There were exceptions to this rule, however: due to national political circumstances the president was sometimes appointed and not elected. This happened in 1907, between 1910 and 1914 (the four first republican Câmaras), in 1917, and 1919 to mention only instances in this century.

This dual system of authority, vested in separate posts and separate persons, with its clear formal distinction between local interests and national (or government) interests ended in 1928 when the post of administrator was abolished. The administrator's main functions were allocated to the president of the Câmara, the latter being appointed by the Government instead of being locally elected.

The main result of this measure has been a tighter government control over the Câmara. The mayor represents local interests to the Government and governmental interests to the concelho. However, since only politically reliable men from the controlling group of latifundists and professionals are appointed as mayors, the degree to which the mayor represents local interests is doubtful. Since 1834, mayors and aldermen have been drawn from the latifundists and their important cilents. But in reading through the minutes, one becomes aware that there has been a change from 'rule by council' to 'rule by mayor'. Before 1928, aldermen sometimes expressed dissent, votes were taken, and there were cases when the mayor was overruled on particular issues. The mayor was always the leading figure but there was an institutional framework for tempering his decisions within the Câmara itself which is now lacking, since aldermen are no longer elected, in a way assuring them representation of the local people. The mayor, who is paid a small salary, personally invites the deputy mayor and the four aldermen to serve with him on the Câmara, although the latter have to be formally elected by the municipal council. Aldermen are not paid and are men of some wealth and social standing in the town: important shopkeepers or brokers, landowners, or senior clerks related to the important families. Nowadays they very rarely come from the villages, although this was not so until the late 1920s. Even then, however, they were locally important landowners. To have a labourer, artisan, or industrial worker on the Câmara would be out of the question. The mayor's position in terms of wealth and status is always higher than that of the councillors. It would be difficult to have a situation in the Câmara in which the day-to-day ranking order was subverted, with an alderman more highly placed in local opinion than the mayor whom he has to obey. The Câmara meets every Wednesday to deal with routine business. An emergency meeting may be called at any time, although this is a rare occurrence. Twice a year there is a meeting of the municipal council, a body which is supposed to represent all the activities and official bodies of the concelho. However, with the exception of the priest who represents the freguesia of Vila Velha, representatives are mainly important landowners or professional men related by kinship or marriage to landowning families. Besides formally electing the aldermen, the municipal council has to sanction the programme of activities of the Câmara and has done so automatically.

It should be noted that, although the Câmara is a much more powerful body than the Junta, it has no jurisdiction over agricultural policies, i.e. it cannot fix prices for agricultural products, provide subsidies, etc. Such decisions are made in Lisbon at the national level and put into practice locally through the Grémio da Lavoura. Since most of its land was alienated during the last century, the Câmara plays no part in agricultural life even as a landowner. In those matters in which it does intervene it is constantly afflicted with money problems. Its normal budget is much bigger than that of the Junta but it could not meet its commitments without subsidies from the State. In 1965 the ordinary revenue was around 1,800,000 escudos (about £25,720). This included revenue from rates, a proportion of general taxation, permits, water-rates, etc. It also received state subsidies of around 1,500,000 escudos (about £21,420)—earmarked exclusively for public works. Mayors always complain about the difficult financial situation in their annual reports.

Since the office of mayor carries only token payment, and in the absence of organized legal political parties that could support a candidate for the post, only a rich man can afford to devote himself to such a time-consuming job. He may remain in office for three terms of four years. after which he has to be replaced. If no one were found in the concelho who met the required conditions of political allegiance to the regime, proper social status, and willingness to take office, the Government could appoint an army officer as mayor. The presence of an outsider to rule over local affairs is very much feared and, although when first consulted all prospective mayors refuse the invitation, someone is generally found in the end to save the community from what is regarded as a serious threat of government tutelage. In fact, there has never been any need to resort to this tutelage, although whenever a mayor approaches the end of his term of office, there is always a fear that it may be imposed.

The difficulty of finding someone willing to be mayor is due to a number of reasons. First of all, most people will say that their own affairs are already as much as they can cope with, and that devotion to the communal good is a fiction invented by those who enjoy the external attributes of power in order to disguise their vanity. In the second place, owing to the complexity and number of problems submitted to the Câmara, it is considered that great skill is necessary to avoid hurting the feelings of friends and relatives. Since decisions have to be taken regardless of the personal consequences, the office holder is immediately open to criticism, which will come from all quarters including his own friends. Given the fact that the latifundists are able to establish political contacts on a purely personal basis, the mayor, although often a big landowner himself, may on occasion not know about decisions to be taken on matters connected with the concelho, when other people may already be aware of them. Shopkeepers and owners of small industries, even if canvassed for the office of mayor after several landowners or professional men have refused, will almost certainly refuse to serve (although there have been some mayors in their position in the past). As they would certainly have to displease some people to satisfy others, they would lose not a political supporter, which is immaterial in present conditions, but a customer. However, tradesmen and shopkeepers often serve as aldermen, since the position of alderman bestows some advantages without such great risks and is not so open to criticism like that of mayor. Aldermen are often suspected of furthering their own interests or of not complying with the rules devised to protect the general welfare. In 1921, when it was forbidden to take food-stuffs out of the concelho without payment of an *ad valorem* tax, a cart with 3,745 cheeses was seized by the Republican Guards and found to belong to an alderman.[13] When the Câmara calls for tenders, prospective contractors who are friends or relatives of the aldermen generally obtain the contract. In 1926 this was so scandalous that local newspapers carried articles about it, and the Câmara submitted its resignation to the Civil Governor.[14] In the early 1960s, the street where an alderman lived was paved, but the new pavement ended immediately after his house. In other words, he had simply seen to the paving of the stretch along which he himself had to walk every day. Finally, since public and private roles are confused in this society and the Câmara's budget is not sufficient to meet all its needs, the mayor sometimes pays for public works out of his own pocket. He derives a certain pleasure and prestige from this, but it may turn out to be expensive. However, this is in the best local tradition. The main square in front of the town hall is embellished with the statue of an important landowner and political cacique of the second half of the nineteenth century who was mayor for over twenty years, having taken office when

[13] LN V, 16 June 1921. [14] LN II 884, 3 Oct. 1926.

the Câmara was definitely settled in Vila Nova in 1851, and built up his own fortune while developing the new town. In 1923 another mayor paid for the paving of one of the squares, and as late as 1961 a council minute[15] thanked the current mayor for the money he had spent on public works.

The notion that the Câmara protects the interests of the rich much more than those of the poor is widespread. The Câmara, although outside the freguesia, is a necessary place of call on many occasions ranging from the payment of local rates and applications for permission to repair a chimney, to requests for public works (until 1956) and enquiries about emigration (since 1964). Poor people queue up to have their affairs settled. Those who have some influence jump the queue and go straight to the secretary or to the mayor himself. The secretary and the mayor are never bribed. Such affairs are settled on the basis of a mutual exchange of favours or, in the case of a very rich man, it is part of his ascribed status that the Câmara should comply with his needs and tastes, provided this does not infringe a major rule, although it may infringe a minor one.

A simple example will illustrate the point: Câmara permission is needed not only to build new houses but also to have any repairs done to an old one. This is, in fact, one of the main reasons that brings people to the Câmara. A wealthy man recently built a new house for his daughter without the authorization of the Câmara. The matter was raised by a small seareiro who, after spending an entire morning at the Câmara in connexion with his own house, shouted: 'You are making me take all this time and trouble because I'm a poor man (*porque sou um pobre*). If I were Dr. Custódio everything would have been settled by now.' He received no reply, but his outburst was considered a disagreeable incident by the mayor, who said that it was perfectly natural for the Câmara to wink an eye (anthropomorphism is a paramount feature of this society) in the case of Dr. Custódio as he was a man of taste and education and consequently should know what he was doing; it would have been inconsiderate to bother such a man with all the red tape involved. But he could certainly not trust uneducated people, who might not only ruin the urban landscape but even build houses that would be unsafe for those who dwelt in them.

[15] 14 May.

Most people who have bureaucratic matters to settle in the Câmara systematically bribe the clerks, the amount of the bribes varying with the relative wealth of the briber and the complexity of the matter in hand. Indeed, if one does not have a friend, a relative or a spiritual kinsman in the bureau—with whom there is already a previous bond based on favours exchanged—bribery is regarded as a means for securing a clerk's personal undertaking to look after one's affairs. Once he accepts the money (usually passed on to him in the course of shaking hands) he becomes personally involved in the matter, which ceases to be an official, abstract problem between a citizen and an administrative body and becomes a problem between two persons. Given the low salaries of Portuguese Civil Servants, for most of them bribes are a reasonably secure way of supplementing their income. As the world of bureaucracy is mysteriously hostile to peasants, a particular clerk may encourage the relationship, requiring more and more money in the process, but there is a generalized local agreement as to the specific amount needed for any particular operation. In the Câmara itself matters have been streamlined: the clerks have agreed among themselves on a schedule of bribes and on the allocation of specific fields of action to each. The secretary himself told me that the Câmara once more 'winks an eye'—although it is unlikely that he himself gets a proportion of the money thus collected.

This brings us back to the fact that although in principle the regulations of local government institutions make no basic distinctions between the rights of different citizens, the relationships between private persons and public authorities vary according to the social status of the person involved, such status being determined by a person's wealth, either in a direct way or through the prestige conveyed by higher forms of education which—with few exceptions—are only available to those who are not poor.

XVI

OFFICE AND OFFICER

THE distinction between office and officer, private person and public function, individual interest and the general good, is seldom clearly grasped and this difficulty of apprehension is found at every level.

In one of the villages a small landowner in his fifties who had once been a member of the Junta and was later put in charge of the sub-post-office, decided to leave the village to go and live on his *horta* ('vegetable garden'). Since a replacement for his post would be needed he began to consider possible candidates, without saying anything to the district postmaster. He eventually made up his mind about who his successor was to be and, on his last morning in the village, he went to the man's house, nailed the red letter-box to the wall, and handed over the stamps and other accessories of office. Under Portuguese law, this action constitutes a serious form of negligence, and the man would have gone to gaol had it not been for the intervention of some wealthy people in the freguesia and the town clerk.

One of the duties of the woman in charge of the public telephone in Vila Velha is to notify persons receiving booked personal calls. Whenever she has to do this, however, she always emphasizes how inconvenient it has been for her to leave her house at that particular time (whatever the time may be), thus converting what is one of her stipulated duties into a personal favour. Mr. Deusdado, the clerk of the Junta, is called upon at almost any hour of day or night to type out certificates—the idea that official departments have definite working hours being quite alien to country people. He runs his department according to his own convenience. People coming into Vila Velha from the villages do not ask 'Is the Junta open?' but 'Is Mr. Deusdado in?' Since certificates must be signed by the chairman of the Junta, who is not available at the Junta office at any precise time during the week, the persons in need of them will take them along to his house after the text has been typed out by the clerk.

When money is involved, the overlapping of office and officer may become more complicated. The treasurer of the Casa do Povo is generally a fairly wealthy local landowner. In bad agricultural years, he may make use of the Casa do Povo's money for personal ends, generally paying it back later. In one such instance, however, the treasurer died while still in debt and since, by agreement with the clerk the loan had not been entered in the books, the clerk had to exact the money from the man's heirs, who were slow with the repayment. There was no legal way for the clerk to prod them without getting himself into trouble.

In Vila Velha there is a dilapidated Misericórdia building which has a four-bed ward and is known as 'the hospital'. Old people who are ill and whose families find it difficult to keep them at home are sometimes sent there by the local doctor. The Misericórdia has a resident employee, known as the orderly, who is supposed to look after the patients on the instructions of the doctor and the directors of the institution. In fact, he runs the place as he likes, occupying rooms that are not part of his official residential quarters, arranging patients' diets and their medication time-tables according to his own convenience, and even beating them on occasion. The patients, who are old and very poor, are in no position to complain, while the directors, who are also local men, know that the orderly should be fired but do not wish to get themselves involved in personal problems for the sake of abstract regulations. The orderly considers himself entirely within his rights and the situation has remained unchanged for more than ten years.

When the law is involved, matters become even more complicated. Trespassing by animals and the ploughing up of common municipal roads and pathways (which was particularly frequent in the years between the partition of the commons and the establishment of a land register in 1950), are infringements of municipal by-laws punishable by fines. The Câmara appointed one or two men, who are known as *zeladores* ('vigilantes'), for each freguesia and who were entrusted with the duty of seeing that there were no infringements of these by-laws. They were all local men, and between 1839 and 1885 the appointments went to the highest bidder at the Câmara's annual auction of the post. He had to cover his expenses from the fines he collected and naturally had to make enough to keep himself during his year of service. Judging from the complaints against the *zeladores* recorded time and again in the Câmara minutes, this was found to be an unsuitable system. As far back as 1879, one of the councillors summed up its drawbacks quite clearly. He alleged that the reputation of the men who became *zeladores* was far from unblemished. Dependent on the 'lack of morality' of the people for a living, the *zeladores* practised abuses when people kept within the bounds of the law because they had bid for their posts 'in order to make a profit and not to incur a loss'.[1] From 1885 on, the *zeladores* were appointed like other Câmara employees but were entitled to a share of the fines.[2] As local men they were still prone to show undue leniency towards their friends and undue harshness towards their enemies or their friends' enemies, and were known occasionally to make deals with the transgressors.[3] The posts still exist but have not been filled since the late 1930s. In any case, their importance had been reduced by the establishment of the Republican Guards in the concelho in 1911.

A similar change occurred with the other police posts in the freguesia. The rural police, recruited from local men and paid by the Câmara, was disbanded. The functions of the *regedor* and his four subordinate *cabos de ordens*,[4] private citizens vested with the authority to take up complaints and make arrests, were severely reduced since complaints are generally taken to the Guards. However, the *regedor*, a man in the confidence of the mayor, has the role of political informer. Since the Guards have only achieved full coverage of the freguesia since 1958, the *regedor* retained his traditional importance up to that time. His role was a difficult one. In the rare cases of fighting between young men, or in the even rarer cases of murder, he was asked to intervene, and the measures he took were seldom challenged.

[1] C.m. 5 Jan. 1879. [2] C.m. 23 Mar. 1885.

[3] Two letters from the Junta to the Câmara explicitly describe a situation of this kind and in the second the Junta asks for the dismissal of two *zeladores* (27 Jan. 1927 and 9 Apr. 1933). On 14 July 1937 the Junta writes to oppose the recent appointment of a *zelador*, on the grounds that he had filled the post before and had been guilty of the faults of which the Junta had previously complained.

[4] Originally responsible to the administrator of the concelho, from 1928 *regedores* and *cabos de ordens* became responsible to the mayor.

In less clear-cut matters, however, this was not so. The following story illustrates the kind of dilemma often faced by the *regedor*. When João Gouveia, a small landowner, was *regedor* in the late 1940s, an old widow came to him with the complaint that a local shopkeeper had killed her cat out of sheer malice. João Gouveia was not only a friend of the shopkeeper but was also probably in his debt. The problem was a difficult one and he stayed awake all night talking the matter over with his wife. He decided not to mention the matter to the shopkeeper and eventually gave the old widow his own cat to settle the affair.

Another difficulty arises from the fact that the exercise of authority is often regarded as a licence to evade the law. Because they are part of the legal framework, *regedores* and *cabos de ordens* consider themselves authorized to manipulate the law. One of the *cabos de ordens* was also one of the most notorious smugglers at the time when smuggling was a flourishing activity (between 1939 and the late 1940s). He escaped scot-free, but the man who was *regedor* at the time had to be dismissed not only because he was caught in the act but also because he kept a military pistol without licence. He was genuinely convinced that as a *regedor* he did not need a licence.

These two problems—the restriction on the use of authority on the one hand and the abuse of authority on the other—are particular instances of the more general problem of the conflict between private and public obligations. Both problems make it clear that outsiders are needed for certain key posts related to the enforcement of law.[5] This is the case with the Republican Guards, judges, and the head of the tax bureau. Local men always lack the independence that is ideally necessary for the

[5] This is an old tradition. In the fourteenth century *Juizes de Fora Parte* ('Judges from Outside the Parish') were created. As outsiders to the towns to which they were appointed they were less subject to local pressures than the ordinary local judges (Justices of the Peace). The law creating the post is quite explicit on this point:

> Locally born judges will by right and reason find many occasions not to carry out justice in the proper manner . . . because natives of the parish will have many friends and kinsmen there as well as many others to whom they are bound by the obligations of partnership or other bonds. Others may have ill feelings and little love for them [i.e. the locally born judges] or may fear them. It is, therefore, right and proper to presume that native-born judges will not perform their office as well as strangers. (Law of 21 Mar. 1349).

The post has now been abolished, but the new judges continue to be outsiders.

discharge of many public functions, but nowhere is this more strongly felt than in the imposition of penalties, most frequently in the form of fines. Characteristically, the most efficient *zeladores* although local residents were often not natives of the freguesia. Nowadays the only local men with a statutory right to impose fines are the Forestry Guards. Given the nature of their job, they cannot avoid exercising this right from time to time. But whereas the Republican Guards always keep the 50 per cent of the fines to which they are entitled, the Forestry Guards give their share of the fines to the local saint and the money is usually spent on the Misericórdia hospital. This places them in a more acceptable moral position *vis-à-vis* the other villagers, and their intervention is regarded as the result of their need to keep their posts rather than as an extension of personal greed. The saint stands for the freguesia. The donation of fine money to the saint is thus a symbolic way of sharing it among all. Even so, Forestry Guards seldom impose fines: they leave this unpleasant duty to the Republican Guards as often as they can.

XVII

LAW AND ORDER

THE GUARDA REPUBLICANA

THE Republican Guards were created in Portugal in 1911 and replaced rural police forces. The Guards strive to maintain law and order in towns, villages, and the countryside in general, both at a criminal and at a political level. Of the forty-eight Guards stationed in the concelho, eight are posted in a neighbouring freguesia.[1] They carry out their patrol duties in pairs, and the freguesia is visited regularly on their rounds. By law they all have to be outsiders. They are generally recruited from among poor country families and undergo additional military training after their conscription service ends. In the villages where they are posted, they do not invite people for drinks in the taverns and do not pass around their cigarette packets before smoking themselves. The Guards are responsible to their own command. In the past, they have lived in houses provided by the Câmara, and there were conflicts over this. In 1922 they almost left the concelho for lack of appropriate accommodation but, although this was costly for the Câmara, they were—and still are—of vital importance for the defence of private property, a point often made during Câmara sessions, in newspaper articles, and in the correspondence of the Syndicato and Grémio. They have to deal with a wide variety of complaints, ranging from trespassing by animals to disputes between neighbouring women. Their rifles are loaded and they may at any moment be called upon to deal with some urgent problem. They see to it that wood, olives, or acorns are not stolen in winter from the big estates. The owners of these big estates maintain patronage relationships with the Guards

[1] The post in the neighbouring freguesia, created in 1958, provides for the patrol of Vila Velha. Up to that time the Guards had to come from Vila Nova to patrol the freguesia. The Junta had often complained and asked for better protection. J.c. 13 Sept. 1930; 12 Mar. 1935; 26 May 1935; 10 June 1949; 4 June 1954; 31 May 1955; 7 June 1956.

and at Christmas time make them and their families gifts. In return they exact a strict protection of their interests. In 1949 a committee of landowners went to the station commander at Vila Nova to ask for stronger action to be taken by the Guards to counteract the endemic thefts of acorns and olives. The local newspaper commented that without stern measures the people would overstep the boundaries of the law. *A justiça branda faz o povo rebelde.*[2] When they are called by latifundists and rich proprietários to intervene in some labour dispute or in a disagreement over sharecropping arrangements, the Guards make a prompt appearance. Since politics in a general sense are practically non-existent in the freguesia nowadays, the Guards are not called upon to intervene in this particular field, although they have occasionally gaoled drunks for having loudly criticized the Government. They are basically feared and disliked but obviously cannot be the object of open hostility.

Although they themselves are outsiders, their colleagues elsewhere may be sons of the freguesia. When these sons of the villages come home on leave, they wear ordinary clothes and mix freely with their former companions and with the local Guards, thus providing a kind of bridge between local civilians and military outsiders. Although most local men will express their reluctance to embark on a career of this nature—since any kind of police work is equated with some form of oppression—and may say they would not have the courage to do such a job, the fact that girls do not seem to make this discrimination in choosing their future husbands has contributed to the popularity of the career.

The Guards, patronized by the wealthy, may in their turn provide patronage to the poor. The following is a case in point. Francelina, the daughter of an innkeeper, was betrothed to a mason, and her future husband was thinking of emigrating to France. The Corporal of the Guards, carrying out his routine patrol of the freguesia, usually stayed at the inn, and the innkeeper often refused to accept payment. Some months before her marriage the girl unexpectedly invited the Corporal to be godfather at the wedding. The invitation was accepted. A few months after the wedding, the husband made up his mind to emigrate and applied to the provincial civil government for

[2] 'Mild justice makes a rebellious people.' LN II 786, 30 Oct. 1949.

a passport. When the request eventually came through to the Guards for corroboration, it fell to the Corporal to confirm his statements. At the time (1963) it was very difficult for a mason to obtain a passport, so the man had declared himself an innkeeper. This was, of course, not true, but as godfather, the Corporal let the statement pass and the passport was issued.

This was a manipulation of a traditional patronage mechanism, both for a new end and with a new type of patron. The move was so transparent, however, that it led to comment in the village. The Corporal remained unperturbed by the gossip and felt that the invitation had been a mark of respect and esteem for him. In some ways he became more closely linked to the freguesia, but his position was resented by those who felt that he had compromised his function by too blunt and open a show of favouritism. Situations of this kind seem to have been more frequent in the past.

One month after the first Republican Guards had been stationed in Vila Nova, all the men had to be replaced following charges of corruption over the imposition of fines.[3] In 1912 the local newspaper complained that there were not enough Republican Guards since the arable land in the concelho had increased, and as Guards were not replaced frequently, they soon came to be on intimate terms with the local population. The article concluded: 'Familiarity of this kind does not make for respect.'[4] It is likely that the new institution had not yet engendered the *esprit de corps* that it later came to develop. For although the Republican Guards are not as free from local pressures as they should ideally be, general complaints of the above nature are no longer made.

There are still situations which have to be kept secret and which greatly hinder the possibility of independent action by the Guards. The more obvious cases are those involving arrangements between Guards and shepherds. The Guard owns a few sheep in the shepherd's flock which are looked after by the shepherd and the two men share the proceeds from the sales of wool and milk. Since many of the matters referred to the Guards are related to grazing rights, and since it is part of a Guard's duty to look out for infringements of grazing regulations on his rounds of inspection, arrangements of this kind place the

[3] LN II 124, 2 Nov. 1911. [4] 14 Feb.

shepherd involved in a privileged position. They have, therefore, to be made in great secrecy, since the Guard could be transferred elsewhere or even dismissed if any complaint were made. But since it would be difficult to prove, the plaintiff could find himself in a difficult position and, to my knowledge, such complaints have never been made.

Thus, even the Republican Guards, who are outsiders by law and supposedly do not mix with the population, are susceptible to attempts to integrate them, both at a high and a low level, into the local network of social relations and interests. However, their own social relations are always confined to a narrow circle and while they mix with some elements of the population they do not receive the approval of all. It is felt that they are manipulated for particular purposes and are used by some members of the community against the community as a whole.

Since the Guards are largely dependent on favours received from individual persons who fall mainly within the latifundist group, it is not surprising that they should be regarded as instruments for ensuring the security of this group. In many instances they are looked upon almost as employees of the latifundists, although they are paid by the State. Indeed this is even expected as part of an unfair but unavoidable order. However, when poorer people—shepherds, shopkeepers, or small landowners—enter into patronage bonds with Republican Guards, they are singling themselves out from their group and establishing alliances which will always be regarded as having the sole purpose of securing leniency in legal matters. These rare cases are, therefore, regarded as instances of collaboration with the outside force of the State—with implicit harmful effects for the rest of the community—rather than as signs of the Republican Guards' integration into the community.

THE COURT

For judicial purposes the freguesia is part of a *Comarca* ('judicial district') with a court of justice in Vila Nova. As in the case of other Comarcas in this scantily populated province, the jurisdiction of the Vila Nova Comarca covers three concelhos.

Nowadays only civil and criminal lawsuits are brought to the local court. Litigations arising out of breaches of agreement between employers and employees, are handled by a special labour court in the provincial capital. Political offences—'offences against the security of the State'—which, in fact, may include anything from attempted revolution to verbal expressions of opinion are not tried locally either. We have seen that in 1911 the leaders of the rural strike were tried in Vila Nova. But as a result of legislation passed by the present regime all political offences are dealt with by special courts in Lisbon and Oporto where the briefing is entrusted to the political police. This procedure is designed to prevent any undue leniency (from the point of view of the prosecution) because of local pressures on the ordinary judges of the Comarcas. It also provides a convenient legal basis for the Government to choose the judges appointed to the special courts.

In the local court, the judge and the public prosecutor are outsiders, and the clerical staff of the court includes some local men but has outsiders as well. They are all appointed by the State and are responsible to the Ministry of Justice. Until the beginning of the century, lay judges or local justices of the peace, elected by popular vote, were responsible for judging minor offences (*transgressões*). As was only to be expected, difficult situations arose and favouritism was often expressed in their judgements. The elected Justice of the Peace in Vila Velha was usually a local proprietário or shopkeeper, and, when the Republican Guards came to the concelho, favouritism assumed a new form: the Justice of the Peace would often quash the fines imposed by the Guards[5] and some cases eventually had to be brought to the ordinary courts.[6] When there were conflicts between latifundists and local small proprietários over rights of way or grazing lands, the Justices of the Peace, being freguesia men, tended to favour the local proprietários. This can be inferred from the petitions lodged with the Câmara by latifundists who asked for such cases to be tried in the ordinary courts. Nowadays, when cases of this nature are not settled by the Guards or by the Câmara, they are always taken to the ordinary courts.

[5] LN II, 262, 25 May 1914.

[6] C.m. 31 Dec. 1858; 14 Feb. 1910; 1 July 1914. The jurisdiction of Justices of the Peace changed several times during the last decades of their existence. The minor offences described seem to have been within the competence of Justices of the Peace up to 1893, from 1907 to 1910, and from 1911 to 1914.

For routine hearings there is only one judge, but in some of the more important cases three judges sit on the bench, the other two coming from nearby comarcas for the purpose. There is at present no trial by jury. It is not difficult to hazard a guess that, given some of the characteristics of this society, trial by jury would often imply a gross miscarriage of justice. Apart from the reports of old people who told me how embarrassing it was to be a juryman and how some juries favoured 'a' or 'b', I have no evidence for making a definite statement on this point, but the sentences given in two cases tried in 1925 and reported in a local newspaper, may give some indication of the unpredictability of the freguesia's juries. A man who had stolen olives was sentenced to five years' imprisonment, whereas a man convicted of capital murder was given only one year. The newspaper gave no details, but the difference between the sentences is striking.[7]

Judges may not remain in office for more than six years in any given Comarca, and only rarely do they stay in one place for such a long period. While in the Comarca they are members of the local upper class and are often invited to dinners and parties given by landowners. Their contact with the rest of the population, except in their professional capacity, is slight. Ill-paid and overworked, judges nonetheless have a reputation for integrity, although attempts to bribe them may be made. In the late 1920s a court clerk in the Vila Nova Comarca was brought to trial, accused of having received money from litigants who were convinced that the money would be given to the judge hearing their cases.

However, a judge is not free from local pressures or attitudes. A few years ago, in a complicated case of inheritance involving the grandchildren of a deceased landowner and his widow (a young woman whom he had married in his old age), the court's verdict favoured the widow. Since this was an expensive lawsuit, three judges, one of whom was the local judge, signed the verdict. One of the grandsons, a local professional man in his late forties, severed relations with the judge over the case and refused to shake hands with him in public. Since this was tantamount to calling into question the judge's integrity, the judge brought an action against the man, who was found guilty

[7] LN II, 807, 16 Feb. 1925.

and fined. He is still convinced, however, that the judges in the original litigation had been bribed.

Going to court is considered a great nuisance and complication, and *andar metido em justiça* is an expression frequently used to describe the whole process. This can be loosely translated as 'being entangled in justice'. To the people of the freguesia 'justice' does not mean the same as it would mean to an educated Portuguese. Nor does it mean what the word 'justice' signifies in English. It conveys the notion that a person has become involved in an unknown, hostile, and money-consuming world with its own set of rules. It also implies that, in the hands of lawyers, court clerks, and judges, whether the case is lost or won, a man undergoes an ordeal from which he emerges certainly the poorer and usually the wiser. The rules of this world—which are identified by most people with the rules of the state—often bear little relation to the rules according to which peasants feel themselves to be right or wrong in a given dispute. And if and when they become involved with the law, the fact that according to their own set of values they are sure they are right, does not offer them any guarantees as to the final verdict of the court. The dangers of the courts are held in such awe that the explanation given in the villages for the difficult financial situation of an important local proprietário was that on his wife's death he had been 'hit by an inventory of minors'[8] (*tinha apanhado um inventário de menores*). This was quite ludicrous when considered in terms of the cost of such proceedings and the wealth of the man concerned.

The idea that justice is something that belongs to the world of the rich—the latifundists, professional men, and important proprietários—and that a poor man, simply because he is poor, will not find justice in court is widespread. In fact, opportunities for a direct legal confrontation between a labourer and a wealthy landowner—if we except summary suits for non-payment of house rents—seldom arise. But in the only two civil-law cases in the local court tried between 1955 and 1965 in which labourers and landowners were involved, the labourers won both. In both cases the plaintiffs' claims that they were natural sons of

[8] Mandatory by law when a husband or wife dies leaving sons or daughters under twenty-one, an inventory of the deceased's estate is made to prevent misappropriation by the surviving spouse.

deceased landowners were upheld. Since then, landowners have been heard to say that the courts favour the poorer side in such cases for demagogic reasons. It is obvious, however, that if social stratification does count it is the other way round, even in a court of law, where judges address defendants and witnesses from the lower social groups in a tone of voice different from the tone they usually adopt in the case of people from their own group and generally much more harshly.

Despite all these qualifications the court seems to be a fairly independent body. With the exception of the cases involving the young widow and the aggrieved grandson, I heard of no explicit accusations nor even any suggestion of corruption, although in minor matters the court clerks are systematically bribed.

XVIII
THE COLLECTION OF TAXES

LIKE judges and the Republican Guards, the head of the tax office is an outsider. The post is a difficult one to fill since the holder is responsible for determining the amount of tax to be paid by landowners, shopkeepers, tradesmen, professionals, industrialists, and others, and some of them are bound to protest at his assessment. Traditionally, the head of the tax office receives Christmas gifts of pigs, olives, olive-oil, and similar items from important landowners, the value of the gift varying with the landowners' wealth. This does not prevent disagreements from arising, and if the small or medium landowners or shopkeepers generally give in to the tax collector, things may go very differently with the latifundists. I know of two cases in which, after a disagreement, landowners appealed directly and personally to a higher-placed official in Lisbon, who settled the dispute in their favour. To evade taxation by all possible means—which range from bribing the inspectors to concealing produce—is, of course, a traditional activity. In 1899 a meeting of producers and buyers of agricultural products was held in the Syndicato to consider 'the surest way of protecting themselves from taxation (*fisco*) when it happens to be vindictive and treacherous (*vingativo e traiçoeiro*) as is more often than not the case'.[1] There is also a reference to the problem in a Junta minute for 1911. After an agricultural survey conducted by questionnaire, the Junta remarks that 'the results of the survey are possibly not an expression of the truth, since in some of the statements of the honourable landowners a certain reserve is noticeable which probably indicates their mistrust, from which we conclude that some of the statements are inaccurate'.[2] With the passage of time, statistics were feared less, but the Grémio still has problems and whenever it asks for precise information about crops the answers received are always inaccurate. The small producers, still afraid that their replies will be used for tax purposes conceal the true figures while the big producers often exaggerate them for the sake of ostentation.

[1] LN, I 14, 22 Mar. 1899. [2] J.m. 14 May 1911.

Since the information is sometimes necessary in order to determine future policies, gross mistakes may be made.

As far as taxes are concerned, the Syndicato and the Grémio have time and again lodged protests against new taxes or against what seemed to them an unfair implementation of existing tax measures. Although in minor matters the bribing of tax office clerks may help both small and big landowners, in more important matters there is little they can do. The latifundists usually manage to get matters settled in their own interest either individually, or collectively. A true test case took place in 1964. The Government promulgated a decree creating a new tax on 'the agricultural industry'. The tax applied only to those with 'taxable incomes' over 30,000 escudos (about £430), which meant that only two landowners resident in the freguesia were subject to it, and only about thirty in the whole concelho including several latifundists owning land in the freguesia. The decree provided for a more detailed estimate of real income than was generally required. Estimates of income were to be provided by a committee presided over by the head of the tax office and including one other civil servant and a representative of the landowners, who in the event was a latifundist and a member of the Grémio board of directors. The committee met twice and, at its first meeting, the latifundist agreed with all the estimates made by the others. At the second meeting, however, held on the following day, he made a point of recording his dissent in every single case. He felt the need to explain the change: 'I have old friends here', he said, 'and although I think you are being more than fair, I would lose them if I did not object.'

The latifundists were incensed by the new tax, which was attacked on three counts: (a) that farming was already in such difficulties that it required subsidies rather than further taxes; (b) that it was unrealistic to try to make any accurate assessments of incomes from agriculture, in view of the poor standards of book-keeping even on the big estates; and (c) that the tax was unfair in the sense that it was discriminatory and affected only the wealthy. This last point was strongly emphasized by the president of the Grémio. The mayor, himself a latifundist, tried to persuade the head of the tax office to decrease the estimates he had made, and publicly insulted him over his refusal to comply. He then wrote to the Civil Governor of the province stating that the head of the tax office was creating a climate of social and political unrest, which in the Portuguese situation, is a very serious charge indeed. Other pressures were brought to bear, and a few months later the man was quietly removed to another concelho supposedly at his own request, but in fact at the suggestion of the Ministry.

Meanwhile landowners all over the province had used their right of appeal against the estimates made. The freguesia's latifundists submitted appeals, but the two local proprietários did not. While the appeals were pending, the Government, under pressure from latifundists throughout the province, suspended the tax.

It is significant that it should have been the latifundists who appealed and not the two proprietários. Both proprietários were known to be heavily in debt and one of them had even been sued by a creditor. Both felt, however, that an appeal would involve expensive legal proceedings and that the outcome would be judged not on the merits of the case but in accordance with the influence of the appellants. They ultimately benefited from the suspension of the tax brought about by the latifundists' efforts, but they did not consider that their own intervention would have been either necessary or useful.

In this episode we find a repetition of the situation that arose over the problem of the allocation of labourers: in individual cases even latifundists may occasionally be forced to submit to local administrative decisions which they consider to be against their own interests but, as a group, they manage to use their influence (which extends beyond the freguesia or the concelho) with the higher levels of the administration to restore the *status quo*. However, despite the fact that they seem to manage to keep taxes at levels acceptable to themselves, latifundists never stop complaining about their straitened circumstances. When handing over office in 1965, the Director of the Grémio made the following remarks: 'Working the land, which was once an honour, has now become a degradation, such being the position to which it has been relegated by the current trends of opinion, which seek to subvert and trample upon those who, by the sweat of their brow, support, feed, clothe, warm and, comfort the very people who look askance at the true props of their existence.'

XIX

POLITICAL POWER AND CONTROL

THE bodies surveyed in the previous chapters are allegedly designed to serve the common good. It is clear, however, that the latifundists are often able to manipulate the working of these bodies for their own good and when this does not coincide with the common good there is an evident conflict of interests.

In some instances, however, the latifundists' interests have coincided with those of the community. During the civil war, which took place in the first half of the nineteenth century, the Câmara[1] was composed of some of the wealthiest men in the concelho.[2] Like most other Câmaras at the time, it supported the absolutist faction which controlled the Government and made periodic demands for certain supplies (cereals, olive-oil, firewood) required by its army. These demands became more frequent as the war neared its end, culminating in the Liberal victory of 1834. Between 1830 and 1834 the Câmara was asked to provide supplies on eight different occasions. In all but one instance, it refused, alleging that there was a dearth of food for local consumption. Although the Government's requests were often strongly worded, the Câmara did not yield.[3] Whether the concelho had been reduced to subsistence level or not is immaterial here. What is relevant is that important decisions were taken by the Câmara which certainly benefited the community as a whole.

In 1856[4] in reply to inquiries made by the Ministry for Home Affairs, the Câmara stated that although there were still large stretches of uncultivated land in the concelho, it would be impossible to undertake the permanent settlement of migrants

[1] At that time, the seat of the Câmara was in Vila Velha; the concelho first moved to Vila Nova in 1838.

[2] This can be inferred from the register of tax payments for 1828.

[3] C.m. 13 May 1830; 23 July 1832; 20 Feb. 1833; 27 Aug. 1833; 31 Dec. 1833; 24 Jan. 1834; 14 Mar. 1834.

[4] 1 June.

from the north of Portugal, a measure contemplated at the time by the Government in an attempt to prevent or decrease emigration to Brazil. In view of the subsequent evolution of the area and the frequent periods of unemployment that we know to have occurred, this was again a decision that favoured the community as a whole.

A railway was a local ambition. From the end of the last century until its eventual inauguration in 1927, latifundists fought for it, through the Câmara, the Syndicato, and local members of Parliament, with a persistence rarely encountered locally. For them, it was a matter of obtaining fertilizers more cheaply and more quickly and assuring a speedier delivery of their products. But all producers benefited and so, of course, did the landless population. In 1916, with the country at war, the Government exerted pressure to channel as much local produce as possible to Lisbon. This provoked strong reactions from the Câmara, the Syndicato, the local press, and the population in general, and the Câmara managed to stop consignments at a certain stage. But one of the wealthiest latifundists in the concelho apparently with the agreement of the Civil Governor of the province, tried to smuggle out a considerable quantity of wheat. When this became known, the population tried to prevent its dispatch with such violence that the Republican Guards had to fire on the crowd and several men were wounded. This was done, however, only for the sake of maintaining law and order because the authorities, including the Administrador de Concelho, who represented the central government, together with all the other latifundists were on the side of the people. The more conservative of the two local papers at the time went to the lengths of stating that, given prevailing conditions, poor people (*o povo*) were right to take action.[5]

On other and less dramatic occasions the latifundists, while trying to further their own interests, were also acting as spokesmen for the community, whenever they asked for an increase in wheat prices for instance (as they often still do), or for a relief in taxation.

But on many other occasions this was certainly not so. Although they fought for the railway at the end of the last century, this was only after the introduction of fertilizers and

[5] LN II, 360, 12 May 1916.

protectionist legislation had created a boom in wheat cultivation. Earlier, as in 1859, the Câmara had refused to contribute to the building of the railway that was beginning to penetrate the province, for fear that the area would lose manpower. This attitude prolonged the delay in opening up communications between the concelho and the rest of the country.[6] And, in 1856, after refusing to accept permanent settlers, it went on to suggest that temporary migrant labour for the harvest would be welcome, a proposal that was certainly not in the interests of local labourers. In 1899, the Syndicato joined in a successful fight against a project for the irrigation of the province. We do not know whether the project would have achieved its aims, but its purpose was a diversification of crops which could have provided work during the seasonal unemployment periods. On various occasions over the last sixty years, the Syndicato and the Grémio have urged the Government to prevent the temporary emigration of labour to Spain or France during the harvest season. In 1964 this took a more active form: the Câmara created difficulties for the man who tried to emigrate to France for the sugar-beet harvest under a government-sponsored scheme, and successfully limited the numbers of those who eventually left.[7] In 1961, the major latifundists in the province put successful pressure on the Government to prevent the implementation of an agrarian reform law.

Over other matters the conflict of interests was even clearer. We have already considered some significant aspects of labour problems in the last hundred years or so, but attempts by landowners to secure cheap manpower found other expressions: in 1965 the mayor refused permission for a factory for manufacturing cotton garments to be built in Vila Nova. The reason for the refusal was the fear of losing female labour, both in the fields and in the wealthy households. In the paper-mill outside Vila Velha, employing men and women from two concelhos, wages are kept lower than in the industrial centres by agreement with the local authorities.

Perhaps the clearest recent example of the conflict of interests

[6] 29 Aug.

[7] There were sixty-five applications from men in the freguesia of Vila Velha who satisfied the conditions of being over twenty-five, married, and literate, but the Câmara allowed only ten to leave.

between latifundists, big proprietários, and their clients on the one hand and the rest of the population on the other is in the field of education. Up to 1965, there were no official secondary schools in the concelho. There was only a private *liceu* or grammar-school teaching up to the fifth form (the full secondary-school course, leading to university entrance, is seven years), and industrial schools, which provide secondary technical education but do not lead on to the university, were completely absent. Such schools are normally attended by boys and girls whose parents are not wealthy enough to send them to university but who can afford to pay for a few years of education beyond primary-school level. A large proportion of the school-age population in the concelho fitted into this category. In 1965 the Ministry of Education decided to establish an industrial school in Vila Nova but, as it could not pay for the building, local financing was needed. One of the town's wealthiest families owned a suitably large house which had not been used for more than fifty years and, when first approached, agreed to consider the matter. A petition, signed by more than a thousand people, was handed to the head of the family to demonstrate the general unity of purpose. In spite of this, however, the family eventually refused to allow the house to be used.

The reasons behind this refusal were the object of much speculation. Eventually it became widely believed that some of the main latifundists, who were friends and cousins in various degrees of the family concerned, had pointed out that, after a few years of technical education, none of the boys would go back to agricultural work, a situation which, coupled with the increasing migration to industrial areas, would lead to severe labour difficulties for their agricultural concerns. An unexpected reaction followed the refusal. Vila Nova has three main 'recreation societies': the 'Club' for the latifundists, professional men, top clerks, and one or two wealthier shopkeepers; the 'Artística' for better-off artisans, shopkeepers, small clerks, small proprietários, and a few industrial workers; and the 'Atlético' mainly for labourers.[8] The board of directors of the Artística

[8] The largest and most active society is the Artística. The Club and the Atlético are on the decline. Rural workers who have become industrial workers have left the Atlético for the Artistica. With improved communication facilities the rich latifundists and their families can enjoy a more intense social life in Lisbon. They are still members of the Club but they do not go there often and their attitude towards

decided that it would give up the ball-room and some other parts of the club's premises to the Ministry of Education for the installation of the industrial school. Obviously children from the groups of the population from which the Artística draws its members stood to benefit most from the school, which the children of the latifundists, professional men, and rich proprietários would never attend, and which most labourers could not afford.

Comments on this episode were quite pointed: the 'rich' had once again tried to foster their own interests, even if this meant damaging the interests of the rest of the people. The fact that the Artística's decision also represented a sectional interest, which was perhaps not as wide as that of the community as a whole, was overlooked. What was new in this episode was that for once the latifundists did not manage to get their own way. In all the other instances which I have examined they were successful in protecting their interests, and an analysis of the administrative decisions taken by the different local bodies we have described invariably reveals the latifundists' ability to manipulate them.

Such a result in this case was possible only because the Artística is not an administrative body but a private association and the problem at issue was sufficiently delicate to prevent possible pressures from being brought to bear on individual directors by members of the latifundist group, and important enough to justify a refusal to yield to such pressures, had they been exerted. But perhaps the most decisive factor was the fact that the Artística had governmental sanction.

The administrative bodies are fully controlled by the latifundists who may intervene directly at all levels, or indirectly through their more eminent clients—professional men and top clerks. This intervention ranges from filling posts compatible with their rank from among the latifundists themselves to using their employees (*criados*, literally 'servants') for the humble posts, as we have seen in the case of the presidency of the Casa do Povo.

Some of the administrative bodies are partly local and partly integrated into the national framework, with regulations

it is condescending. Membership of the Club is still sought by shopkeepers or brokers in the process of enriching themselves who are sometimes accepted as members through their mutual patronage relationship with other men born into the upper group whose wealth is shrinking.

laid down in general codes. Conflicts are bound to arise over this ambiguity and in some cases the issues are important enough to need a radical change of policy by the national government rather than a partial disregard of the laws at local level. We have seen this in cases involving the Casa do Povo and the tax bureau.

In less important matters, but still at the locally high level of the Câmara—as also at that of the provincial civil government—a legalistic framework has to be preserved, while fostering local interests which may at first seem to contradict current legislation. The structure of these administrative bodies provides the machinery for the solution of such problems. By diligently searching through the legislation, the secretary of the Câmara and the secretary of the civil government, who are always career Civil Servants (the latter is required to have a law degree), generally manage to find a loophole that will make the demands of the mayor or the Civil Governor appear to come within the bounds of law.[9]

At a more basic level, however, even these legal manipulations are unnecessary. As private citizens, the latifundists can always have matters settled more easily than other people. When any document is needed, they can get it without having to leave their houses to go to the appropriate office. They can have identity cards made out at home, since the official is only too glad to take them the forms and other items needed, including the ink-pad for finger-prints. The Republican Guards are ready to come at their first call, sometimes for such matters as a disagreement with a sharecropper over the division of the crop, and will always side with the latifundist.[10]

[9] The man who was Civil Governor at the time of my field-work used a revealing phrase when taking matters of this kind to the secretary: 'Dr. So-and-so, will you make us a law?'

[10] The Republican Guards are required by law to take up any complaint lodged with them. But in trivial matters poor plaintiffs do not receive any better treatment than those against whom the complaint is lodged. The Guards may not be sure at the outset whether the complaint is genuine and both plaintiff and alleged wrongdoer are suspect. Once the genuineness of the complaint has been established, the methods of dealing with the latter, embody the following underlying assumptions, common to other forms of police procedure in Portugal:

(a) All suspects are guilty until they can prove the contrary.

(b) Those who arrest them or conduct the interrogation feel themselves entitled to mete out part of the punishment, which, because they are in principle guilty,

As members of the governing boards of the several bodies described, latifundists exercise extensive personal control over the clerks employed. A letter written by the Grémio in reply to an inquiry as to whether or not it had a written statute of internal regulations is illustrative in this respect. 'This Grémio da Lavoura has no statute of internal regulations. Only a few indispensable orders are given in writing. All matters concerning the staff are left to the discretion of the directors—leave of absence, sickness benefits, financial allowances, etc. In other words, in this Grémio da Lavoura we still live under a "patriarchal" régime—and with the best possible results.'[11] (quotes in the original). This 'patriarchal' régime may take curious forms. Some twenty years ago, a young clerk embezzled a small amount of money and was later found out. Instead of taking the matter to the police or to the courts, the directors made him write and sign a confession, which was kept in the safe of the Grémio. This same man helped me to find my way among the disorganized archives of the Grémio. A local latifundist (who had been a director of the Grémio at the time of the incident) had told me: 'Alfredo will help you there. Tell him that I have recommended you. He will do anything I ask.' While not always in so dramatic a form, all clerks are, for one reason or another, morally obliged to and dependent upon some of the members of the latifundist-professional group, whose instructions they carry out. Their loyalties lie much more with these private persons than with the general principles on which their functions as civil or corporative servants should be based.

A common characteristic of the political institutions we have discussed is that all of them normally operate in forms requiring the use of the written word. And the world of the written word seems to the peasant not only distinctly mysterious but superior. It is mysterious because he does not know its basic rules, i.e. he either cannot read or write at all, or, although considered literate for statistical purposes (with three or four years of formal

suspects are thought to deserve. This is the rationale behind general police violence against suspects, of which the violence of the Republican Guards is only a particular instance. However, the complaints of the wealthy are never regarded as open to doubt and if a wealthy man is caught in any infringement of the law—a traffic offence, fishing without a licence—he is treated with respect and seldom fined.

11 G.c. 19 Mar. 1945.

education), lack of practice may have made him forget the little he had learned and he is barely able to write his name or at best is able to spell out a newspaper headline. In the freguesia this is particularly true among the group of labourers and share-croppers. Even the proprietários who can read and write, however, feel ill at ease when confronted with paper work. The latifundists, on the other hand, have all had much more formal education, and some have university degrees.

The world of literacy is, thus, not only mysterious but also powerful. The entire structure of the administration and the formal organization of political control by locally powerful individuals is channelled through the written word.

People are aware that there are degrees of literacy, and prestige is attached to the literate in a hierarchical manner corresponding to the hierarchy of power within the administration. Important posts are usually held only by people with university degrees, and to be a *senhor doutor* (a title given in Portugal in ordinary usage to anyone holding a first degree) is to have reached the top rung in the ladder of prestige. Within the hierarchy of literate prestige, the peasant who was taught to read and has simply continued to read a few books and newspapers is placed at the bottom. During the last years of the monarchy and in the republican period (1910–26) there were several political parties, the press was free, and newspapers were more abundant, and a few men in this situation were able to acquire a much more general knowledge of political and historical matters than is now generally available to illiterate people. They were men who 'knew a lot' (*sabiam muito*) but there are very few of these men left, and amongst the younger generation none are in this position. No one, in present conditions, can play the political role that was once open to such men, while the radio and television are cutting people off from the type of experience represented by reading. The men 'who knew a lot' are still remembered and the few survivors are respected, but they have ceased to play any significant role.

On the next rung of the ladder of prestige established by literacy stand the junior clerks and officials who draft the minutes of the meetings of the Junta or Misericórdia, and the few shopkeepers who, like the clerks, can read and write letters for other people. Since practically everybody under eighteen can now read and write, there are hardly any families that need such outside help, with its accompanying risk of uncovering family secrets. But up to a few years ago, the practice was widespread, and the few literate people in the freguesia whose help was sought consequently possessed a considerable amount of information on other people's lives, a circumstance which gave an added importance to their function. Even today, bureaucratic difficulties are often taken to such people for advice, and, because of their familiarity with the written word, their opinion on these matters is accepted with a deference that is not given to less literate, and sometimes wealthier, local men.[12] Literate men who do not become clerks in the administration often occupy posts such as that of *regedor*, or *cabo de ordens*, or are put in charge of sub-post-offices.

Schoolteachers occupy the next place. They have traditionally played an important role in political life. Indeed during the last years of the monarchy and during the republican period, the concelho's more vocal anticlerical radicals and left-wing Democratic Republicans were schoolmasters. In present conditions, schoolteachers often hold political or administrative posts. The present secretary of the Câmara began his career as a schoolmaster. In the last fifty years or so, however, schoolteachers in the freguesia have been women, a circumstance which has considerably reduced the possibilities of playing a political role by occupying an administrative post. These women teachers enjoy as much prestige as a woman can in this society, but live a rather secluded existence and are not prominent in political life.

At the top of the ladder we find the *senhores doutores*. Medical doctors and lawyers are the two main categories, but everyone with a first degree acquires the prestige conveyed by this form of address. They derive power from the key posts they occupy in political and administrative life at concelho, provincial, and even national level. Thus, in the eyes of the peasants, knowledge and power, government and university, are closely related.

[12] Matters relating strictly to traditional agricultural practices are an exception. As could be expected, peasants consider themselves better informed on such matters than anyone else, regardless of differences in formal education. But most of these literate men are sons of small landowners who worked in the fields when young. They are thus vested with a dual authority that allows them to express their opinions on matters ranging from crop practices to international politics.

Although the *doutores* are known to have acquired different skills through their training, they are thought to share some basic knowledge which may vary in amount but is not really specialized. I was asked more than once whether my first degree (which is in medicine) has made me 'know *more*' than Maria (Maria is a local girl who was taking a degree in Germanic languages). People often asserted that Salazar's degree must certainly be the best, and enabled one to *know* more and would ask whether some opposition figure had taken the same degree.

This identification of power and literate knowledge which peasants see in operation at freguesia and concelho level and suppose to exist at the higher levels of government, together with the fact that such knowledge can be acquired at secondary school and university, accounts for the extreme importance of education in a peasant's eyes. To give a son an education which will enable him to have a career as a civil servant, a schoolteacher or, in rarer cases, as a professional man, is an important goal in the lives of the proprietários and an almost impossible aspiration for everyone else. Some proprietários contract heavy debts in order to give their sons an education. The progressive raising of educational standards in the country has meant that higher educational qualifications are required for any job, while the decline of local agriculture has created a need to find new jobs, which serves to reinforce the situation. At the turn of the century, sons of local proprietários and wealthier seareiros would, after leaving school, learn a craft (shoemaker, tailor, ironmonger) as a safeguard against the hazards of agriculture. Nowadays they are generally sent to *liceu* or some industrial school.

Through the 'knowledge' conveyed by education, a man finds his way to better-paid jobs and positions of political control. The entire administrative machinery is staffed by people whose place in the hierarchy corresponds to their literate qualifications. At the lower level, an abrupt line is drawn between white-collar workers and the illiterate or semi-literate population of the rural freguesia.

The social importance of an education, the relationship between the possibility of acquiring 'book learning' and the economic and social group into which one is born, and the prestige attached to the art of writing are all brought out in the confessional remarks made by a retired Corporal of the

Republican Guard: 'I don't have a bad life, but I could have had a better one. I should have been a lawyer. By inclination and vocation I should have been a lawyer. But my poor parents had no money, and the only education I could get was primary schooling. But even today I enjoy writing... The most intelligent man I ever met was a Sergeant at headquarters in Lisbon. He could write with both hands at the same time.'

All that has been said about the importance of the written word and the fact that even the smallest matter, dealt with by official institutions, more often than not involves an almost unbelievable number of documents of various kinds (certificates, forms, etc.), should not convey the idea that there is an efficient bureaucracy. There are always two levels at which to approach these matters: the official, legal level which involves all the red-tape mentioned above, and the personal, which is the really significant level at which things can be made to work. For someone trying to have matters officially dealt with, the first approach is a necessary condition, but it is almost certainly not sufficient. Personal intervention has to play its part.

This is, of course, the basis of the whole system. The abundance of legal dispositions on any matter is designed to preclude the possibility of any legal loopholes, but it is assumed that in most cases these dispositions will not be enforced and that matters will be speeded up by by-passing some of the provisions. If all regulations were observed, the life of the country would be paralysed within twenty-four hours. What is achieved through the control of the several administrative institutions at various levels—from the Ministries in Lisbon to the Juntas de Freguesia and Casas do Povo—is a selective application of the law for each particular case. What a successful patron generally manages to achieve for his client is not that the law should be applied to him but that it should not be. Even if all the respective forms have to be completed, the several bureaucratic steps are shortened and more direct routes are taken. When involved in any sort of problem with one of the official institutions, a person's main concern is rather to find a patron than to attempt to clarify a point or substantiate a claim at the legal level. What matters is the personal intervention of powerful men and not the internal coherence of bureaucratic rules. The legal level is, however, necessary, and nothing would be possible without it. For those who are unable to find a convenient patron it may involve considerable delays, and the outcome is unpredictable.

An official who is not subject to the influence of a patron, or, even worse, one with a grudge against the person who needs his services, can make life very difficult indeed without breaking the law. What he usually does is to insist on the strict enforcement of all the legal provisions on the matter. Indeed, this is one of the main uses of the law: to force the enemies of those who can control its application to obey it to the letter.

To find efficient patrons nowadays is often difficult or even impossible for labourers and sharecroppers. This means that both at the open and formal level, because of their illiteracy, and at the personal level, because of their lack of suitable connexions, they are in an unfavourable position. The search for a patron may thus become vital.

PART FOUR
PATRONAGE

XX

THE CONCEPT OF PATRONAGE

THERE is no Portuguese word in common usage that covers all the different operations which can be described under the heading of patronage.[1] This reflects the fact that the people involved do not see these operations as parts of a whole, or instances of the same social institution, but as different categories of action. These different categories are, however, responses to needs of the same kind: the needs resulting from the awareness that the number of things in life to which one may have access is very small and that most of the things to which one aspires are obtainable only through privilege. This privileged situation is, in its turn, attainable only through the protection of someone close to the ultimate source of the benefit needed. To secure such protection, a personal bond has to be created. The whole network of patronage is one of exchanged favours between private individuals often subsumed under the institutions of spiritual kinship and friendship. At a spiritual level, the cult of particular saints shows characteristics that are similar to those of the worldly patronage system.

This exchange of favours is, of course, unbalanced. In the give and take of patronage, one of the parties is in need and initiates the whole process by asking for a favour. If the favour is granted, it has to be paid for. But the payment that the client can afford is objectively less valuable than whatever he has been favoured with by or through the patron. For reasons

[1] The Portuguese word *patronato* exists, but it is very seldom used in any sense akin to the meaning of the word 'patronage' as employed by social anthropologists. In Vila Velha I never heard it used, and only once did I see it written, with a meaning that was close to the English (anthropological) sense. In a Junta minute for 1852 commenting on a protest made to the Câmara about the Junta's alleged unfairness in allocating plots in the commons that year, it is stated that the different plots had been 'chosen by lot' and that there could therefore not have been any *patronato* (J.m. 23 May 1852). In the context *patronato* reads as 'corruption' or 'favouritism'—which is indeed how most patronage operations are seen by outsiders, although this is by no means always so, as there are forms of patronage that have open and public aspects.

discussed later this imbalance has become more pronounced in recent years.

Implicit in the general acceptance of patronage is the notion that society is wrongly organized in some basic way and that individual rather than collective efforts are the only means of attempting to avoid this predicament. This is well illustrated by the Portuguese word so often used to describe the approach made to someone in a position of power (prospective employer, examiner, judge, public or private administrator) so as to ensure a favourable outcome. The word is *cunha* or 'wedge'. A wedge is the temporary, *ad hoc* solution found by individual cunning for a problem resulting from the looseness or other inadequacy of a mechanical structure of some kind. It is not an attempt to remedy the structural defect, but to make do with it as well as possible by obtaining a counteractive effect. The use of the word *cunha* in social contexts is based on an analogy derived from a day-to-day material reality. The technological level of the country is much lower than that of developed western societies, particularly in the countryside where still the wedge is often a necessary makeshift for repairing a traditional tool or mechanism. There are remarkable difficulties in obtaining spare parts for modern manufactured articles—from tractors and reapers to electric irons and sewing-machines—and as a result many disorders are ingeniously dealt with by the owners themselves using wedges of some kind or comparable aids.

To ask for a *cunha*, to obtain a *cunha*, to insert a *cunha*, are common operations—the necessary accompaniment to examinations, applications for jobs, legal trials, and many administrative and bureaucratic procedures. Whenever competition is involved—in the case of a civil-service promotion, for instance, or the securing of a permanent job in a factory or on a farm—selection takes place as much at the level of the *cunha* as on the basis of the specific skills allegedly to be assessed. To obtain the best *cunhas* one needs the best patrons. One may hear statements such as: 'for that purpose the best *cunha* you can get is Mr. So and So.' There is general agreement as to the efficiency of different people as *cunhas* and, just as in London there are experts on the Stock Exchange, so in Vila Velha there are experts on the best value to be had in *cunhas* from particular persons for particular purposes at any given time.

During the course of a lifetime the need to find a patron is likely to be a frequent and recurrent phenomenon. A poor man requires the consistent protection achieved through a permanent patronage relationship. The few people who are well placed in life will, of course, grant more favours than they ask for and will thus be patrons more often than they are clients.

XXI
SPIRITUAL KINSHIP

SPIRITUAL kinship is a permanent and closed relationship. It has an institutionalized formality of ceremonial nature which is not found in friendship or in the cult of the saints.

Spiritual kinship is entered into at two critical moments of life: baptism and marriage. When a baby is born he should be baptized, baptism being regarded as by far the most important of the sacraments. Even when there was no resident priest in the parish people tried to arrange for their children's baptism.

Through baptism the child gains admission to the body of the Church, and the soul is redeemed from original sin. A non-baptized soul will remain for ever in limbo. However, it is not only this spiritual disability that people refer to when they speak of someone who has not been baptized. They say: '*Quem não tem padrinhos morre mouro.*' ('If you have no godparents you will die a Moor'). There is no reference in the saying to the sacrament as such but to the *padrinhos* (i.e. the two godparents, generally a male and a female, who accompany the child and his father to the church for the baptismal ceremony). Whereas the sacrament itself introduces the child to a proper spiritual world, the *padrinhos* are in fact also sponsoring the child's entrance into society and this is an important implication of the ceremony. Even children of the few convinced atheists, who are not baptized in the church but simply registered in the civil registry, have *padrinhos* since the word is applied to the two people who accompany the parents to the registry as witnesses. This is both a rare and a recent phenomenon and people will point out that *padrinhos de registo* ('registry godparents') are not as good as *padrinhos de água benta* ('holy-water godparents'), thus emphasizing the importance of the spiritual side of the ceremony. However, the same word is used, and the worldly roles of *padrinhos de registo* do not differ from those of *padrinhos de água benta*. In some rare cases, a child may have a spiritual *madrinha* ('godmother') in the person of a saint as well as human *padrinhos*. This happens when the delivery is difficult: the midwife then sends to one of the local churches for the gown of a female saint or of one of the images of the Virgin Mary to drape over the shoulders of the mother in order to speed and ease labour. If the child is a girl she will bear the name of the saint or of the particular invocation of Our Lady who came to the mother's aid in this way.

But most children have only human *padrinhos* whose ideal role is to provide aid and support in the material world. The words *padrinho* and *madrinha* literally mean 'little father' and 'little mother'. Since a person who has no *padrinhos* is said to die a Moor and no mention is made of the soul going to limbo, it is obvious that the saying does not refer simply to a metaphysical distinction between Christian and non-Christian. Other expressions in current use—*vida de mouro* ('a Moor's life') or *um mouro de trabalho* ('as hardworking as a Moor'), both of which imply difficult conditions—point to the fact that to be a Moor was not only to be non-Christian but to live at the lowest level of society, working for little reward and often as a slave. Moreover, up to the beginning of the nineteenth century, in order to be eligible for posts in the administration and other corporate bodies (viz. the Misericórdias), the applicants had to provide 'proof of cleanliness of blood' (i.e. excluding Jewish and Moorish blood), the scrutiny of his family background going back four generations.[1] People in the freguesia are no longer aware of these implications, but the word *mouro* is frequently used in such contexts. Not to be baptized is therefore seen as both a spiritual and a social handicap.

Ideally, *padrinhos* should aid their godchildren on any occasion and help them through the hardships of life. One of the traditional duties ascribed to the *padrinhos* is to take the place of the child's parents in case of need. In fact the reciprocal term for *padrinho* is *afilhado* (literally 'taken as a son'), but adoption has taken place only in very rare cases, and in all those known to me the *padrinho* was himself childless. The main agricultural 'house' of our region is owned by the descendants of an *afilhado* of a man who had made his fortune in the nineteenth century. There

[1] This was mentioned as a condition for membership of the brotherhood of the Misericórdia in an 1820 statute modelled on one of the statutes of the Lisbon Misericórdia.

are other cases of adoption of *afilhados* but as a rule this does not occur; the *padrinhos* may give financial help if they can afford it, but they will not adopt the orphan.

Ideally the tie created by the establishment of a spiritual kinship relation is of a sacred and almost familial type as strong as that of consanguinity. People kiss the hand of their *padrinhos* and *madrinhas* and seek their blessing, a form of behaviour generally reserved for the mother and father. When *padrinhos* are chosen among close kin (cousins or uncles), the *padrinho–afilhado* relationship will superimpose itself on the pre-existent kinship position to determine the relative terms of address. The parents of the child and the *padrinho* become *compadres* (literally 'coparents') and so do the *padrinhos* who address each other by the reciprocal terms *compadre* and *comadre*. The relationship was also subject to the rules of incest, which further emphasizes the almost familial aspect of the institution; but if this prohibition was ever respected, it no longer is, although people who are engaged or have a namôro are never invited to be godparents to the same child. When people address each other as *compadre* or *comadre*, the emphasis put on the form of address varies according to circumstances: poor people who have rich *compadres* will be eager to use it in conversation, thereby including themselves in the near-familial relationships of the rich *compadres*. For the opposite reason the latter will be more reluctant to use the form when addressing those who are poorer. Obviously a person has only one *padrinho*, whilst a *padrinho* generally has several *afilhados*, and anybody may have quite a few *compadres*. From a purely formal point of view, the more specific and unique the relationship, the more it is emphasized.

At the marriage ceremony both the bride and the groom should be accompanied by their baptismal *padrinhos*. If the latter are no longer alive, they should be replaced by their sons or daughters, but this is not always the case, and new *padrinhos* may make their appearance. They share some of the reverence accorded to baptismal *padrinhos*, although the relationship is of a much more profane nature (there is for instance no asking for blessings or kissing of hands).[2]

[2] Spiritual kinship may be established at another moment: confirmation (*crisma*). This is rare, and when it happens the reason is to be found in the need to sanction a patronage relationship at a moment when there are no births or marriages in the family.

Spiritual kinship may be used to reinforce existing kinship ties. Some people emphasize that this is how it should always be, i.e., people who are not kin should not be asked to be *padrinhos* to a child. That this is the ideal way is by no means generally agreed upon, although in practice one finds this pattern prevailing. When this is not so, however, the need to find *padrinhos* will probably mean the creation or reassertion of a patron-client bond. In a few cases a friend of the husband (or a female friend of the wife), rather than someone from a higher social group, may be invited, this being a symbolic inclusion of the friend in the kinship network. But in the majority of choices outside the family it is someone of more importance and wealth than the child's parents who is invited to become a godparent. These invitations raise several problems—the first being to choose a *padrinho* and a *madrinha* who are socially compatible. On the one hand it is thought that to choose *padrinhos* who do not belong to the same social group (labourers, sharecroppers, small landowners) would be to subject the wealthier godparent to a situation that could be considered to show a lack of respect and consideration. On the other hand, if a member of an equally wealthy family is invited to become the other godparent it might seem there were doubts about the powers of patronage of the first family. What generally happens in these cases is that the two *padrinhos* come from the same wealthy family or, if not, the second godparent will be a member of the child's family. These invitations were, on the whole, easier to make, and hence more frequent, up to some twenty or thirty years ago owing to the large number of *concertados* still employed at that time. Ideally no one should refuse to help to bring a new soul into Christianity. But even at the risk of incurring spiritual penalties, refusals do occur. To avoid this, labourers approaching a latifundist family are careful to make inquiries first, through someone they know in the 'house', if they are not employed there themselves. The second problem, of another nature, is the village talk, whenever requests of this kind are made and particularly if they begin a cycle of patronage between the prospective patron and client families. Some will invoke the tradition that *padrinhos* should be drawn only from the family, others will accuse the child's parents of vanity (*vaidade*) for having sought protection in such high places. Comments are particularly harsh when there has been a real breach of custom. This happens when wealthier people are invited to become *padrinhos* of marriage in the place of the living baptismal *padrinhos*.

The system of favours involved in spiritual kinship is sanctioned by the religious aspects of the institution that ideally give its operations a stable and respectable frame. It is both a system for obtaining concrete advantages and a way of self-identification and promotion. In some cases it is a way of maintaining bonds that, like family bonds, are ideally transferred from one generation to another. A peasant stated that his family had always had the best tracts of sharecropping land on a big estate, because they were *afilhados da casa* ('godchildren to the "house"'). In fact, his mother was the daughter of a general manager in the 'house', and one of her brothers had been sponsored at baptism by the owner before the turn of the century. This bond, established some seventy years ago, was sufficient for the whole family to consider itself *afilhados da casa*. Reciprocity in these cases is far from being the rule. The present owners of the 'house' do not feel that they have any special duties towards the families of godsons of two or three generations back.

The superimposition of the set of roles created by spiritual kinship on roles created by other social relations may be carried to extremes. A fairly wealthy landowning family employed a young servant girl whose sister was the *afilhada* ('goddaughter') of one of the nieces of the landowner's wife. Instead of addressing them as *minha senhora* and *Senhor X*, as her status as a servant required, she consistently called them and their sons *padrinho* or *madrinha* to the point of causing embarrassment in the presence of guests. The form of address was intended to emphasize that, although she was employed as a servant, the bond connecting her to them was of a higher and less transient nature than that between master and servant, employer and employee.

Like family or kinship bonds, spiritual kinship bonds cannot be severed—as can those of friendship. Persons may break off a relationship, but they retain their relative formal positions. In the above case, however, the bond was certainly much more important for the young servant than for her employers and she became so troublesome that she was eventually dismissed.

Spiritual kinship as a means of bridging social distance in a personalized way and securing benefits of an exceptional kind for those sponsored is, therefore, far from guaranteed. First, the relationship does not often occur between the top and bottom social groups (except in cases of some male and female servants and, when they existed, of long standing *concertados*). Spiritual kinship bonds outside the family are in fact more often found bridging consecutive strata of society—from latifundists to local landowners or proprietários, and from the latter down to small sharecroppers or labourers. Secondly, by its very nature, it cannot be a widespread form of efficient protection. Although important landowners and their wives and children[3] were frequently invited to become godparents at christenings, the number involved was very small when compared with the total numbers of those who were born or married. In fact, this was necessarily so, otherwise the privilege associated with the relationship would of course disappear. Thirdly, the institution is declining. Locally resident landowners may sometimes still be invited to become godparents by people of the freguesia—although latifundists living in Vila Nova are seldom asked nowadays. Their response to these invitations varies according to their outlook on life. Those who are trying to streamline and modernize their farms or even to disentangle themselves as much as they can from direct farming do not wish to be saddled with the burden of several *afilhados*, with its traditional obligation of providing various forms of help, including employment. And in the present political situation, they do not need a large body of followers for electoral purposes. Those who are involved in traditional farming and find themselves caught up in a process of gradual agricultural decline enjoy being asked to become *padrinhos*, since for them this is an assurance of a local prestige that is slowly fading. The very few who are moving upwards are also pleased to be asked to act as godparents and will talk about their commitments in this respect. An innkeeper who is making some money out of the tourist trade in Vila Velha, some of the men who are now moving between the freguesia and France, and some of the better-off industrial workers belong in this group. To be invited to be a godfather underlines the new importance of their position and although the direction of their

[3] Since the spiritual kinship bond ideally connects not only godparent and godchild but the latter's whole family to the godparent, it is very frequent for a small child to be invited to act as spiritual sponsor, thus securing an active relationship for a longer span of time.

financial and social movement is the opposite to that of the declining group, their situation in this context is similar. The innkeeper's wife once said: 'we are often invited now *porque temos esta vida assim.*' (Literally 'our life being what it is', i.e. because we have become people of consequence). Just as those who have, or whose children have, important godparents will mention them in conversation or address them as *padrinho* or *compadre*, so those who enjoy being invited to be godparents will speak about their *afilhados*. '*Afilhado* João came in yesterday', one of them will say, this being a mode of expression not commonly used. The need to assert that they have godchildren (*afilhados*) is in itself indicative of the insecurity of their position. The importance of the relationship in these cases is much more of an expressive than of a useful nature. The amount of protection that declining proprietários can afford to give is small and will tend to become even smaller. And those who are moving upwards do so in an increasingly changing, mobile, and secular society, where the obligations of spiritual kinship tend to vanish and long-term commitments are difficult to fulfil.

But however much on the decline the institution may be, the rationale behind it is still justified. A man by himself is always in a potentially weak position, and the poorer he is, the weaker is his position. Support must be sought, and the first and most obvious institution that provides this support is the family. But a labourer's family will, in any case, be a poor and uninfluential group and, even if a man is a proprietário, the same applies, with little qualification. Only the very rich latifundists of Vila Nova can ignore these contingencies—they are the *padrinhos* of other people and *afilhados* only among themselves, and mainly within their own family.

Spiritual kinship stands between the ascribed formal pattern of relationships determined by kinship and that of the voluntary, less formalized relations deriving from friendship. Like friendship it is a voluntarily created bond, but like kinship it is, theoretically, sacred and irrevocable. *Compadres* come somewhere between *parentes* ('kin') and *amigos* ('friends'). The interchange of favours between *compadres* cannot be interrupted as easily as that between friends, and the removal of the avowed basis of the relationship from a purely emotional ground to a ceremonial one makes for its ideal strength. Other factors, besides the eagerness of clients to enter into bonds of spiritual kinship with their patrons, are indicative of this strength. A traditional ritual that has almost completely disappeared since the 1930s, but of which people still talk, points to the importance of *compadrio* (the relationship between two *compadres*). The two Thursdays before carnival are known as *Compadres Thursday* and *Comadres Thursday* respectively, and on these days a joking relationship was tolerated with verbal abuse from men to women and practical jokes from women to men. The special relationship created between those who abused and those who were abused was seen as *compadrio* in an obvious reversal of the seriousness and weight of the social commitment of the normal situation—a reversal that had to do both with the respective roles of the sexes and with the almost sacred nature of the *compadrio* relationship. At another level the word *compadrio* is often used in a derogatory sense to denote a patronage situation, when the person talking is an outsider and thinks general norms are being distorted to serve the private ends of a small group. The members of this group do not necessarily have to be *compadres* for the word to apply. One also occasionally hears the remark: '*Isto é um país de compadres*' ('This is a country of arrangements between *compadres*.') Finally the word *padrinho* may be used by extension to describe any sponsor. Such is the case when an amateur bull-fighter becomes professional. An already established professional who becomes his *padrinho* sponsors him. In this case, as in the original religious situations, the *padrinho* sponsors a man who is going through a *rite de passage*. But in ordinary usage this connexion may be lost and *padrinho* may become synonymous with protector, a sense present in the remark: 'He went far in life because he had good *padrinhos*.'

Spiritual kinship may be seen as a method of further extending a man's web of kinship relationships in a select direction. The full observance of the rights and obligations thus created is qualified, however, by particular situations, as in the case of kinship relations. And a man will often have to seek support, not from his kin or spiritual kin, but from his friends.

XXII

POLITICAL FRIENDSHIPS

IN January 1900 the recently elected local M.P., a very wealthy university graduate and a latifundist, paid visits of thanks to the several villages of the concelho. The local newspaper carried a report of the visit paid to one of the villages on 18 January. The streets were decorated with flowers, the population joyfully acclaimed him in the streets, a fireworks display was put on, speeches were exchanged, and he had meals at the houses of eight different *influentes*.[1] He arrived in the late morning and in the evening he went to a nearby village 'accompanied by 209 friends' (*acompanhado por* 209 *amigos* [sic]).[2]

Both the number and its precision are remarkable. The large number immediately excludes the notion of friendship as basically a reciprocal emotional bond; the precision implies that the reporter counted them. The reporter was the editor and owner of the paper, a personal friend and political supporter of the M.P., and when stating the figure 209 he was publicizing the importance of this man, who could move around with such a large clientele.

These friends were clients who benefited from the potential or actual protection of their interests, by their patron the M.P., and repaid him by guaranteeing the necessary number of votes whenever elections were held. In most cases, a chain of individuals in a position to do one another reciprocal favours came between M.P. and voter.

Between the Regeneração (1851) and the Republic (1910) the party system of the Portuguese constitutional monarchy found local expression in the division between the two main latifundist families in the freguesia. Each backed one of the two main parties and provided the poles around which two clienteles were established.

[1] *Influentes* were the local *caciques*—small landowners, shopkeepers, or schoolteachers, who could control a number of voters in the elections.

[2] LN I 48, 21 Jan. 1900.

A similar situation was found at the wider level of the concelho. Between 1860 and 1880 the main supporters of the two political parties were two brothers-in-law who had severed relations. Their respective descendants remained in traditional opposition to one another until 1910. The two families had their respective cluster of clients, and personal rivalries thus found an institutionalized and external way of expressing themselves.

The manipulation of votes was carried out in the freguesia by two different 'pyramidal' groups having at their apex the heads of the two main latifundist families. Permanent employees and godsons of these families voted with them as a matter of course. Among these spiritual kinsfolk were locally important proprietários, some of whom were descendants of former managers or sub-managers of one or other of the two big 'houses', and as a rule they continued to give their political allegiance to their former masters. But there was a large number of people with whom direct ties were not pre-established and who had to be won over by more active means in order to secure their votes and the votes they could in turn muster for the candidate of one or the other of the two parties. Payments for votes could be made in several different ways, according to the social position of the persons concerned. The most important method was, perhaps, the allotment of land for sharecropping under better conditions than those generally prevailing. It is said today that some men were able to get much better deals in their sharecropping arrangements with the latifundists *por causa dos votos* ('on account of the votes'). These small proprietários who sometimes farmed up to thirty or forty hectares of land on the big estates were able to guarantee not only their own votes and those of their sons, but also those of labourers they employed during the harvest season and of some of their poorer relatives. In some extreme cases the latifundists gave away houses in the villages together with adjoining tracts of land for the same purpose. Near one of the villages there is a small cluster of plots adjoining the estate of one of the latifundists which now belongs to several different families, and was allegedly created by a partition of part of the estate in the 1890s carried out to secure political allegiance.

Shopkeepers were attracted by the guarantee of a wealthy customer for their shops—and they themselves commanded the votes of their poorer customers who were nearly always in debt to them.

There was still another common way of mustering votes. Up to 1910 those who were drafted to the army could avoid going by paying an indemnity. For poor people who could not afford the indemnity the local latifundists often offered to supply the money in return for votes. In 1900 the sum of 150,000 *reis* was needed for this purpose and it was reckoned to be worth three votes. Each vote thus cost about 125 times a labourer's daily wage at that time.

These three methods of securing votes were common enough to be remembered by many people or known from tradition, but it can reasonably be assumed that there were other situations in which help from the powerful could be obtained by those in need of it in return for their votes.

The Republic brought about great changes in this system. Exemption from conscription on any grounds other than physical fitness was abolished in 1911. However, this was not the most important change. The abolition of the old parties and the formation of new ones—although some of the new parties absorbed previous adherents of the old—considerably altered the political picture. In our freguesia one of the two main latifundists remained royalist and ceased to intervene in parliamentary politics. The other, at first a conspicuous republican, soon recognized that the Parliamentary Republic did not suit his interests best.

This is an important point. Although a few latifundists in the concelho remained monarchists, most of them did not, and the mayor and deputy mayor of the first republican Câmara, which took office on 7 October 1910, were two of the wealthiest men in the concelho. For a short time it seemed that the republican parties would create the same cleavage of society from top to bottom, allowing the latifundists to retain their political control within a parliamentary framework through the traditional patronage mechanism. But republican propaganda proved a double-edged weapon for the latifundists. As in the case of the working class in most other parts of the country, the labourers in the province had been attracted to republican ideals, and it was partly as an outcome of these ideals that the 1911 strikes were possible. For the first time landowners and labourers were in clear-cut opposition within a political framework.[3]

Reading through the court records of the trial of the local strike leaders, one becomes aware that 'the Republic' had quite a different meaning for landowners and labourers. The strike was at one and the same time organized and repressed in the name of the Republic. The official letters written to the Lisbon police by the Administrador de Concelho, and the written messages exchanged by the accused during the strike, end with the same Republican greeting: 'Health and Fraternity'. Witnesses testified that some of the accused had assured them that the strikers would win because the Government was on their side, that it was, in fact 'their Government'. While Republican newspapers in Lisbon seriously suggested that the strikes were provoked by monarchists to create difficulties for the new régime, and while this was also hinted at by the prosecution (although not proved by the evidence), one of the accused declared that he had always been a Republican, that the local M.P. knew him well and that the fact that he had been gaoled could only be attributed to the machinations of a monarchist plot.

There were obviously two conflicting 'Republics': one in the minds of the landowners and the other in the minds of the labourers. To the latifundists this must have been a first warning of the potential dangers of the new regime.

The latifundists had been divided among themselves along the party lines of the last decades of the monarchy and those who did not withdraw from politics in 1910 adhered, for a time, to different republican parties. But in 1926, they either openly supported the new regime, or at least did not oppose it. The political evolution of the first republican deputy-mayor (who was one of the leading latifundists in our freguesia) is particularly illustrative. He had been an active propagandist for the Republic and held office in the Câmara between 1910 and 1913. In 1917, however, he gave financial support to the right-wing coup that

[3] An adequate history of the first Portuguese Republic, from the 'propaganda years' to its eventual collapse in 1926 has still to be written and in the absence of an over-all survey, it is very difficult to generalize about facts collected in a limited area. Some are worth recording here, it being understood that they are not presented as a chain of cause and effect, but simply as local illustrations of what may have been a more general trend.

installed the dictatorship of Sidónio Pais[4] (as a reward for which he was made, briefly, Civil Governor of Lisbon) and in 1929 he became the first president of the local branch of the União Nacional (the only legal party of the new regime).

The Spanish Civil War further strengthened the adherence of the latifundists and big proprietários to the regime. In 1945 only two of them signed a petition for free national elections. When this petition (which was widely circulated in the country) was taken to the latifundist who had been the first republican mayor in 1910, but who had retired from politics with the advent of the new regime and enjoyed great moral prestige and a reputation for liberal views, he stated that although he agreed with its contents he could not sign it because this would upset his family and friends. From then up to the time of my field-work in 1965, on none of the several occasions of brief political agitation preceding elections did any of the latifundists and big proprietários support the opponents of the regime. The vertical political cleavage of the last decades of the monarchy had become a horizontal one.

Between 1910 and 1926 the political patronage associated with the *Regeneração* began to decline and its nature changed completely after 1926. The withdrawal from legal politics[5] of some of the big latifundists and the creation of the new republican parties undermined the established chains of political patronage centred on the main local figures of the monarchy parties. Some of the new republican supporters, whose loyalty to their party had made them locally important political figures, were not latifundists but clerks, schoolmasters, shopkeepers, and lawyers, who mustered a clientele in Vila Nova but were unable to command the same number of followers in the rural freguesias as the previous latifundist *caciques* had done. Elections continued to be held, but fewer voters came forward, and the final figures were often obtained by placing 'dummy'

[4] Sidónio Pais (1872–1918), mathematician, army officer, politician, and sometime ambassador to Germany, was President of the Portuguese Republic between 5 Dec. 1917 and his death by assassination on 14 Dec. 1918. His presidential régime, which he called 'The New Republic', was the most articulate attempt to impose autocratic right-wing rule in Portugal between 1910 and 1926. Some of its features were later developed by the 'New State'.

[5] Between 1910 and 1926 any monarchist worth his salt was plotting more or less actively against the republican regime.

votes in the ballot box. In 1922 a local newspaper draws a nostalgic comparison between the sober nature of republican elections and the festivities that marked the monarchist elections.[6] Government instability and the proliferation of parties also created a feeling of progressive political apathy. Only one list of candidates was presented for the Câmara elections of 1919. A local newspaper attributed this to the indifference of the people.[7]

The present regime, established by the *coup* of 28 May 1926, put an end to genuine parliamentary politics with legal political parties. Political patronage changed its nature and took on new forms. In 1937, under the threat of a possible communist regime in Spain, a local branch of the Portuguese Legion was created in Vila Nova. This is a para-military organization modelled on similar organizations in Nazi Germany and Fascist Italy and Spain, that aims to safeguard the regime and prevent political insurrection. Most latifundists, some professional men, and some proprietários joined the Legion, and their employees, administrative clerks, and some small shopkeepers and craftsmen, all of whom were more or less dependent on them, were made to join as well. While the latifundists, professional men, and proprietários were well aware of the Legion's aims and endorsed them, this was not the case with most of the others who joined only because they were ordered to do so. Had they disobeyed they would have found themselves in difficulties.[8] In 1940 a special celebration was held at which the wives of wealthy *legionários* made gifts of food to the families of poor *legionários*. The details of the gifts show that these families were really in need.[9]

In recent years the *Legião* has declined. The patriotic and moral zeal that led to its formation lost some of its urgency with Franco's victory and stable rule in Spain—after some anxiety in the late 1940s—with the realization that the Allies'

[6] LN II 648, 29 Jan. 1922. The successful party provided a huge repast for its poor supporters and there was often dancing afterwards.

[7] LN II 510, 8 May 1919.

[8] A Grémio clerk who signed the 1945 petition for free elections felt obliged to write a letter of apology to the President of the Direction, to avoid a fall from favour in the eyes of the local great, a situation which, among other inconveniences, might have prevented his son—whose studies were paid for by one of them—from getting into the university.

[9] LN II (2nd series) 399, 24 Mar. 1940.

victory in World War II did not mean a swing to the left in western Europe. The numbers coming forward to enlist have abated, and in the concelho of Vila Velha it is almost a defunct body. People who enrolled are still members but para-military training, parades, and other displays, and even the sporting of uniforms or badges, are no longer found.

Nonetheless, the population is still asked to give formal support to the political regime. The government holds a general parliamentary election every four years and (up to 1958) a presidential election every seven years. By agreement with the Câmara, the big latifundists provide lorries and *roulottes* to go through the villages and pick up labourers to be taken to the polling stations. Clerks, shopkeepers, and local proprietários are not herded in this way. They go of their own accord because they would hate to displease the mayor and find themselves in difficulties over administrative matters in the future. All this does not alter the fact that the percentages of voters in the results announced are pre-established. The mayor visits the polling stations a few days before each election and tells the assessors the figures he wants returned to the Câmara.

Political calm is achieved in the country as a whole through the control of information,[10] of education, of access to the Civil Service, and a nation-wide police network of which the Republican Guard is the local expression. Although the province of Alentejo has a reputation for the political consciousness of its labourers, the freguesia itself is remarkably quiet. It is unlikely that it it has been a consistent target for articulate propaganda by the underground Communist Party, and the understanding of political problems by the peasants is very limited. In the 1958 elections only six votes were cast for General H. Delgado, the opposition candidate,[11] and this is indicative of the political isolation of the freguesia. It is not surprising, therefore, that few people are able to take an active political position against the Government. When this has happened, however, their fate has been exemplary. During the Spanish Civil War a talkative

[10] Censorship of the press since 1926 has had the effect of decreasing the number of newspapers and periodicals everywhere in the country. During the Republic, five periodicals were published in Vila Nova, three of them concurrently. There is none today (nor were there any before the introduction of television).

[11] This figure comes from a reliable source which, in this particular case, confirmed the official figure.

labourer who supported the republicans was arrested and sent off to a Lisbon gaol, where he died years later. In less critical moments, repression is not so strong and often amounts simply to a withdrawal of patronage benefits. Some years ago, the foreman of a gang of road-workers who tried to persuade the men under his orders that they should collectively ask for better pay,[12] was swiftly reprimanded by the mayor who threatened him with permanent unemployment in the future if he persisted in this talk. In 1962 a veterinary surgeon in Vila Nova spent a few months in a Lisbon prison accused of having connexions with the Communist Party. He comes from a respected family of landowners in Vila Nova. Out of loyalty to his family, two latifundists agreed to testify to his good character. But when he returned to the town they joined with the other latifundists in blacklisting him as a professional. These consequences of political indiscipline act as a warning against creating situations of the same type and very few openly occur. This is due to a lack of political tradition in terms of ideology and organization and to fear of repression. This fear is clearly felt whenever politics or even wages are being discussed by labourers in a café or tavern. If an outsider comes in, the subject is immediately changed. In front of proprietários or other members of the upper group such matters are also avoided, and only very indirect remarks are made to a newcomer even if he is believed to be, as they say, 'against the Government'. Anti-government politics, whether in actions or opinions, are subject to this negative use of patronage, i.e. the withdrawal of benefits, if certain types of behaviour are not maintained.

The patronage relationship implies that, however unbalanced a patron–client relationship may be, the client retains some bargaining power. The nature of the parliamentary system created this bargaining position: a man could shift his allegiance from one patron to another if he obtained better conditions from the new patron. To a certain extent, this was still the case during the republican period. But under the present regime the situation is completely different. Political hostility to the government in power has to be concealed, and active support has to be shown at critical moments only. When peasants are needed to take part in ostentatious displays such as national elections or

[12] Strikes, it will be remembered, are illegal in Portugal.

occasional 'spontaneous' demonstrations of gratitude to the Government, they are in no position to avoid the moral and material pressures put on them. It is not a matter of gaining anything from their support: better sharecropping deals, better employment conditions, avoidance of conscription for their sons, more customers for their shops—all these are things of the past. It is a matter of not being put in the very difficult situation of being labelled a communist and treated accordingly, a situation which would make life much more complicated in the already cramping conditions with which they have to cope.

It is often pointed out by Portuguese liberals that the present regime destroyed democracy in Portugal. As far as the region under study is concerned this is not true, because democracy—in a western European sense—never really existed there. But it did eventually destroy a system of political patronage which had allowed a very limited degree of power to groups of the population whose economic weakness would otherwise have left them politically powerless. Their limited bargaining power operated at the level of individual interests and not at the more general levels of community, party, ideology, or class. But limited and uncoordinated as it was, it gave clients a certain leverage in relation to patrons which has now disappeared.

XXIII

FROM PATERNALISM TO CORPORATIVISM

THE decline and ultimate change in the nature of political patronage is part and parcel of the decline in what can be called, for lack of a better description, paternalistic relations. Such paternalistic relations or—as latifundists sometimes like to put it—'patriarchal' relations, are often remembered with nostalgia and the ideal model of this patriarchal society seems to be based on recollections of local life before the end of the last century. Basically, what is remembered and often missed is the greater protection given by the rich to the poor or, in a more specific context, by latifundists and big proprietários to the labourers they employed. The former importance of almsgiving seems to indicate that there was an extension of this protection to the poorer groups in general. Indeed, a frequent entry in estate budgets at the turn of the century was a sum of money allocated for charity and beggars.

A progressive erosion of this protection which, while it existed, functioned as a very primitive and incomplete system of social security, has taken place in recent decades. The financial situation of landowners of all groups has steadily deteriorated. Population increase and the end of communal land supplied more hands for the labour market while mechanization gradually reduced the demand. Unemployment and its hardships increased, while private means to fight it were repeatedly proved to be ineffectual. The creation of the Casa do Povo in 1947, with its system of medical and social assistance, gave landowners a further justification to restrict whatever traditional forms of help they had provided for their labourers. Some big 'houses' had provided old age pensions for retired labourers.[1] But as the Casa do Povo had its own pension scheme this practice was

[1] There is no standard retiring age. Some old men well over seventy insist on surviving after having become worthless as wage earners. This is often a burden to their families.

first reduced and has now been discontinued. However, the Casa do Povo can handle only a limited number of cases and as a result there are always a few old men waiting for their contemporaries to die so that they can fill the vacant places for assistance. A parallel situation has developed in the field of medicine. Before the establishment of the Casa do Povo local doctors worked on an *avença*[2] basis, and the very poor were attended free of charge, the 'houses' often providing medicines for their *concertados*. After the Casa do Povo started functioning, however, the *avença* system broke down. Labourers are still treated free of charge.[3] But there are some three hundred families who, because they own land, do not qualify as labourers and have to pay, whereas before many of them would have qualified as poor, or paid an *avença* appropriate to their means. A further point to be considered is that forty or fifty years ago the most expensive item in medical treatment was the doctor's fees. This is no longer so. The difference between the medical treatment available to those who can afford it and the type of attention given to those who cannot is very wide. Moreover, although poor people in the freguesia now receive better medical attention than they did forty years ago, this is by no means so in relative terms (as compared with methods of treatment in current use elsewhere). These are important points, because ill health and disability are among the reasons that drive people to seek the support of patrons of various kinds.

The progressive application of broader-based (in some cases nation-wide) benefit schemes in such matters as seasonal unemployment, illness, and old age has removed from the landowners responsibilities that in the past many would have considered part of a traditional set of duties. This is further emphasized by the comparative decline in their position as a source of employment: the factory and job opportunities elsewhere now have priority in labourers' expectations.

The relationship between landowner and labourer is ceasing to be that of *patrão* and *criado* (the etymologies should be kept in mind: *patrão* ('patron') for the employer; *criado*—'someone

[2] The *avença* was a voluntary annual contribution in cash or in kind for the medical services provided by the local doctor. The amounts paid varied according to the wealth of the person concerned. Very poor families did not pay an *avença* and were treated free of charge.

[3] Although they have to pay for a share of the medicines prescribed.

who has been brought up in the household'—for the employee).[4] Many landowners prefer this state of affairs. Most of them claim a 'rational' approach to agriculture (some also say they have an industrialist approach) which means that they do not employ more men than they consider indispensable at any given time. The following illustrations will show how the 'industrialist' approach may, on the one hand, affect quite marginal fields, while on the other disrupting traditional practices that would have been considered unassailable only a few years ago.

In the past, latifundists allowed poor men of the freguesia to cultivate melons (after the cereal harvest) on small tracts of land. No charge was made for this concession. Some years ago, production was placed on a sharecropping basis and the landowner's share increased with the passage of time from one-fifth to one-half. In 1965 these lands were, in some cases, being rented out by the hectare to people from a nearby concelho who specialize in melon growing and who, being more highly organized, can afford to pay the rent now charged, which is beyond the means of local growers.

In 1965 the buyer of a big estate rented it to a latifundist of Vila Nova who wanted to work all the land himself. He made this known to the eight sharecroppers then working on the estate not by talking to them directly, but through one of his sub-managers who informed them that they would have to leave the land after harvesting their wheat.[5] Their agreement had been made with the bankrupt former owner of the estate and, as was usual in these cases, had been a verbal agreement. The sharecroppers put their cases individually to the sub-manager and finally two of them went to see the latifundist. The other six did not think it was worth their while and in the event they were proved right. The latifundist stood his ground and all eight sharecroppers had to leave the land after harvesting their wheat. People commented that such actions as these could not

[4] As late as 1890 an official census of the population counted *criados* as members of the family.

[5] Sharecroppers usually take land for two years, and if the first year's wheat harvest is poor, they may be compensated for their losses by the crop of oats or barley harvested in the second year. If the administration of the estate on whose land they are working changes hands through selling, inheritance, or new renting agreements after they have begun their first year, traditional custom entitles them to remain on until the end of the second year.

have been taken in the past, i.e. in the days when a sharecopper's vote had a certain value and when the general attitude of landowners was of a paternalistic type. Even if the sharecroppers and melon growers had not themselves been political friends of the landowners they would almost certainly have had friends who were, or else they would have created new and operative friendships. Their voting power could thus have been used as a bargaining counter to secure the required conditions. As this can no longer be done, such men have nothing left with which to bargain, since they cannot afford to withhold their labour.

'Patriarchs' are becoming 'industrialists' while *criados* are becoming proletarian workers. The need for patronage, however, has not become any less pressing. In fact, as in the case of the political changes described above—although for quite different reasons—the change has had the effect of placing prospective clients in an even weaker position.

Although landowners today are less important on a nationwide scale than they were fifty years ago, because of the development of industry and the comparative failure of the wheat effort, they have been the object of consistent protection by the State, particularly since 1899, and their interests have consequently been respected in many different contexts. They are members of landowners' associations and have been able to voice their discontent on many occasions. Agrarian conferences are held regularly; landowner deputies sit in Parliament and there have been landowner ministers. However much the richest individual landowners may benefit from this, the group as a whole is able to enjoy their advantages.

Quite a different picture emerges, however, in the case of the labourers. The worst period for the labourers as a group was probably that between 1880 and 1950. The communal lands had disappeared, death rates were falling, and large-scale emigration had not yet begun. If the conditions of labourers are comparatively better now, this is because most of them have left or are about the leave agriculture. Their interests *qua* labourers are not expressed or represented through any specific body. The labourers' associations of early republican days were abolished by the authorities after the 1911 strike and in the region under study they were never revived.

The structure and functions of the Casa do Povo have already been described. It certainly does not play the role of a trade union.

The weakness of Portuguese syndicatos (or trade unions) is well known. But whereas other occupational groups have managed to bargain collectively for minimum wages and hours of work through their (state-controlled) unions, however unsatisfactory the outcome, farm labourers have not even managed to do this. Their general conditions of work are thus the worst to be found in Portugal. When landowners were relieved of their traditional duties and responsibilities towards labourers, in part as a result of the evolution of their agricultural concerns, but prompted and morally justified by the creation of state welfare agencies, rural workers failed to gain new rights under the new conditions.

The idyllic view of a relatively recent past when landowners protected their labourers and the relationship between the two groups was wholly happy and harmonious is certainly an exaggeration. A Virgilian world of *labor*, *pietas*, and *fatum* exists only in retrospective wishful thinking. References to a golden past are frequently made in agricultural societies and this particular society is no exception. A few facts, however, seem to indicate that there was a system of social relations in which strife and attrition were not so prominent as today. Local newspapers credited the 1911 strikes with the consolidation of the antagonistic position of labourers and landowners and stated that life would never again be as peaceful as it had been before the strikes. Old labourers complain that the present landowners are 'lesser men' than their fathers and grandfathers because the latter gave alms and generally helped the poor. Former generations of landowners also spent more time on their estates and many of them were, in their outlook and way of life, much closer to the labourers than their more urbanized descendants. In objective terms—wages, literacy, diet—the labourers of fifty years ago led a worse life than their present-day counterparts, but the gulf between them and their masters was not as wide. Moreover, unlike labourers today, particularly the younger generations, they had no means of comparison (afforded by television, the spread of literacy, and, more recently, by conversations with emigrants) and were not politically indoctrinated enough to rebel, protest, or even feel in any articulate way the unfairness of their lot.

If the legal and administrative framework of labour relations leaves labourers unprotected and individually isolated, there is no substitute, in the form of private associations, that could create a corporate feeling or build up collective protection. This extends far beyond the ranks of the labourers themselves: it is a general characteristic of this society, regardless of social strata.

In the freguesia there are no co-operative recreation associations (the Clubs are in Vila Nova) and attempts to organize them have failed. A co-operative olive-press was discussed but never established because three or four of the prospective members who produced the most olives assumed that they would have priority over the others,[6] and would run the business as their own. Of the two existing religious lay brotherhoods, one is virtually defunct and the other has lost much of its past importance. The Brotherhood of the Holy Sacrament exists only on paper and, although up to 1910 it played a certain role as a money-lender, it no longer owns any property. The priest tried to revive it in 1945, when almost all the old members had died. He persuaded some young men to join and they filled in the necessary application forms. They never met, however, and it no longer plays any role in local life.

The Brotherhood of the Misericórdia[7] is a less dormant body. It has about forty members who are supposed to elect from among themselves the twelve directors, one of whom becomes warden and the other deputy warden. Nowadays in fact, the directors are chosen in much the same way as are the governing boards of administrative bodies. Before legislation passed in the nineteenth century, the Misericórdia was a reasonably wealthy institution and lent money at moderate interest (in 1860 the recorded rate was 5 per cent; it rose to 7 per cent in 1890).[8] Its

[6] In Vila Nova a prospective co-operative winepress met a similar fate. Several instances of this incapacity for association during the last sixty years could be provided. A local newspaper once pointed out that it had even been impossible to find enough people to go on a day trip to the seaside by coach.

[7] Misericórdias are lay brotherhoods dedicated to Our Lady of Mercy, systematically created in Portugal since 1498. They had provided assistance to the poor and the infirm and are now integrated in the National Health Service. In their prosperous days, the Misericórdias played an important role as money-lenders.

[8] Misericórdia, Books of Accounts for 1860 and 1890.

income is now so reduced that it sometimes has to ask for government subsidies to run the four-bed ward traditionally called 'the hospital', and the consulting room adjoining it (which, since the creation of the Casa do Povo, is practically unused), to pay the orderly, and to keep its church in reasonable repair. The warden is usually a local proprietário. Years ago, some of the members felt that someone with important connexions would be of more help to the brotherhood and one of the latifundists was invited to act as warden. He accepted, but did no more for the brotherhood than his predecessors. At the personal level, some of his fellow members found themselves in a better position to ask for his help or support in their private affairs. However, the notion of the brotherhood as an institution with interests other than those of the personal concerns of its individual members is a distinctly hazy one. Today the main function of the directors is to organize the festival of the freguesia's patron saint, an important but very limited function.

This lack of associations, and the fact that the few that exist are run in accordance with the individual interests of their more prominent members, combined with the decline in political patronage and paternalistic labour relations and the lack of effective trade unions, creates a further need to forge personal bonds. In need or in trouble people can only resort to the exclusive, privileged, and partly secret nature of personal arrangements. They need *amigos*—friends and patrons.

XXIV

PERSONAL FRIENDSHIPS

AMIGOS, 'friends', are necessary to help one 'get on in life', and friendships are often established with this purpose in mind. The meaning of the word in these cases is different from the meaning that an English reader could attach to the word 'friend'. Friendship in Vila Velha is not (or at least not only) a disinterested emotional sharing of feelings, or a pleasant awareness of elective affinities. It is rather a system of exchanged favours, in which a strict account is kept of the transactions. This does not mean that the relationship is not emotionally loaded: expectations, gratitude, and disappointment have emotional components. When a man has received what he considers a great favour, his affection for his protector is genuinely increased; and his anger, when let down, shows that what he had expected from the unreliable friend was a commitment based on feelings rather than on merely practical considerations. Indeed, if 'friendships' are often not of a perennial nature, they are displayed with great exuberance. This exuberance only apparently contradicts the contingent basis on which many of these relationships stand. It is exactly this contingency that leads people to reaffirm and reassert, as often as they can, their friendly commitments. While they last, friendships are conducted with enthusiasm, concern, and fastidious care. Friends have to be punctilious in the attention they pay to each other's lives; instantly ready for emergencies, keen to offer their support in difficult situations (illness, money troubles, defending a friend's reputation against his enemies). Moreover, friendship must also be shown in the uneventful minutiae of daily life.

Friendship, as we usually conceive it, is determined by two things—personal liking, depending on personal characteristics of a more or less permanent nature, and the incidents of life. In Vila Velha the second component is certainly more important than the first. The relationship requires a certain affinity of character and personality as a basis, since people do not often force themselves to accept as friends persons entirely uncongenial to them. For reasons of expediency, however, the future of the friendship depends on the incidents of life much more than on the basic personal characteristics that make the relationship at all possible.

The Portuguese saying *Amigos, amigos, negócios à parte* ('Friends are friends but business is business') reflects the basic ambivalence of the relationship. It is known that commercial transactions (and business partnerships) are bound to create ill feelings and may eventually lead to a quarrel. In any sort of agreement a man is bound to lose some of his ideal independence, and if things are not conducted with the utmost care, this loss may become too obvious and may come to be resented. Consequently, it is better for this type of contract to be avoided by *amigos* if the friendship is to be safe. On the other hand, if a man cannot trust his friends, he would find it difficult to survive. People thus find themselves in a dilemma: whether to conduct their business transactions with 'strangers', i.e. those who, being neither kin nor friend, are potential enemies, since they are not subject to the moral restrictions ideally imposed by friendship as barriers to deception; or whether to enter into dealings with friends, in which case self-interest may overcome the ideal safeguards of friendship. A local swindler (i.e. a man whom everybody considered to be a crook) put it in a nutshell: 'You can only fool your friends', he said; 'who else will trust you?'

Friendships are thus volatile, not because people's feelings are weak, but because individual interests will often be more important than the altruistic restraints ideally imposed on them. Even long-standing relationships, cemented by numerous and important exchanges of favours, are not altogether safe. A case history will illustrate this point.

Joaquim Antonio, a tavern owner, was hired by the Câmara as a pump attendant.[1] In winter time this did not involve too much work but in the hot, dry months of the summer he had to spend a few hours at the pump each day. He had been given the job because he was a good friend and *compadre* of the Junta secretary. The pay was small but regular and he performed the job for several years. He threatened to give it up every summer, but each time a small increase in pay persuaded him to stay on. When Joaquim Antonio's sharecropping tasks or tavern duties

[1] Fresh water is pumped to Vila Velha from a well at the bottom of the hill.

kept him too busy to attend to the pump, he was sometimes helped by a farm labourer turned mill worker. Cristovão was a much younger man and had proved a dedicated friend; 'A man without malice', Joaquim Antonio would often say. He would not accept any payment for his trouble and in the idle hours between shifts he often helped Joaquim Antonio with other small tasks. He was a regular customer of the tavern and Joaquim Antonio and his wife gave him discounts on goods purchased. They also gave him little presents for his children as he came from a very poor family and his job as an unskilled worker in the mill meant that he was not by any standards a prosperous man. A few years ago, when it was rumoured that Cristovão's wife had had an extra-marital affair, Joaquim Antonio and his family took a firm stand against the gossip. Cristovão opened his heart to them and came to them for consolation and guidance. He was 'just like one of the family'.

In the summer of 1967, Joaquim Antonio's wife had a major operation and was in hospital for more than a month. Cristovão worked the pump throughout this period and once more refused to accept any payment. Joaquim Antonio, with a convalescent wife, thought that the work was really becoming too much for him at the pay offered and asked for an unusually substantial wage increase. This was not granted, and he decided to give notice. The Junta secretary approached Cristovão and invited him to take the job at a slightly higher rate of pay than the current figure, but well below Joaquim Antonio's latest demand. Cristovão went to see Joaquim Antonio, and at this point their accounts differ, Cristovão claiming that he told Joaquim Antonio about the offer, while Joaquim Antonio claimed that Cristovão merely asked him whether he had definitely resigned, without mentioning that he himself had been offered the job. However this may be, Cristovão accepted the offer and when Joaquim Antonio heard about it he was furious. When Cristovão next came to the tavern Joaquim Antonio rebuked him in no uncertain terms and their relationship was severed. Joaquim Antonio went to see the Junta secretary, told him that he had never expected such a thing to happen, and that he was prepared to accept the job at the current rate of pay. This had become, by then, impossible. Although Cristovão, in disgust, had submitted his resignation, the secretary had persuaded him to stay on. And whatever the final outcome may have been (the situation had only just developed when I left and things may have changed since then) one thing was certain; the friendship between Cristovão and the Antonios was irretrievably shattered. The years of mutual favours and publicly expressed considerations for each other were completely blotted out. When I reminded Joaquim Antonio's wife, to whom Cristovão was by now the worst of villains, of her former praise for his virtues and pointed out how surprising it was that a shrewd woman like her should have been fooled for so long, she began by quoting a popular aphorism '*Quem vê caras não vê corações*' ('To see a face is not to see a heart'), and went on to say that although Cristovão might have good features, he was a weak man and had been manipulated by the Junta secretary. Why the Junta secretary, an alleged friend of Joaquim Antonio, should wish to slight him now, was not clear. But the whole affair was regarded as a conspiracy from which Cristovão had consciously benefited. When friend deserts friend it is because he has found a more convenient friendship. Joaquim Antonio did not, however, sever relations with the secretary. In private conversations the secretary was alleged to have played a nasty part in the plot, but publicly the blame was placed entirely on the greed and lack of consideration of Cristovão.

It is clear that whereas Joaquim Antonio felt that he could sever relations with Cristovão, he was unable to do so in the case of the secretary of the Junta. In the situation of Vila Velha, the secretary is a far more important person than either Joaquim Antonio or Cristovão, and his goodwill would be needed in many bureaucratic matters. Personal 'friendship' with him, moreover, is not only useful in isolated instances but also conveys a certain prestige. Cristovão and Joaquim Antonio are not in the same group. Although Joaquim Antonio had for some time been a wage labourer, he comes from a family of artisans and small shopkeepers and his present position ranks him well below the proprietários but above the seareiros and labourers. For Cristovão, a former labourer coming from a family of labourers, his present mill job has meant a rise in the social scale (once, when discussing his wages, he said: 'A mill worker should not live like a labourer') but he is still very close to the poorest group. It was easy for Joaquim Antonio to discard him;

and since their difference in rank was not very great it was equally easy, in a way, for Cristovão to accept the situation, without attempting to win back the favour of Joaquim Antonio. In due course, Joaqium Antonio will find rationalizations to justify his attitude towards the secretary. In similar situations, where a relationship has to be maintained by the weaker party, out of need, these rationalizations are harder to find but are sought nonetheless. Only a marginal number of people will openly disclaim their self-respect in such cases. Conversely only paranoiac personalities will try to remain aloof from the entanglements of patronage.

Patronage has been described elsewhere as 'lop-sided' friendship[2] and this description would apply here. There are variations in the extent of the 'lop-sidedness', ranging from an ideal where friends would be equals to situations of blatant asymmetry where the word *amigo*, if retained at all, no longer carries any equalitarian connotation. These variations cannot be measured in any exact way but they are obvious to the observer. In the case of Vila Velha patronage relationships are often very asymmetric.

At all levels of society equals are potential rivals—for material gains as well as for the less quantifiable accretions of prestige—and this is more pronounced at the lower levels. Once adolescence is over, a period during which a man's friendships are dictated more by feeling than by interest and his friends are more often found among members of his own social group, 'friendships' tend to be rearranged and to become the means, for the majority of those in need, to seek protection from the few who can afford to give it. What separates this type of friendship-patronage from outright charity is the ideal claim to some form of reciprocity, however unbalanced, on the part of the client. Gifts are duly presented to efficient patrons, although their material value is generally well below the value of the favour obtained by the patron. The patron certainly does not need these gifts, and there is little bargaining power left to clients whose prospective patrons are lazy, clumsy, or merely uninterested.

We find only two particular groups of patronage relationships in which the client retains some power over the patron. These

[2] J. A. Pitt-Rivers, *People of the Sierra* (London, 1954), p. 140.

are the relationships between administrative clerks and members of the public and those between shopkeepers and their customers. Instances of the first have been described in the section on political structure and may be summarized here as follows: in relation to latifundists, big proprietários, and professional men the clerks can only offer their personal efficiency and their speed in solving specific problems. In many cases they have attained their present positions through the patronage of latifundists and they may need the latter's help again at any time. In relation to the rest of the population, however, the clerks assume a role of patrons who guide people through the intricacies of the administrative written word. In this case the client is not completely defenceless. The gifts in cash or kind with which he repays his patron and, in offices where there are several clerks, the choice of the particular patron, are based on the clerk's efficiency or reputation for competence in dealing with the type of case in hand. Moreover, since a considerable part of the clerk's income is derived from these relationships, he has to satisfy his clients. The relationship is, however, limited to this particular field. It cannot be extended to others and cannot become a link in a more general and articulate system related to a political life that no longer exists.

The case of shopkeepers and their customers is subject to the same limitation.[3] The wives of labourers and small sharecroppers accumulate debts in the shops from which they buy during the year, and their husbands pay off all or part of their debts after the harvest. Outstanding debts often accumulate for years and constitute a permanent problem for local shopkeepers. The shopkeeper acts as a patron by providing credit, but he also secures a customer by doing so, since the client knows that should he take his custom to another shop, he would have to settle his debts immediately. There is less pressure to pay if he continues his account. It is in the interest of the shopkeeper to keep the customer, particularly since in the absence of fixed prices the more in debt the customer is, the more the shopkeeper will charge him, by securing a high interest on the money he is

[3] The term used to describe the customer of a shop is *cliente* ('client'). Patron (*patrão*) is the owner of the shop. Customers do not 'patronize' shops—they become the clients of their owners. Although in many urban areas analogies with the patronage situation would not be legitimate, this is not so in the villages, where customers are, in most cases, clients of the shopkeepers.

owed. The customer, for his part, knows that he is in no position to complain. A prosperous shopkeeper is sometimes invited to act as godfather to a child or to become godfather at a wedding by labourers who hope, in this way, to gain privileged treatment. Such treatment may be repaid by providing labour free, or at a reduced charge, when work is required on the plots that most shopkeepers own but are unable to cultivate entirely by themselves. Moreover, most shopkeepers know how to read and write and can be of help in problems where the written word is involved. The village post-office and telephone are usually on the premises of a shopkeeper. Some shops also act as meeting-places where men and women chat about village affairs, and shopkeepers are thus better informed than other people. A shopkeeper's signature is officially required to support claims for a residence certificate, and shopkeepers often act as referees when formal proof of identity is required from a peasant who has not bothered to secure an identity card. In the case of the more important shopkeepers of Vila Nova, there is another traditional facet of patronage relationships: poor women from the villages who shop in the town, often obtain discounts or 'gifts' by favouring them sexually.

By lowering their prices, shopkeepers are able to secure some patronage for themselves. The following incident illustrates this. One of the odd functions of the local priest is to report the wine made in the freguesia to the National Wine Board for tax purposes. A shopkeeper in one of the villages made wine for years without being reported because the priest was a friend of his. One of the implications of this friendship was, of course, that the shopkeeper would sell the priest goods at cut prices. The two eventually fell out over the rent of one of the church plots and their relationship became more distant. From then on, the shopkeeper stopped making wine because he could no longer count on the discretion of the priest.

Cases of this type are rare, however, and the shopkeeper's position towards his fellow villagers is more often that of a patron than that of a client. Any shopkeeper has a large number of such patron–client relationships. Detailed evidence of this is provided by the court proceedings in bankruptcy cases. One of the problems of the trustees in cases affecting shopkeepers is to recover outstanding debts from poor customers. When a small grocer in one of the villages became bankrupt in 1964, the individual debts owed him hardly exceeded 1,000 escudos (£15) but more than thirty of his regular customers were in his debt. The situation shows the risks taken by shopkeepers, particularly when a poor-crop year restricts the amount of cash transactions over the counter and indicates the balanced nature of the shopkeeper–customer relationship.[4]

[4] The relationship of a shopkeeper with his debtors may become strained and the tangle of local loyalties may severely impair a man's business success. Not surprisingly, more than half the shopkeepers in the freguesia were not born there and these are certainly the most successful. An outsider, even if he has been a resident for many years, is freer to act: he is not expected to show the same lenience to his debtors nor indeed the same fairness to his customers in general, as a local man should.

XXV

PATRONAGE AND SOCIAL CONTROL

In many situations of patronage the client is subject to various forms of moral pressure against which he has no defence, since there is little or nothing in material terms that he can offer in return for the favours he receives. What is asked of him is often a conformity to what the patron regards as convenient moral standards. The client is expected to abide by these even if they often clash with his interests and the organization of his life. In more general terms, the upper group (latifundists, big proprietários, professional men, priests) use patronage relationships to impose on people of lower groups standards of behaviour which they consider to be most suited to them.

The use of patronage as a means of social control of one group by the other is mainly found in three particular fields: religion, family, and politics.[1] These are the fields in which observance of what members of the upper group regard as the traditional values of the society is of most importance if the society is to be saved from the danger of slow moral disruption or violent change. The political aspects of this use of patronage have already been discussed. The religious aspects are closely related. The alleged lack of religious feeling among the peasants of Alentejo has been for many years a problem both for the Church and for the latifundists. This 'lack of religious sentiment' is thought to be evident in the small attendance at mass and other Catholic ceremonies and practices. The organized structure of the Church is divorced from the religious life of the population, and both priests and latifundists try to impose on labourers a more frequent participation in the rites of the Roman Catholic Church.

The clearest instance of this is the following episode. Between 1958 and 1964 the priest of Vila Velha distributed wheat flour, powdered milk, and butter, provided by an international charity organization, through a local committee of latifundists'

[1] This is coherent with one of the mottoes of the regime: 'You cannot question, God, homeland, or the family' (*Deus, Pátria, Família*).

wives, among the poor mothers of the community. The distribution should of course have been free. What, in fact, happened, was that the priest gave the groceries free to women who attended daily mass and exacted a small fee from the others. He managed to bring a few of them to the Church in this way, but never more than five or six. And in 1964, when the distributions were discontinued, even these five or six ceased attending mass.

In 1950 one of the latifundists offered to pay the men working on his estates for any Sunday work they undertook, provided they agreed to go to mass and to keep away from the taverns afterwards. This was, however, such a reversal of the usual way of spending Sundays that the scheme did not last more than a month. Another latifundist promoted the marriages of labourers in the private chapel of his estate and offered a gift of money as an incentive, so that the period of courtship during which sinful sexual intercourse could take place would be shortened. In one case, when the bride-to-be insisted that her trousseau was not ready, the young man was forced to marry another girl chosen by the latifundist himself. The last of these marriages was solemnized in 1960.

Since the latifundists do not live in the freguesia itself, they are unable to enforce observance of religious practices for those who work for them. But the male and female servants in their Vila Nova houses have to attend mass and, in some cases, particularly in the case of women, have to join in the daily evening prayers. This religious observance was not part of their lives in the villages, but they have to comply with the master's wishes in this respect if they want to keep their jobs. A master–servant relationship is not necessarily a patronage relationship, but servants are, in this case, important links between their families and their employers. The latter's help will often be sought in the case of family need and such assistance may range from outright charity to intercession with the local authorities, court officials, or prospective employers.

The latifundists are responsible for a higher proportional attendance at Sunday mass in Vila Nova than in the villages. The congregation is made up mostly of women: the wives of local administrative officials, small shopkeepers, and labourers, although a few men also attend. In 1964, when some of the members of the upper group were invited to join instruction sessions known as 'Courses in Christianity' (*Cursillos*), they promptly brought their employees with them, and a few small shopkeepers and small clerks felt obliged to attend.

Both in the freguesia and in Vila Nova such actions are attempts to secure a firmer control of the population through the Church. They are not very successful: in fact their effect in the freguesia itself is negligible. But in one way or another these callings are repeated from time to time. From as far back as people can remember, the Church has been identified with the rich and with right-wing policies, and the latifundists are well aware of its potential role among the labourers. It should be noted that whereas all latifundists' wives are very pious women, this is not true of the majority of their husbands—who seem, indeed to look at religion through Marxian eyes, albeit with approval. The poor need it, they say, and should have more of it.

Attempts to enforce conformity with traditional morals are also made in support of a moral family life. This may take an open religious aspect—as when pious ladies from Vila Nova managed to persuade some old couples who had been married only in the civil registry[2] to go through a proper Catholic marriage. But the moralizing intervention of the wealthy in the family life of others is often concerned with less ceremonial matters. A few illustrations will help to make this clear. The estate manager of a latifundist had been married for fifteen years but the marriage was childless. Despite his reputation as a philanderer, he had become very much attached to a young woman who had borne him a child. The wife was very upset by this, and refused to give her permission for him to recognize the child. He confided in his employer who, relying on the superior authority conferred by his wealth and university degree, harangued the wife over the telephone, and eventually obtained her consent. The argument he used was that, although the husband had undoubtedly sinned, he was now trying to do his moral duty and that she, as a true Catholic, must exercise her charity to forgive and help him.

As could be expected, Christian charity is not invoked in the same way if the guilty party is the wife. In 1965, the wife of a labourer who had already been suspected of extra-marital

[2] Between 1911 and 1945 there was no resident priest in the freguesia.

affairs in the past, ran away with a travelling salesman, only to return a fortnight later to her parents' home in one of the villages. The husband, who was employed on a big estate, had continued to live in his house on the estate. Although the affair had provoked a good deal of scandal, he was prepared to take his wife back, since he was a poor man and not in very good health. We know that adultery is often tolerated by labourers. But in this case the scandal had been too great and had reached the latifundist's ears. He informed the labourer that he would be fired on the spot if he took his wife back. The labourer waited six months until his annual contract ended and returned to wage labour so that he could live with his wife again. The scandalous nature of the adultery was the main reason for the action taken by the latifundist. His wife—and all the other women in the upper group—would have been very annoyed if he had allowed such a sinful woman on his estates and he therefore tried to force the labourer himself to accept the standards of the upper group. This story is in sharp contrast with the first, the difference lying in the fact that in the first case, the adultery was committed by a man and in the second by a woman: the adultery of a husband is not regarded as a sin.

This complacency towards a man's sexual misbehaviour may be qualified. We have seen how frequent and accepted it is for wealthy men to have poor married women as mistresses. Not only are these affairs accepted but they are considered a reason for boasting among friends. They enhance rather than impair a man's prestige. If the situation is reversed, however, reactions are quite different. A few years ago it became known that the wife of a Vila Nova lawyer had a lover, and her husband duly took her back to her parents. The affair had apparently lasted for more than six months and was made public when a servant gave the lovers away. The lover was not a member of the upper group: he came from a family of small landowners and earned his living as a horse trainer and dealer. His work had brought him into close contact with the latifundists and their more prosperous clients: he would often sit at their tables in the café and was sometimes invited to their parties. He was a well known philanderer and the accounts of his philandering among peasants' wives were much enjoyed in café conversation. In this case, however, the reaction was different. By having become involved with a woman from the upper group he had infringed the order of society in a much more violent way than in his other affairs. And instead of earning admiration for his escapade he was openly rebuked. Two of the latifundists severed both personal and professional relations with him. Others merely severed professional relations and he was privately admonished by several members of the upper group. The reason always given was that he had broken the rules of friendship. Yet these rules had never been invoked in cases when the husband–friend was lower down in the social hierarchy. The incident affected his prestige and his professional life, and his chances of reaching a higher position in society were seriously impaired.

These are illustrations of the enforcement of traditional values in situations affecting the family structure. They are somewhat exceptional situations but their exceptional nature helps to clarify how patronage is used to reinforce the order of society as seen and supported by the upper controlling group.

It is true also that patronage helps to alleviate some of the difficulties that poverty, and the illiteracy associated with it, create for the majority of people. In less dramatic but more frequent situations in life—finding work on the estates, in the mill, or elsewhere, the solution of legal or bureaucratic problems, illness when hospital treatment is needed—the power of latifundists and professionals or priests as patrons is always sought. The price, however, is the compliance with the political, religious, and familial (or perhaps one should say sexual) values that the patron considers suitable for his clients.

The social conditions that create the need for patronage are perpetuated by patronage itself. The basic assumption behind the search for patronage is that the individual can only get what he needs from an unjustly organized society by opposing its apparently hostile and inefficient mechanisms (designed for the common good though these supposedly are) with a series of operative personal relationships with those who are in a position to manipulate the mechanisms of society most effectively. To fight the injustice of society in this way can only produce results in personal terms and stifles any attempt to change general conditions. Moreover, in acknowledging the power of a patron by asking for his favour, a man is not only accepting the order of society but trying to use it for his own benefit. The fact that this order is seen as unjust by most of those who live by it is not an objection to the exercise of patronage, but a positive sanction of it. The actions of patronage, because they are often secret and privileged, may also be seen as not entirely honest by those who take them, but this dishonesty is justified in their eyes by the wickedness of the world in general, which is over-emphasized for the purpose. The gap between ideal norms and actual behaviour is thus progressively widened. Ideal norms in any society are often seen as unattainable goals. They have something of the nature of an algebraic limit. But in this society, in many cases, no effort is made to attain them any longer and the moral advantages that could be gained by adhering to ideal norms are offset by the practical advantages of doing what everybody else does.

Society is wrongly organized and every individual suffers from this; but every individual is, at the same time, responsible. Membership of this society implies complicity in the general decay of morality rather than co-operation or co-citizenship. This complicity contains elements of mistrust and deceit and the fear of being exposed. It qualifies the agonistic values of the society. A clear instance of this is provided by the way people boast. Boasting is a ritual exercise for evenings spent in the tavern, particularly on Saturdays when more wine is drunk. But straightforward boasting is rarely practised because its results are self-defeating. If a man tells stories in which he is the triumphant hero, the winner of fights or arguments, he will acquire a reputation for vanity and be regarded as a liar not to be trusted or respected. Skilful boasting is done in the opposite way: a man will relate in great detail how in his youth he was badly kicked by a bull in an amateur bullfight, how he was deceived by the gypsies in a mule deal, how he got lost the first time he went to Lisbon (or nowadays to Paris). In these cases he will be praised for his courage, his honesty, and his adventurous nature. The vanity of his audience will not have been wounded by tales of exceptional deeds that most of them would feel unable to accomplish and would tend not to believe. By displaying his failures he is providing evidence of the difficulties in a man's life and of the hopelessness of most human endeavour however gifted a man may be. And he is safeguarding his position against the threat of ridicule or a more openly hostile attitude.

The difficulties surrounding solitary undertakings and the need to be discreet about possible success for fear of retaliation of various kinds are woven into the fabric of patronage. They demonstrate that, however much each patronage operation may be regarded as a single effort by those involved, it is really part of a system of comparable operations. A balance has to be achieved between the extent to which patronage may be used in any particular instance, and the degree to which it would be wise to denounce any particular instance of it on moral grounds. The accuser is bound to need moral tolerance at some time or other. Once this is admitted, it is also implicitly admitted that some general norms have to be disobeyed in practice and everyone shares part of the responsibility.

This is probably true of all societies with highly developed systems of patronage. However, the particular type of patronage we have described has a moral implication which is of the utmost importance for the understanding not only of the freguesia but of contemporary Portuguese society in general. It has been emphasized that the disruption and eventual end of party politics changed the nature of political patronage and deprived of their bargaining power the groups of society in which the clients in patronage relationships are generally found. This means that a patron's decision whether to act or not in a client's interest is left very much to his own discretion, since no retaliation can be taken against him. The moral consequences of this are far-reaching. The exchange of favours—however unequal these may have been—has almost disappeared. The essence of a favour lies in its reciprocity, even if such reciprocity is incomplete. Deprived of any capacity to reciprocate, but still needing the intervention of a patron, a man is reduced to begging for favours. The only thing he can offer in return is his moral dependence and we have seen that this is often exacted. The cost of buying material advantages through moral submission may be extremely high. A *pedido* ('request') may have to be made several times because the prospective patron has been forgetful or lazy. If the matter involved is not very important a man's pride will often prevent him from taking it any further after one or two failed attempts, but if it is important to him, he has little choice. People who are known to ask for the patronage of wealthier individuals too often or to ask for too much, acquire a reputation for shamelessness. Yet anyone seeking patronage has to be shameless to some degree. Given the economic stratification, the administrative structure, and the political system, there are no adequate mechanisms in the natural world for dealing with many difficult situations in life. *Pedidos* constantly have to be made. And as an old woman put it once: 'What I ask for is not a favour: it costs me my shame.' (*Isso que eu peço não é favor: minha vergonha me custa.*)

PART FIVE
RELIGION

XXVI

THE RITES OF THE CHURCH

I

PATRONAGE mechanisms are extended to the supernatural world through the establishment of a relationship with the saints. The cult of saints is part of the body of beliefs, concepts, and images of the Roman Catholic Church which shapes the religious life of Vila Velha.

The relative importance of religious rituals and religious thought in people's lives is certainly less now than it was in the not very distant past. Nevertheless, it is probably still greater that in the urban areas of modern industrialized Europe. The major yearly festivals, which help to affirm and reassert communal feelings, apart from having a religious pretext, still retain a basic religious meaning. The bells in the church tower still herald dawn and evening and announce christenings, marriages, and deaths. A special tolling of the church bells informs people in the freguesia that fire has broken out.

The landscape of Vila Velha is marked by the traditional importance of religion. The town is organized around a square where the parish church, visible for many miles, towers over the hill. There are nine other churches and chapels in and around the town, but only one is still used for worship; the others are now in ruins. No church has been built since the seventeenth century. The small village churches are always situated in a prominent place, and some of these still hold special feasts in honour of their patron saints, although for the rest of the year they are generally closed. Between the lower slopes of the hill of Vila Velha and one of the villages, the massive shape of a former monastery of the Bare-foot Augustinians, in its ugly and sad seventeenth-century neo-classical style, is a reminder of the past importance of religious orders. It provides a plausible setting for the stories of friars, all of them derogatory and most of them certainly apocryphal, still told by the fireside on long winter nights. And whenever an abnormally dry spring threatens the cereal crops, prayers are said to the Virgin in the monastery church.

The overwhelming traditional importance of the Roman Catholic Church is clearly evident in popular speech. When time is reckoned, the religious and the agricultural often replace the lay-urban official terms. The month of June is seldom called by its name: people refer to it as *São João* (St. John's day is on 24 June) or *Ceifas* ('harvest'). Events may be said to have occurred 'at olive time' (*tempo da azeitona*) or during the months of St. Francis (October), *Santos* (from All Saints day on 1 November) or *Natal* (Christmas), but very rarely will the terms *Outubro*, *Novembro*, and *Dezembro* be used. Agricultural contracts, which traditionally extend from 15 August of one year to 14 August of the following year, are said to last from St. Mary to St. Mary; and livestock contracts extending from 29 September of one year to 28 September in the following year, are said to extend from St. Michael to St. Michael. The auction of communal land rights took place every year in the parish-church porch; and until the late 1920s harvest arrangements were made between landowners and labourers during the feast of St. Stephen. It is rare nowadays to hear the greeting 'May God Our Lord grant you a very good morning (or evening, etc.)', but *Até amanhã se Deus quiser*—'Until tomorrow, God willing'—is the universal form of evening farewell. Exclamations of sorrow, surprise, or anger often take a religious form: *Valha-me Deus* ('God help me'). The word 'God' is often replaced by the name of one of the many saints and evocations of Christ and the Virgin Mary. *Jesus*, *Nossa Sonhora*, *Credo* are exclamations frequently heard in many different contexts. Beggars evoke the love of God when they beg for alms. If something too impious or too brutal is said, the speaker will often be told that God will punish him. Farewells often take the form: *Vai com Deus* ('Go with God'). When dead relatives are mentioned their names are followed by the phrase *Que Deus tem* ('in God's care').

All these are fairly obvious points, and little of a striking nature concerning religious attitudes can be deduced from them. A deeper analysis is needed to understand the place of religion in the lives of the people of Vila Velha. For this a broad distinction must be made between practices and rituals directly connected with the Church and its ministers, and those that do not require their direct participation. Both fall within Roman Catholicism, but they find different expressions and have different implications. We begin with the first group.

II

The freguesia of Vila Velha forms a parish. Mass is celebrated in the parish church of St. Mary every morning at eight o'clock, but only two or three old women bother to attend, and even these, particularly in winter, may stay away. The priest and verger (always a young boy) are often alone in the church.[1] Afternoon mass is said every Sunday and is attended by schoolchildren of both sexes who are taken by their schoolteacher, and by a few women, mostly young and single, who treat it as a social occasion for dressing up. The presence of the girls has recently attracted a few young men, but by and large men stay away from mass.[2] Attendance by married women is also infrequent. Every alternate Sunday the priest visits each of the two more distant villages to celebrate late-morning masses and finds much the same type of attendance. A few years ago, when a small church in another village was opened for worship, the priest included it in his Sunday itinerary. But since the village has no primary school attendance was so low that he threatened to cancel his visit if fewer than twenty people were present at mass, and eventually had to carry out his threat. Early in 1965, the priest had a loud speaker fitted to one of the bell-towers of the parish church and uses it to preach to the population and say prayers before celebrating the daily mass. He winds up the morning's ceremony by emphasizing that people can no longer claim the traditional excuse for not saying their prayers regularly —that since they had not been taught the prayers they did not know them off by heart—and exhorts them to fulfil their

[1] Since 1960, the Archbishopric of Evora has sent out forms to the parishes to record the main aspects of the cult. In the space for 'average attendance at daily mass' the Vila Velha priest answered '0' (zero) in 1960 and has not filled in any figure since.

[2] Men spend Sunday in the taverns. The different attitudes of men and women are expressed in a popular quatrain:

Lá porque fui à Igreja	Because I went to church you say
Chamaste-me cabeça ôca.	That I'm an empty head.
Tu meteste-te na cerveja	You frittered your day's wages away
Gastaste a jorna toda.	On drinking beer instead.

Christian duties. Despite these efforts, the loud speaker has failed to persuade more people to attend mass.

Men and women from Vila Velha and the two nearby villages regularly attend Christmas Eve mass but nowadays hardly anyone comes from the more distant villages, although I was told that this was not so in the past. During the mass, women sit in the centre nave of the church, while some of the more respected men (the local doctor, one or two proprietários, the Junta clerk) sit in the front pews with their families. Other men stand at the back or take seats in the right nave of the church and go in and out during the mass. Since it is usually very cold at Christmas time, they stamp their feet on the stone floor, some talk in loud voices, some smoke, some are clearly intoxicated. When the mass is over, the priest holds up the image of the infant Jesus for the congregation to kiss. Women and children move forward first and form an orderly queue but when the men's turn comes, they rush up noisily to plant a perfrunctory kiss on the foot of the image.[3] After mass, everyone goes home to the traditional Christmas-eve supper.

Mass and supper mark the two moments of the Christmas celebration. The supper is strictly a family reunion and even families who do not attend the mass respect this traditional Christmas custom.

The separation between church ceremonies and profane celebrations is even more explicit at Easter. The Portuguese word for Easter is *Páscoa*, but it is seldom used and some people do not even know its meaning. The religious ceremonies are called *Endoenças* (Roman Catholic rites during Holy Week). The brilliance of the *Endoenças* once performed in Vila Velha is often remembered. They were apparently celebrated every year until the beginning of the century, but they gradually became rarer and the last full performance took place in 1935. Priests from outside were called in to participate in the ceremonies. Episodes from the Passion were enacted with local people taking part and some old women still remember having played the role of Veronica, St. Mary Magdalen, or one of the three Marys. I was told that the men who played the roles of Joseph of

[3] During the Easter of 1923, when the Archbishop of Evora came to preach at the church of Vila Nova, it was difficult to hear his voice because of 'the loud voices (*vozeirão*) of the crowd, characteristic of these ceremonies' (LN II 707, 18 Mar. 1923).

Arimathaea and his friends had to cover their faces to avoid abuse after the performance, since the people thought they were the Jews who had crucified Christ. An old woman, who had agreed to sing me her part in the performance—*O vos omnes qui transitis per viam*—had to climb onto a chair with her arms widespread, holding a large handkerchief in her hand, before she could actually begin. For a few moments she was back in the role she had played some thirty years ago and became Veronica once more. For the younger people, the performances are simply tales told by their elders and there is no move to revive them.

The religious plays involved lengthy preparations, with many rehearsals and, quite apart from their expression of religious commitment, provided a lively form of entertainment at a time when the freguesia was cut off from the rest of the world, before the introduction of radio, television, and the itinerant cinema. With the decay of religious tradition and the growth of modern communications-media providing new forms of entertainment, traditional church festivals involving the participation of laymen and women began to decline. One aspect of their *raison d'être* was largely undermined, and after a time, they disappeared altogether.[4]

The 'profane' Easter celebrations take place on the afternoon of Easter Monday when villagers and townspeople turn out for the traditional picnic meal eaten in the fields around the town and villages. The meal should include lamb,[5] but for economic reasons this is often omitted. The Easter picnic is a great occasion. It is known as the *Festa das Flores* ('the Feast of Flowers') and is celebrated every year notwithstanding the disappearance of the Easter church rites in recent years. Men stay away from work, dances are often organized, and many people return to their homes only after nightfall.

At Christmas and Easter both the church ceremonies and the traditional festive meals are expressions of religious life. The Christmas-eve supper celebrates the family and is a reminder of its spiritual dimension. The Feast of Flowers is a communal feast in which kin and neighbour participate and in which the

[4] Nowadays the church is open during Easter but the images are covered. The procession of the Holy Ghost takes palce on Easter Sunday. In 1965 eleven women and five men followed it, and three of the men were outsiders visiting the town.

[5] This was originally a religious observance (cf. Exod. 12:15) but the religious significance of the eating of lamb has been completely lost.

ideal brotherhood of man is implicit. On both occasions, however, there is a clear distinction between what takes place in the church or under its guidance and what does not. This distinction recurs throughout the religious life of the freguesia and on one particular occasion even leads to open contradiction between the two forms of religious expression. During the last days of the carnival when there are organized dances in the different villages every evening, the most important are held on Ash Wednesday, which is the first day of Lent in the church calendar. The relative independence of tradition and liturgy is clearly evident.

III

Rites de passage in individual lives—christenings, weddings, and funerals—are communal occasions; friends and relations gather, food is eaten, and wine is drunk. The relative importance of the intervention of the Church on these occasions varies.

Baptism is the sacrament to which people in the freguesia attach most importance, even if it is sometimes performed only several months after the birth of the child. Between 1911 and 1944, when there was no resident priest in the parish and few people could afford—or few thought it worth their while—to send for a priest from a neighbouring parish to celebrate a marriage, officiate at a funeral, or baptize an infant, parents took the opportunity of having their children baptized whenever a priest was called to Vila Velha to marry or bury one of the wealthier people or to officiate at a religious ceremony.[6] The children baptized on these occasions were sometimes more than ten years old, but their parents still felt that the sacrament was needed. Very few were allowed to 'remain Moors'. There are two explanations for this which are not mutually exclusive. One is that baptism is regarded as a far more important sacrament than marriage or religious burial. The other is that it was cheaper to have a child baptized than to have a religious wedding-ceremony or funeral. Unlike burial, baptism does not have to be performed at any precise time.

[6] Throughout this period, Christmas mass was always celebrated by a visiting priest, Easter rites only sometimes. The local feast of Our Lord of the Cross, on the second Sunday of September was always celebrated.

IX. Waiting for death

X. Going away

Nowadays marriages are always celebrated in the church. I know of no civil marriage contracted by people in the freguesia since 1945. In the thirty-four years when there was no resident priest, however, only one hundred marriages were celebrated in the parish church (an average of 2·94 per year). Between 1945 and 1965 there were 588 church weddings. Of these, 179 were the religious solemnization of civil marriages contracted between 1911 and 1944, making a yearly average of 19·47 for the remaining 409 religious marriages contracted in the twenty-year period.[7] Even without a priest people preferred marriage to common-law liaisons and between 1911 and 1944 weddings were held in the civil registry of Vila Velha. The registry has now been abolished and anyone wishing to contract a civil marriage has to make at least three trips to Vila Nova. By contrast, a church wedding is simplicity itself: the engaged couple have only to tell the priest, who will deal with all the bureaucratic details himself. Another reason why marriages are celebrated in the church is that the wedding feast can then be held locally, whereas this would be far more difficult to arrange if the ceremony were held in Vila Nova. Since the local importance of the feast is paramount, this is an important consideration. Moreover, in recent years even the very poor brides tend to want 'white weddings', and this would not be considered appropriate in the case of a civil marriage. On the whole, a church wedding is considered more proper nowadays than civil marriage.

Funerals are nearly all religious. No records are available of the religious funerals that took place in the period between 1911 and 1944, but there is no doubt that very few people sent for a priest to conduct funeral rites, and that those who did so were among the freguesia's wealthier residents. Nowadays the only non-religious funerals are those of persons married by civil ceremony only and those of suicides.[8] For the funeral rites, the

[7] It must be pointed out that the need to solemnize long-standing civil marriages was not a spontaneous one on the part of the couples involved but the result of pressure from the pious ladies of Vila Nova. Most of these marriages took place in 1950, when the image of Our Lady of Fatima was carried in pilgrimage throughout the country and passed through the freguesia. The promoters of such marriages were particularly zealous that year.

[8] In these cases the priest does not attend the funeral, the church remains closed, and the bells do not toll for the dead. But this does not reflect the attitude of the population. Indeed, the funerals of suicides are amongst those best attended. A Junta minute for 1937 (14 May) is quite clear in this respect. The Junta decided to

priest accompanies the procession and says the last prayers for the dead over the grave. He is often called on the evening before the funeral to say prayers over the corpse. The house is full of relatives and neighbours, and old women accompany the priest in his prayers. The display of grief is continued at the funeral the next day. Until the beginning of the present century, women would stand by their windows during the funeral procession and weep as the coffin passed by. This is no longer traditional, but funeral processions, still pass through the main square on their way to the cemetery, even when there has been no church service. In such cases, the funeral procession makes a special detour to pass through the square. The intervention of the priest is part of the traditional display of grief for the dead: his presence lends the funeral the solemn quality that it would otherwise lack and, as in the case of marriage, a religious ceremony is considered more proper than a burial without the presence of a priest. However, priests are seldom called to administer extreme unction to the dying. This emphasizes the fact that the intervention of the priest is regarded as unnecessary in the intimate aspects of religious life.

A comparison of the periods 1911–44 and 1945–65, indicates that, by and large, the people of the freguesia opted for a religious or a civil ritual to mark their *rites de passage* in accordance with the availability of each. This availability was determined by administrative conditions beyond the control of the local population. Most people avoid problems by adapting themselves to the prevailing political, ideological, and administrative conditions. This was well summed up by a local proprietário who had been married by civil ceremony in the 1920s. 'There is really no difference between being married in church and married in a registry. What matters is to behave according to the existing law' (*a lei que há*). And 'the existing law' in the 1920s had made it easier to marry in the civil registry than in church. In his comment, Church and State were equated as controllers of public behaviour. The metaphysical difference between a sacrament and a profane contract was not even considered.

In conclusion, it can be said that although people in the

pay the grave-digger for 'the work of digging a grave for an unfortunate [female] beggar who committed suicide "by means of the water of a well" [sic], and waived all civil-registry or other expenses which should have been paid to the Junta'.

freguesia do not rebel when they are deprived of religious rituals conducted by a priest, they prefer a religious ceremony when it is available. The special importance attached to baptism relates to the fact that both in spiritual terms and in terms of worldly patronage, baptism is a more critical moment than marriage or extreme unction and religious burial. The participation of priests in religious life seems to be necessary only during the most important celebrations of the Catholic calendar—Christmas, Easter, and the Exaltation of the Cross (which is celebrated as the major local feast) and for christenings, weddings, and funerals. The local priest put it in a nutshell: 'For them (the local people) religion is baptism, marriage, and burial.'

XXVII

PRIESTS

THE DECAY OF FAITH

THE freguesia's estrangement from the Church and its ministers is often attributed to the fact that from 1911 to 1945, with a brief intermission in 1939, there was no resident priest in the parish. Following the republican law providing for the separation of Church and State, Church property was administered by the parish Junta in 1910 and from 1911 to 1938 by an appointed committee in Vila Nova. In 1910[1] the mayor wrote to the Junta advising it to spend as little as possible of its budget on religious practices and this advice was certainly respected, very few religious ceremonies being performed. Although the republican law allowed the Misericórdia to assume responsibility for religious practices, this was not done. In 1913, on an order of the Administration of the Concelho,[2] the cemetery was secularized and the crosses were removed from its gates (in 1915, however, permission was granted to reinstate these). In 1925[3] the Administrator of the Concelho wrote to the Junta to enquire whether it would be inconvenient to do without a priest for a further year and the answer was that there would be no inconvenience. Although this was an official letter, sent by one republican official to another, the fact is that even after political conditions had changed and the administration had become more sympathetic to the Church (i.e. after 1926), the people of the freguesia never petitioned for a resident priest.

Despite the fact that there has been a permanent resident priest in the freguesia since 1945, no noticeable improvement in relations between Church and people has taken place. The situation is no different in the nearby parishes. Although the three other parishes in the concelho have had resident priests since as far back as people can remember,[4] the low rates of

[1] 2 Dec. [2] 6 Mar. [3] 14 Sept.

[4] It should be noted, however, that only 186 of the 385 parishes in the Archbishopric of Evora had vicars in 1965.

attendance at church ceremonies in these parishes are very similar to those of the freguesia. Indeed, the Church considers the whole province to be a *região de missão*, a region where missionary effort is needed to counteract the lack of religious enthusiasm.

If, as the number of ruined churches seems to indicate, there was far greater religious fervour in the past it certainly began to wane before 1910. Church records prior to 1910 had been removed from the parish and what evidence I have, therefore, had to be gathered from other sources. It does point, however, in one direction. In the sixteenth century, Vila Velha, with a much smaller population, was divided into four parishes. By 1758 there were only two: St. Mary of the Lagoon and St. James, and, when the parish of St. James ceased to exist in 1836, St. Mary of the Lagoon became the only parish in the freguesia. It is significant that no important bequests have been made to the local Misericórdia since the beginning of the eighteenth century. It managed to make ends meet, however, until the late nineteenth century. The first serious complaint concerning lack of funds is recorded in the 1892 minutes, and refers to the ruinous consequences of the shift of investment into government bonds forced upon it by the Government.[5] The Misericórdia fulfilled an important role in providing assistance to the poor and the infirm, but brotherhoods with more specific religious aims fared less well. The Brotherhoods of *Almas* ('Souls') and the *Santíssimo Coração de Jesus* ('the Sacred Heart of Jesus') became extinct in 1876, and the Junta took over what remained of their capital.[6] In 1864 the Brotherhood of the *Santíssimo Sacramento* ('Holy Sacrament') was rich enough to pay the deficit in the yearly accounts of the Junta,[7] but by 1896 it was in such financial difficulties that it could not afford to pay for the candles that it usually provided for the church.[8] Is still exists on paper, but it is completely ineffectual.

The attitude of laymen towards these and similar institutions was not unlike their attitude towards secular bodies. On numerous occasions during the last hundred and fifty years the Misericórdia treasurer has complained against the number of *foreiros* ('leaseholders') who have failed to pay their dues. In

[5] M.m. 17 Apr. 1892.
[6] J.m. 2 Jan. 1876.
[7] J.m. 25 June 1864.
[8] J.m. 14 June 1896.

1840 the committee of laymen responsible for the upkeep of the chapel of *Nossa Senhora da Orada* ('Our Lady of Orada') committed so many abuses in relation to chapel property that the Câmara was obliged to dissolve it, and decided that from then on it would have to keep a vigilant eye on chapel accounts.[9] In 1869 the committee entrusted with the upkeep of the chapel of *Nossa Senhora do Carmo* presented such confused accounts to the Junta, and it was discovered that there had been so many abuses by the treasurers who had served on it, that the Junta found itself obliged to insist on the presentation of proper accounts within a period of twenty days.[10]

In 1852 some sacred objects were stolen from the church, among them the reliquary for taking the viaticum to the sick. Since the reliquary was considered to be of 'prime necessity' the Junta decided to sell some lesser church objects in order to raise money to buy a new one.[11] In 1901, however, the priest complained to the Misericórdia that a number of people had died without his knowledge in the Misericórdia hospital and had not, therefore, received the last sacrament. He asked that in future he be promptly notified on such occasions.[12] This incident shows that the 'necessity' which had led the Junta to act so promptly in 1852 seems to have become far less important by 1901.

The changing response of the faithful to the demands of the faith is perhaps best illustrated by the following story. Up to the last years of the nineteenth century, the feast of St. Anthony, which falls on 13 June, was always celebrated in the freguesia with the income derived from two cows which were allowed to graze on the commons. When the commons were partitioned, a proprietário undertook to keep the cows on his land free of charge. Upon his death in 1892, however, his heirs refused to fulfil this obligation and the Junta was obliged to look for free grazing land elsewhere.[13] After many difficulties, a woman was finally found who agreed to keep the cows on her land.[14] But a few months later the Junta was advised that it would have to find another place for the two cows since the woman was not

[9] C.m. 30 Sept. 1840.
[10] J.m. 9 Sept. 1869.
[11] J.m. 16 Sept. 1852.
[12] M.m. 4 Aug. 1901.
[13] J.m. 24 Nov. 1892.
[14] She was, incidentally, the daughter of a priest.

prepared to keep them for more than another fortnight. She said that her own cows gave her quite enough trouble and that her charity and devotion to the saint 'were well satisfied with one year' (*com um ano fico satisfeita*).[15] She was persuaded to keep the cows for another year, but insisted that the Junta pay her, at what it considered too high a fee.[16] When the woman died a few months later it proved impossible to find anyone who was willing to take the cows at a fee acceptable to the Junta. Finally, the Junta was granted permission to sell the cows and the feast of St. Anthony ceased to be celebrated.[17]

Soon after the priest left the freguesia in 1911 there was an outbreak of vandalism and a group of schoolboys staged a hanging with the images of some of the saints.[18] To avoid any repetition of such acts, pious women removed the remaining statues and images from the church and kept them in their homes. When they were asked to return them years later some showed great reluctance, and indeed, a few images were eventually sold to antique dealers by the women concerned or by their heirs. The carved and gilded decorations of the church of St. James have been removed along the years and used as firewood.

All these incidents serve to show that, while the absence of a priest between 1911 and 1944 certainly played a part in the 'decay of faith' in the freguesia, it was by no means the main cause. Even today, when there is strong official support for the Church, the permanent presence of a priest has not brought about a revival or strengthening of the part played by the Church in the religious life of the freguesia. The reasons for this can be understood more readily once the different roles of priests have been examined.

THE WORLDLY ROLE OF PRIESTS

Before 1910 the local vicar was also the president of the Junta and this gave him an important administrative position. The present priest is the Junta's representative on the municipal council. Elsewhere in the country priests often occupy key political posts. Even during the republican period a priest was Administrator of the Concelho of Vila Nova in 1918.[19]

[15] J.m. 10 June 1893. [16] J.m. 7 June 1894. [17] J.m. 14 Oct. 1894.
[18] Two of the people involved, now old men, told me this story.
[19] LN II, 448, 17 Jan. 1918.

The vicar of Vila Velha has bought some land and rents it out together with several church plots. He is in a better financial position than most people in the freguesia and lends money on interest, as some of his predecessors are said to have done.

Although priests are generally outsiders, their 'outsideness' is of a particular kind: they are outsiders in the sense that they were not born and bred in the freguesia but, in terms of local status, education, and personal relationships, they belong to the upper group of society, together with the latifundists, professional men, and wealthy proprietários. They consequently lack an outsider's ideal independence and are regarded as members of the upper group: they are educated, they own land, and they act as administrators, and for most of the time they behave no differently from other educated landowners and administrators.

As landowners, they rent out their land and try to obtain the highest possible rents, exacting regular payments and showing little understanding for the difficulties of their tenants or sharecroppers.

As administrators, priests are no different from other administrators. From 1836 to the second decade of this century, the Junta minutes often record financial irregularities in Junta accounts, which are discovered by the newly elected members when they examine the financial records of the outgoing Junta. On at least two occasions the president-priest was directly blamed for the discrepancies.

Their relationships with the latifundists are similar to those of other professional men and affect them not only as persons but also as priests. In Vila Nova, latifundists are among the few men who perform their Easter obligation and in certain cases the priest goes to their homes to hear their confessions. (This may be looked upon as a symbolic moment: it is not the rich man who goes to the house of God to ask for forgiveness and expiation, but God's minister who goes to the house of the rich where, as a guest, he forgives or condemns.) During my stay in Vila Velha one of the latifundists often attended the Sunday afternoon mass in Vila Velha, and on one occasion, before announcing the time of the mass on the following Sunday, the priest turned to the latifundist and asked him in respectful tones what time he would prefer.

These connexions may take other forms. A wealthy outsider decided to have a house in Vila Velha rebuilt, and the priest was placed in charge of all payments to local workers. When the workers asked for certain wages the owner, who was accustomed to the higher wages of the city, agreed in principle to pay the rates asked. But, as any profane agent would have done, the priest thought the claims were exaggerated and wages were paid at the local rate. This incident aroused strong feelings against the priest but his action was not interpreted in terms of an alliance between local priest and outsider against the community. What people said was that he had been 'cruel to the poor' and had taken the side of the rich against the poor or that he was 'not a friend of the poor'.

So close is their association with the rich, that priests may even be suspected of activities that would seem to be totally unbecoming to their position. A priest was suspected recently of acting as *procureur* to a latifundist and, although this was certainly untrue, it is significant that the rumour could have arisen at all. The subservience of priests' manners in talking to people richer than themselves is unfavourably compared with their frequently harsh and rude ways towards the poor. Certain popular sayings reveal the gulf between priest and community, between the poverty of the people and the wealth of the priest: 'A good meal with good wine makes a man feel like a priest'; or 'fat as an abbot'.

The picture of the worldly priest is incomplete without reference to his relationship with women. Nowadays it is much rarer to find priests who have liaisons with women than it was up to some thirty years ago, but the tradition is so lively that rumour has it that the present priest, who shows no interest in women, may well be a homosexual. Formerly, priests often established permanent liaisons and for all but legal purposes had wives and children. This troubled the ecclesiastical authorities but was openly accepted by the local population. In 1915 when the Archbishop of Evora ordered a 'married' priest in Vila Nova to leave his family for the sake of decency, the latter refused to do so for precisely the same reason. People approved of his behaviour and condemned the Archbishop's suggestion as thoroughly immoral. 'Married' priests were not frowned upon, because it was thought that, as 'family men', they would not try to seduce other men's wives or daughters, a contingency regarded as more than likely.

Some of the descendants of these stable liaisons are still alive. The freguesia's richest latifundist is the grandson of a priest as are four of the rich local proprietários. A fifth is married to the granddaughter of the same priest. Vila Velha's main family of proprietários at the turn of the century was also descended from a priest who had been vicar of the parish in the mid-nineteenth century. Such cases further integrated the priests into the upper groups of the community. Indeed, the present local priest, while telling me about the unusual faith and devotion of the proprietário's wife mentioned above, remarked quite naturally that this could probably be attributed to the fact that she was the granddaughter of an ordained man.

Patronage is closely bound up with the different worldly roles of the priest. Priests use their influence to promote the interests of their friends and may make life difficult for persons they dislike. It is widely believed in Vila Velha that a local man, who has joined the Republican Guards and is almost constantly in a state of drunkenness, has not yet been dismissed because the priest is a close friend of the man's family and has used his influence. Nowadays, a recommendation from a priest is an important asset when seeking employment or when attempting to find short cuts in administrative procedure. By granting or refusing such recommendations the priest exercises his powers of patronage. In this respect he is no different from any top clerk, professional man, or latifundist. Finally, priests have steadily supported the present government's policies. There are a few exceptions, but there was none in the parish nor was any known in the neighbouring parishes.

Superimposed on these worldly roles of the priest is his spiritual role as a minister of God. The administration of the sacraments and the celebration of those religious ceremonies which call for his presence, have already been discussed. To these functions is added the hearing of confessions, in which the clash between the priest's worldly and spiritual roles becomes more critical.

Very few people go to confession, either at Easter and the other times specified in the religious calendar, or because of personal moral problems. Schoolchildren and couples about to marry are obliged to confess, but apart from these, not more than a dozen women in the freguesia and even fewer men go to confession every year.[20] The women are mostly old and have unfortunate personal lives. The unpopularity of confession cannot be understood without taking into account the reputation of priests in their worldly roles and activities. People do not accept that a categorical change takes place during the confession and that the priest becomes a minister of God with power to hear their sins and condemn or forgive them. Moreover, his involvement in the life of the community makes it totally impossible to trust him, in purely human terms, as an independent person whose discretion and better judgement can be respected. Objections to confession are made on the same grounds as objection to any form of breach of secrecy in important personal matters. 'The priest has nothing to do with my life' is usually the first explanation offered for not going to confession. The nature of the priest's ministry is not understood.[21]

ANTICLERICALISM

In view of the priest's worldly roles, it is hardly surprising that he is not a highly respected figure. He is accorded some of the blame heaped on the rich, but in much stronger terms, since it is thought that there is a clear inconsistency between what he preaches about love, charity, and the brotherhood of man and what he often practises. It is pointed out that actions such as philandering, money lending at high interest, exaction and bargaining when renting out plots, and generally siding with the rich against the poor, are totally unbecoming to the ideal position of a priest. Although he is given the respectful treatment reserved for the upper group in face-to-face contact, behind his back he is never referred to as *o senhor padre* or *o senhor prior* but simply as

[20] In 1965, eleven women and two men went to confession in the freguesia. The number is higher in Vila Nova but the resident priest still finds it unsatisfactory, in particular in the case of men. I was unable to obtain exact figures from him: 'about one-third of the women and some sixty men' was the most precise information I could elicit. The men are drawn mostly from the group of latifundists and their clients.

[21] Indeed the word *padre* has such unpleasant connotations that priests do not use the word to refer to themselves in conversation. Instead they say *sacerdote*. The use of this more sophisticated but less precise term cannot be otherwise explained.

o padre or *o prior*[22] and derogatory terms are often used in conversations about him.

Jokes, anecdotes,[23] gossip, and avoidance of most church ceremonies are the only means through which popular anticlericalism can be expressed. In part, this is because of the authorities' refusal to take a lenient view of more direct forms of expression, but mainly because people cannot afford to ignore the secular roles of the priest, however much they may dislike him and what he stands for. He is after all a vital link in many chains of patronage and, although his involvement may be condemned as contrary to his ideal position of independence, it nevertheless creates bonds with various people at different times. An intellectual view that places the priest against the community is therefore difficult to sustain. This impossibility of placing the relationship between priest and people in any clear-cut category gives popular anticlericalism the peculiar characteristics it has come to assume.

During the republican period (1911–26), and particularly in its early years, anticlericalism was open and outspoken. It was an anticlericalism of the literate encouraged by government policies, anticlerical books, pamphlets, and newspaper articles. Its main proselytes were found among local schoolteachers, shopkeepers, and a few landowners, rather than among labourers. As a result, it affected Vila Nova more than the rural parishes, and even there its promoters did not find the support they had expected among the mass of the labouring class. At no time were there acts of violence against priests or pious people which might have been expected, given the political

[22] The omission of the word *senhor* is a sign of disrespect when referring to someone by his professional title. An engineer or a doctor would be referred to as *o senhor engenheiro* or *o senhor doutor*.

[23] The defects of priests, monks, and the Church in general are part of traditional lore in the form of satirical anecdotes in prose or verse. An old landowner, known for his nastiness, has been nicknamed 'the Jesuit'. When speaking of the hard conditions of agricultural work in their youth, old labourers often say *Muita Inquisição a gente sofreu*—'We suffered a dreadful inquisition' (the Holy Office is currently known in Portugal as 'The Inquisition'). There is a house in Vila Velha known as the 'House of the Inquisition' which is pointed out to visitors as the place where 'prisoners were tortured by Jesuits', although there is no evidence to support the claim that any branch of the Holy Office was ever established in the freguesia. When a party of nuns visited Vila Velha men commented: 'This is what pays best in Portugal', voicing their belief that nuns, monks, and priests cunningly make their living without having to earn it.

climate of the period. On at least one occasion, women took a stand against the anticlerical administration: during Easter 1913,[24] the Procession of the Cross was banned in Vila Nova. That evening a group of poor women took the image out of the church and, with scornful looks for the priest who had refused to accompany them, carried the statue in procession through the town. Seventeen women were arrested, tried and, convicted. The authorities claimed that a monarchist plot was behind the procession and their reluctance to accept the incident merely as an expression of popular sentiment is evident in the report of the Câmara session held the day after the incident. The minute states:[25]

It is hard to believe that only the feminine element—and the lowest among it at that—should be imbued with the faith that dignifies the true believer.

The 'anticlericalism from above' of the republican period was replaced by the 'pro-clericalism' of the authorities after 1926. However, this stand had as little effect on the rural masses as the opposite attitude had in 1910–26. The anticlericalism of the peasants is of a non-ideological, non-intellectual nature and relates not to matters of principle but to the practice of everyday life which both nourishes it and checks its outspoken expression. In some cases it appears to be closer to the literate urban form of anticlericalism and is accompanied by expressed religious scepticism, which could be called agnosticism, and even more rarely by an atheistic outlook. These attitudes are inconsistent, however, with the systematic appeals made by such men for the intervention of the saints, either directly or through their womenfolk, whenever they find themselves in trouble.

The key to this lukewarm brand of anticlericalism, always present and yet never open and violent, is to be found in the attitude of women. As women are more religious than men they find more reason to blame the priest for his shortcomings in carrying out the duties of his ministry. In some cases they may even consider that not only is the priest *not* a mediator between man and God but that he is a positive obstacle and he may be thought to care less for religious matters than lay people do. When the priest played a popular tune to try out the loud

[24] LN II 194, 7 Mar. 1913.

[25] C.m. 17 Mar. 1913.

speaker, indignation was widespread. The use of light music for this purpose and the fact that it poured out all over the parish from the bell-tower seemed to some of the women a form of blasphemy: *Ainda se fôsse musica grave* ('It could have been serious music at least'), they commented.

These attitudes may be called pious anticlericalism. They are well expressed in the qualification old women sometimes make when referring to a priest who had an exceptional reputation: 'He was a priest', they point out, 'but he was a very religious man.'

Priests are caught, therefore, between two forms of anticlericalism: the anticlericalism of men, often associated with anti-Catholicism and anti-religious views, and the anticlericalism of women, stemming from concern with religion in general and Catholicism in particular. The existence of this second type of anticlericalism helps to explain why the first type is so undramatic and peaceful in its manifestations. If the priests were to gain hold over a sizeable part of the population it is likely that opposition to them would be stronger and would come violently into the open in moments of conflict. But this is not the case today. They belong to the upper group but their role among its members is not one of spiritual leadership, but rather of temporal subordination. Nor can they be accused of controlling the community through the mechanism of confession. And the fact that the most significant aspects of the community's religious life, preserved and fostered by women, are outside the scope of the priest's activities, makes these aspects more acceptable to the men, and the position of the priest more tolerable.

Priests seem to have adapted themselves to these conditions. In 1912, when the republican government decided to put priests on the government payroll, most priests regarded this measure as a curtailment of their freedom: they refused to accept the government stipends and came into conflict with the authorities. In the country as a whole, only 370 priests accepted the measure, while 3,608 refused to comply with its provisions. Naturally there were regional variations. The district of Braga in the extreme north-west, generally considered the most devout region in Portugal, had 993 priests at the time, and only four of these accepted the stipend. In the Alentejo, the districts of Evora and Beja were known for the traditional lack of devotion of the population. In Beja 115 priests accepted the stipend and 62 refused it, and in Evora the figures were 176 and 42 respectively.[26] Priests seemed, therefore, to respond to the general tone of religious feeling in the area to which they were posted. Given their involvement in secular life, this is hardly surprising. Nor have the circumstances changed. The term 'mission area' clearly implies that the vicars of Alentejo are not obtaining the results desired by the Church, and few exhibit any outstanding missionary zeal. If they did, it would probably make their lives more difficult, since their zeal would tend to polarize the communities in which they live. As long as they do not have a militant body of followers their opponents will remain relatively passive.

The priest of Vila Velha certainly lacks, or is not prepared to exercise, the missionary zeal that would increase his congregation. He cares for his plots of land, his loans, his friends, and his relationship with the ladies and gentlemen of the upper group. He also performs the rites strictly prescribed by his office, and there the matter rests. By showing this restraint he certainly does not mobilize all the religious potentialities of the freguesia, and may incur the displeasure of some of the women. But at the same time he guarantees his own peace of mind. The enmities aroused by his secular roles will thus not be galvanized in an open anticlerical front. The price of this safety, however, is a reduced participation in some of the significant aspects of religious life.

[26] LN II 176, 31 Oct. 1912.

XXVIII

SAINTS (I)

THE religious life of Vila Velha cannot be assessed only from popular participation in the official practices of the Church. God's protection and help in the unpredictability of life is often sought through other channels. Since life is full of difficulties and hazards for most of the population, to come through, men and women have to rely on their worldly patrons, on their health, and on their luck. Indeed, a usual form of greeting is *Saúde e sorte* ('Health and luck'). The importance of luck (*sorte*) is paramount in this society of scarce resources and sharp social stratification. The nature of the crop is a matter of luck and it is luck that determines many personal matters: financial success (the first prize in the Portuguese lottery is known as *a sorte grande*—'the big luck'); the success or failure of marriage, and hence the social prestige related to the hazards of marital life; the outcome of dealings with the administration; and health itself. Health is a matter of chance in any society but when the means available to treat and fight disease are scarce and very inefficient, chance plays an even greater role.

To ensure the successful outcome of any endeavour, the help of human patronage is sought and in previous chapters we have discussed some of the forms this takes. But a man's luck is part of his destiny (*destino*) and his destiny is ultimately determined by God. There are matters in which human patrons will be enough to ensure a satisfactory outcome to problems, but in others divine help must be sought to complement more worldly forms of support.

The term divine patronage aptly describes the search for, and the acceptance of, divine favours in this society. God is a distant and awesome figure to whom direct approaches are seldom made. As a man once said. 'I can cope with the saints but I want no dealings with the One Above.' What he meant was that it would be too risky to involve the Almighty in the bargaining and cheating that accompanies both earthly patronage and the fulfilment of vows made to the saints. The saints, the Virgin Mary, and Christ—in their many invocations[1]—act as mediators between men's needs and God's will.

As in worldly patronage, favours are asked for on an individual basis and, as in worldly patronage, they have to be paid for. In this case payment takes the form of fulfilling vows made. Mothers often offer vows for the sake of their children's health, and a saint may sometimes be asked to intervene on behalf of a third party, but such requests are still individual personal enterprises. Since families do not adopt any one particular saint as their sole patron, individual members of the same family often make vows to different saints. The individual nature of the relationship expressed through the vows is evident in the fact that some women develop a close and somewhat exclusive relationship with their favourite saints. Other people are aware of these relationships and a woman may be asked to pray to *her* saint on behalf of her friends who feel he will be better disposed towards her. 'He knows me well', she will say as she eagerly agrees to their request.

It is significant that very few vows are made for the purpose of ensuring a good crop. As we have seen, climatic conditions vary extremely from year to year and the rainfall is particularly unpredictable, seldom following the pattern needed for a good harvest. This would seem to create the need to ask for God's compassion. But the weather is the same for all and, although there are variations in the quality of individual harvests, they do not differ dramatically from the general trend for that year. In the conditions of extreme stress created by drought, general prayers are said and drought processions are organized. But to offer individual vows would imply that the person making them would be paying for everybody else if the request succeeded, and straining his relationship with the saint, for the sake of others, if it failed. It would therefore be foolish for anyone to embark upon such an action.

Like patronage requests, vows often have a partly secret nature. The word to vow is *promessa* ('promise') and what is

[1] Christ and His Mother are below God. Our Lord of the Cross, the image to whom most vows are made in the freguesia, intercedes with God, His Father. The mystery of the Holy Trinity bothers few minds. There is no special cult of the Holy Ghost, and Christ is simply the Son of God.

promised to the saint as payment for his favour is never confided to others before the vow is fulfilled, because this would render the process ineffectual. The favour asked from the saint is sometimes kept secret too, both before and after payment. These transactions take place between the faithful and their saints and no satisfaction is given to outsiders. Outsiders learn about them when they hear that a mass has been celebrated as payment for a vow, when they see someone lighting an oil fire in the bottom of a broken bucket at the door of a church or when people are seen hanging money or gold on the robe of the image of Our Lord of the Cross before it is carried in procession on the day of his feast. These are traditional forms of payment for favours received. But the nature of the operations involved is the business of those who make the vows and is not published—although in cases of illness or military service in Africa they are obviously well known to everybody and there is no point in concealing them.

Women make vows far more often than men, and when the latter do so, it is often at the instance of their womenfolk. Women know much more about religion than men: not only about prayer and the rituals of the Church, but also about all the details in the lives of Jesus, the Virgin Mary, and the saints, the specific merits of each saint, the cases in which their help may be sought, and the practical details involved in seeking it. The assurance of divine protection for the community is therefore almost entirely the task of the women. Their fathers, brothers, husbands, and sons are often unwilling to take the necessary steps to secure this protection on their own, and they may even boast about their impiety. When faced with a crisis, however, they invariably have recourse to the women's talent for dealing with God and His mediators.

The realm of the sacred is the women's preserve and their prerogative extends to its dark side likewise: only women may be agents of the evil eye.

XXIX

OLD WOMEN AND THE EVIL EYE

SOME women acquire with time a deeper and more specialized knowledge of sacred matters and are summoned by unrelated people to deal with difficulties of several kinds. There are three or four such women in any village. They have all passed the menopause and most of them are very poor. They enjoy a somewhat mixed reputation: those who regard their abilities as purely beneficial respect their powers and praise the kindness of their souls, whereas those who consider their activities harmful fear them or even suspect them of being witches. These differing assessments have to do with the relative position of those who make them. The same old woman will be seen by some as virtuous and by others as wicked (or, rather, as an agent of God or of the Devil), the reasons for such views being at any moment based on their position in the changing network of friendships and enmities that underlies village life. None of them is considered as holy or is supposed to perform miracles; they are mere officiants and, when the desired intervention is supposed to have occurred, it is attributed to the saint whose aid has been invoked and, ultimately, to God.

They are most often called upon to lay hands on the sick and recite prayers for them, or as they say to 'make the blessing' (*fazer as benzeduras*) after having diagnosed their condition.[1] Many ailments, both in adults and children, have prescribed healing rites.[2] The blessings consist of the laying on of hands and the invocation of one or several saints or of the Holy Virgin and of the hand of God: 'May God's hand precede mine and

[1] This blessing may be performed at a distance in exceptional circumstances. When the local doctor was ill he was blessed by one of these old women without his knowledge. To be effective, however, the blessing must be done with the person to be blessed in sight. If the sick person is not in view no results can be expected.

[2] I listed fifteen but there may well be more. The diagnosis is usually made by the family or the sick person himself and one of the old women is called to confirm it and bless the patient. She may make a different diagnosis and perform a different blessing accordingly. Her verdict in these matters is final.

serve as physic.' They are performed a given number of times—the number is always uneven—at intervals that vary with the type and seriousness of the illness and may be spread over weeks.[3] These blessings are not restricted to humans; sick domestic animals may also be blessed. Nor are they only supposed to fight off some evil supernatural intervention generally the result of the evil eye. Indeed in most adult cases the illnesses are known to be of natural origin and the purpose of the blessing is to achieve a cure by supernatural means.

Children are more often supposed to be victims of harmful supernatural action than adults. They are frequent victims of *quebranto* (a spell not deliberately inflicted by the 'evil eye') and *mau olhado* (a spell deliberately inflicted by the evil eye).[4] A child suffering from *quebranto* may simply be the victim of extreme affection with no conscious feeling of envy on the part of the person responsible, or may be suffering as the result of a look given by a woman during menstruation; in *mau olhado* envy was clearly felt by the person responsible for the spell.[5]

Given the high rate of infant mortality registered until very recently, many children were supposed to have died from one form or another of the evil eye and although there are fewer child deaths and their illnesses are less frequent nowadays, children are still protected against the evil eye. From the first few months of their lives they wear around their necks and have sewn to their clothes small medals of saints, prayers printed (with the imprimatur of the Archbishop) on small bits of paper, some of them written backwards, a *figa* (an amulet in the shape of a clenched fist with the thumb clasped between the index finger and the second finger) against *mau olhado*, and a small

[3] The uneven numbers preferred are: five (for the wounds of Christ), seven (for the sacraments), and nine (for the number of months Our Lady carried Jesus in her womb).

[4] When a child (or for that matter an adult) is ill and the evil eye is suspected, an old woman is called for, to confirm the diagnosis and prescribe the adequate rites and prayers. The diagnosis is ascertained by pouring some drops of olive oil in a bowl of water; if the oil does not remain above the water as it normally should, the evil eye is confirmed. Prayers are said to God and the Holy Virgin and the patient's forehead is touched with water from the bowl, the sign of the Cross being made.

[5] Some women will say that *quebranto* is only a result of the influence of the moon without any human intervention, although this is a less current view: *A lua nos cria, a lua nos mata* ('the moon makes us, the moon breaks us'). For the majority, expert and laywoman alike, *lua* ('moon') is the name given to a different condition for which there is a different form of blessing and which has nothing to do with *quebranto*.

horn against *quebranto;* the star of David may also be found. At puberty these protections are removed, since the likelihood of suffering from the evil eye is more remote, although it happens nonetheless. I was told that in the past, men would leave the horn of a bull on the fields they had sown to protect the crops from the envy of neighbours but I could find no surviving instance of this custom.

In all cases of evil eye there is considerable speculation among the victim's relatives as to the identity of the guilty party. In the case of children suspicion generally falls on the mothers or older female relatives of neighbouring children. Streets are the village playgrounds; children of different families play together in front of their houses and in good weather mothers often sit on the doorstep nursing their infants. This gives rise to several forms of competition. The manners, clothes, and cleanliness of the children are compared, and so are their few toys. The introduction of manufactured products has accentuated this rivalry: a mill worker may bring home a toy bought in Vila Nova which a labourer will less often be able to afford for his children; or his wife may buy ready-to-wear clothes from a travelling salesman. Modern baby-foods are now being introduced and the few young mothers who can afford them are only too willing to display these tokens of prosperity and city custom.

This small-scale prestige game gives rise to much emulation and comment. The less one can afford any of the material marks of prestige, the harsher the comments, particularly when it is thought that those who exhibit such tokens should, in principle, be likewise unable to afford them. Timing is very important: the first new toy or the first new fabric to be seen in the neighbourhood will arouse more envy.

When a child falls victim to the evil eye, an immediate review of neighbourly relations takes place: the recent past is scrutinized and manifestations of envy on the part of some neighbour are soon discovered. The envy may have been clearly expressed, or, more frequently, it may have taken the form of an exaggerated contempt. Relations with the suspected neighbour are not severed, however, nor is any supernatural means of fighting the evil agent resorted to. Suspicion and ill-feeling grows inside the afflicted household but is not directly and publicly expressed. If there has previously been friction between two families and a child in one of them falls ill, the women of the other family will be suspected more readily than anybody else. And since children are often ill and the diagnosis of evil eye is often made, almost every woman has at one time or another been suspected of being an agent of the evil eye. The matter is further complicated because any menstruating woman is a potentially harmful agent, even if she is far from intending to cause any harm.

When the victim is an adult, previous disagreements and tensions will also come out into the open and the persons involved will be charged with having cast the evil eye. Accusations are sometimes made against female affines after arguments over inheritances. Since men do not have the power and sisters are thought to be less likely to cast the evil eye on each other, it is the sisters-in-law[6] who take the blame when situations of this kind arise. There are other instances in which accusations of evil eye may be made. Any tensions between two persons may lead to them. When a young bride had a hysterical honeymoon in which she was unable to enjoy her husband, this was attributed to the evil eye and suspicion fell on her young aunt, who had strongly opposed the marriage because, rumour had it, she was secretly in love with her niece's fiancé. When André, an old labourer, was dying, he attributed his final illness to the evil eye cast on him by the wife of a shopkeeper whom he claimed to have seen receiving forged money some years before. Landowners' wives will sometimes attribute small misfortunes in their households to the evil eye of former servants who had left their service with a grievance or to some gypsy woman who had come to beg and was sent away empty-handed.

The evil eye, particularly in its effects on adults, is decreasing in importance. As I was sometimes told, *A gente agora está mais esperta; já não se ouve falar tanto disso* ('People are getting cleverer now; one does not hear so much about these things any more'). As in many other instances, the opening up of the society has brought about a change. More modern and efficient ways of dealing with disease are beginning to be known and applied. General literate knowledge is increasing. Migration is disrupting

[6] The word *cunhada* ('sister-in-law) has somewhat nasty connotations in Portuguese. *Cunhadas são unhadas* ('sisters-in-law have long nails') the saying goes.

the traditional networks of relations in which tensions were sometimes resolved or expressed through charges of casting the evil eye. In the wider society the forces that led to these accusations are diluted and lose their pre-eminence.

When Serafim emigrated to France with his wife and two-year-old daughter, the child's health improved so much that the mother removed the amulets the child had worn around her neck to ward off the evil eye because she felt they were no longer necessary. A year later when they returned to their village for a month's holiday, she made the child wear the amulets during their stay because she knew that their comparative prosperity would give rise to envy. On their departure, the necklace was once more put away. Who would envy them on the train or in Tours? This disruption of traditional forms of community life brings about the disruption of the institution of the evil eye which was based on tensions arising from these traditional forms.[7]

As long as the evil eye still exists, however, the old women's expertise in dealing with it is of vital importance. But their functions are much wider. As we have seen, their blessings are also in demand for illnesses of natural origin in humans and domestic animals alike. They know the incantations and prayers to be made in many other difficult situations: ensuring the constancy of a sweetheart or the success of a journey, for instance. They dictate prayers to the young men who are now going to Africa as soldiers, and these are written down and kept to protect them during the war. They are on very familiar terms with the saints. Whereas other women are often afraid of touching the image of Our Lord of the Cross, these old women are quite at home with it and dress it for the annual procession.

Most of them practise midwifery. This includes not only the technicalities of rural obstetrics but also the performance of the religious rituals; they say prayers to St. Anne and St. Joachim, and decide whether to send for the gown of a female saint if the labour is difficult. The midwife carries the child to the church for baptism and becomes the *comadre* of both parents and godparents. As well as bringing people into this world, they help to see them

[7] It is significant that rich women are never accused of casting the evil eye on poor ones. If they are displeased they have open ways of expressing their anger.

off properly to the other. They dress the dead, empty the earthenware jars of water in the bereaved household—so that the soul will not be kept in them—and join in the priest's prayers if he is called in.

All these roles are religious roles. The various rites and the wording of some of the prayers are different from the rites and prayers used and approved by the Church, but they are directed to the same God, to the same invocations of His Son and His Mother, and to the saints of the Roman Catholic pantheon. Moreover, the fight against the evil eye is a fight against the Devil.

These old women officiate in the same religion of which the vicar is priest. They do not celebrate masses, hear confessions, or administer sacraments, but in the day-to-day struggle to propitiate God and fight off the Devil, when a human mediator is needed, they and not the priest are called in to fulfil this role, because they and not the priest are supposed to have the feeling and knowledge required. They are, so to speak, unordained priestesses, but their training is simply specialization in the general knowledge and feeling on religious matters common to all women.

XXX

SAINTS (II)

WOMEN are the first link in the chain of patronage between men and God. The saints, Christ, and the Virgin Mary are the second.

The intervention of saints is seldom asked for in isolation: in most cases it is combined with attempts to gain the protection of worldly patrons. A case history will illustrate this point. Marcos Fernandes, a seareiro who usually avows himself a non-believer, suffered from a pain in the leg. He went to the local doctor who diagnosed sciatica, prescribed some pills, and gave him a course of injections. But the pain did not subside. An old woman carried out the ritual blessing but he continued to suffer. At a certain stage he learned that an *amanhador* (a kind of rural osteopath) in a nearby town cured these pains by 'burning a nerve in the ear' and he was considering a visit to him, when a friend told him the name of a doctor in Lisbon who was apparently well known for his expertise in such cases. He asked a doctor in Vila Nova (from whom he rented a small plot) to give him a letter of recommendation to the Lisbon doctor with a request for the consultation to be free. In Lisbon he and his wife stayed with his wife's sister who was a prostitute. The Lisbon doctor confirmed the original diagnosis but, on the suggestion of his sister-in-law, Marcos Fernandes consulted a second doctor who was one of her regular customers and would, therefore, charge him a reduced fee. This doctor told him that he had a hernia which required an operation and offered to perform the operation for a special fee but pointed out that Marcos Fernandes would have to spend some time in hospital, which could be very expensive. Since free hospitalization required a certificate of poverty, to which Marcos Fernandes was not entitled, his next steps, back in the freguesia, took him to the Junta. He was a *compadre* of the Junta clerk and was therefore able to obtain his certificate of poverty without having to bribe anyone. He was admitted to the hospital in Lisbon where he gave pork sausages and cheeses to one of the male nurses to ensure better treatment. He noticed that two men admitted after him also suffering from hernias were operated on before him, but he attributed this not to some medical urgency but to the fact that 'they must have been rich'. Eventually he underwent a successful operation. Before going to Lisbon, and on the insistence of his wife and daughter, he had promised three masses to the *Senhor dos Passos*,[1] one to be said after the operation, another six months later, and the last after one year. The first two were duly celebrated but he was reluctant to pay for the third. His leg no longer hurt him so he felt there was no need for another mass. He himself attributed the cure to the cleverness of the doctor who had made the right diagnosis, but his wife would point out that the vow to the *Senhor dos Passos* had been of equal importance (if he had not made the vow her sister might not have thought of recommending him to the right doctor, and even if she had, he might not have discovered the root of the trouble, and then again the operation might not have been so successful, etc., etc.). She insisted time and again, that he should have the third mass celebrated and, although he always maintained he would do so, he kept postponing it and was therefore, according to his wife, in grave danger of risking the serious displeasure of the saint. This form of cheating had already lasted two years when I left.

This is not a unique story. In many cases of need or illness, natural and supernatural agencies are brought into play in

[1] Our Lord of the Cross is the most important local saint, who is patron (*orago*) of Vila Velha and, by extension, of the whole of the freguesia. It should be noted that the parish is named after St. Mary of the Lagoon, to whom the parish church is dedicated and that the old parishes, now abolished, were dedicated to St. James, St. John, and St. Bartholomew. The Saint and his cult are therefore not directly connected with the Church's administrative framework. The small church dedicated to him is incorporated in the Misericórdia, which organizes his annual feast but he does not belong to this institution, either in people's minds or in practical terms. The Misericórdia's accounts are kept apart from those of the Saint's feast. This was so, even when the Misericórdia was a powerful body: in a book of accounts for 1818–20 we read that the Saint owes the Misericórdia a certain amount of money (13,036 reis), which the Misericórdia had probably laid out to cover the deficit for his feast in the previous year. The Saint does not stand for a branch of the official Church nor for any particular brotherhood or sect: he belongs to the town and its people.

His reputation for gaining divine favours is strong and long-lasting (see Appendix IV). The church dedicated to him was built in 1680 and on its site stood an inn to lodge pilgrims built with funds from a private donation (*Livro de Bens da Misericórdia*, 1855, fl. 1).

very much the same way, since they are not regarded as being mutually exclusive. Marcos Fernandes gave more weight to the operations at the natural level, while his wife considered that the supernatural element was essential, but both agreed that one could not have been effective without the other. Old women's blessings do not preclude consultation with a doctor and neither precludes recourse to the saints. Women from the villages who come to Vila Velha with a sick child often visit both the doctor and the *Senhor dos Passos*. Conversely, very old people who have become a financial burden to their families are literally allowed to die: the doctor is not summoned and no promises are made to the saints on their behalf.

This pragmatic view of relations with the other world is better brought out in matters in which the relative chances of success of the two levels of patronage may be assessed beforehand. One or the other is then resorted to in accordance with this assessment. Military service provides a good illustration. Until very recently conscription could easily be avoided through worldly patronage. Until 1911 it was possible to buy exemption from military service and we have seen that this was an important element in political patronage. From 1911 onwards, however, exemption from military duty was granted solely on grounds of physical disability. For some years the committee responsible for assessing physical fitness included, besides the army doctors, important local men, and their patronage was always sought to ensure that they managed to dodge the draft. When the committee's composition became purely military, matters became more complicated, but with the introduction of new links in the chains of patronage, suitable persons were eventually found to ask the relevant doctor or colonel the favour of 'freeing' a young man from the army. Pious mothers would also make vows to their favourite saints—but these were small vows and it was at the natural level that results could really be expected. Gratitude was thus due to the relevant personality in the chain of patronage. A professional man or a latifundist is sometimes referred to by a poor peasant as the person who 'freed' him (or his son) from the army.

In 1961, when rebellion broke out in Angola, the situation was radically altered. The need for conscripts became overwhelming and only the crippled, the blind, and the insane have been exempted from military service. It is now useless for anyone—let alone a poor peasant—to try to bring pressure to bear on the members of draft committees. Since then, a new type of ex-voto has begun to appear in the church of the local saint: framed photographs of young men in uniform with a dedication to the saint are placed in the chapel when they leave for Africa. Patronage has changed levels and emphasis. Vows are not offered in return for the saint's intervention in the case of conscription, since this is as difficult for divine powers to achieve as it is for human. But survival in the war is a different matter, in which the will of God can manifest itself in individual cases and the saints can therefore be asked to intercede. When a young man eventually returns from Africa his mother says that the Saint has brought him safely home.

In 1752 a swarm of locusts threatened Vila Velha. The priests, the mayor, and other high officials, followed by a large crowd, came out of the town to meet it carrying the image of *Senhor dos Passos*. At the sight of the image, the locusts changed direction and vanished over the horizon.[2] But in 1902 when the region was again threatened by locusts, the saint was not brought out. Instead the Syndicato directors wrote to the General Director of Agriculture in Lisbon asking for technicians or advice so that, should the locusts arrive, they could fight them 'with the means that science and experience have proved to be the most useful'.[3]

So far, science and experience have not found any means of producing rain and when unusually-prolonged spring droughts threaten the fate of the cereal crop *ad petendam pluviam*, processions and collective prayers are still held. Such a drought occurred in 1965. Almost everyone in the freguesia joined the procession,[4] including some of the latifundists who seldom appear on public occasions. People recalled that in previous years rain had sometimes fallen immediately after the procession but this was not the case in 1965. It took the mercy of God about a fortnight to manifest itself and by that time only the most pious women still believed that the rain was the result of

[2] '*Memórias Paroquiais* (Lisboa, 1758), Paróquia de S. Tiago de *** Arquivo Nacional da Torre do Tombo.

[3] S.c. 10 Apr. 1902.

[4] In other and more important towns of the province similar processions were held in which the Civil Governor, generals, and mayors took part.

prayers and the procession. This will not preclude the organization of a procession when there is another severe drought. The designs of God are inscrutable and because He has once failed to come to the aid of His creatures it does not follow that He will fail them the next time. Besides, since the prayers are addressed to an invocation of Our Lady—her image is carried with those of other saints in the procession—she may have considered that they were not properly couched or may even have failed in her advocacy.

The use of saints as intercessors with God allows the blame to be put on them when results are not achieved. It has been pointed out that relationships with saints are often very familiar: some of the more pious women even have nicknames for their favourites. In talking about their vows to the saints people often refer to the latter as if they were human beings: powerful but moody, found more reliable by some than by others, and on occasion deserving mistrust and contempt. This humanization of the saints allows for delays and cheating over the fulfilment of vows—Marcos Fernandes' procrastination in paying his vow is far from unusual—and the saints may even become partners in actions of dubious morality. A case of this kind happened a few years ago. A latifundist had brought a lawsuit against some small landowners over right of way on his land. To settle the matter, evidence on traditional custom was necessary. The village elders maintained that the latifundist was wrong but a very old woman testified that in her youth things were as he now claimed them to be, and since she had always lived very close to the right of way in dispute, he won the lawsuit. It was rumoured afterwards that the latifundist had given her a considerable sum of money. He also erected a small monument to his favourite invocation of Our Lady, to whom he had made a vow over the matter, on the contested spot.

Cases as publicly known as this one are rare, but indirect evidence suggests that the aid of the saints is sometimes invoked for the purpose of gaining the better of rivals in such matters as the division of an inheritance or preferment for a job. This measure is often accompanied by more worldly precautions such as the bribing of clerks, or the subtle slandering of rivals.

The type of relationship between human beings and saints that we have described suggests that although faith in their powers may be strong, they are not themselves regarded with awe and do not command great personal respect. The vows offered in payment are indicative of this: masses, lights at the church doors (*luminárias*), small amounts of money or payment in kind, inexpensive gold jewellery, framed photographs, wax limbs, the recital or prayers, abstention from some items of food, or, for younger members of the community, staying away from such pleasant social gatherings as a dance or a feast. The material and physical sacrifices offered to the saints do not extend beyond these small concessions. Vila Velha is on top of a hill but no one has yet vowed to climb it on his knees—a form of promise frequent in the north of Portugal. Nor do vows take the form of other kinds of self-inflicted physical violence.

Devotion to the saints is widespread and occupies an important place in people's lives. But it is not an exalted, burning, mystical form of faith. Saints are very close to humans, and this closeness is established through the exchange of favours which becomes a form of complicity. As in earthly patronage, a permanent account is kept between the faithful and their saints. This involves calculations, expectations, and deceptions at a very matter-of-fact level, and does not allow faith to take wing in mystical experience.

God is above the saints. Even Our Lord of the Cross is considered to be below God and is asked by people to intercede with God on their behalf. Saints may advocate the interests of humans (in some prayers the word 'advocate' is explicitly used, as in prayers for rain which are said to one of the invocations of Our Lady) but all are ultimately dependent on His will. This supremacy does not imply, at least in one respect, a qualitative difference from the saints. God is certainly an anthropomorphic God. There is little doubt in people's minds that He is a bearded patriarch. How powerful and omnipresent His will is thought to be is a difficult matter to assess. Great variations in belief are found here—from the men who declare themselves atheists to the very pious women who assert that everything that happens in life is an expression of God's will. But this is very difficult ground as we know: men who avow themselves atheists may offer vows or have them offered on their behalf, or ask to be blessed by an old woman. It would seem, however, that for most of those who believe in Him, God is certainly not felt as an overwhelming, constant presence. Man's salvation lies in God's power, but the confession to redeem any sins that would make this salvation difficult or impossible, seems to be regarded as unnecessary. His forgiveness is taken for granted and therefore little thought is given to it in ordinary life, or indeed even when death is near since the last sacraments are rarely sought. People either do not believe that Hell exists, or they do not believe that they run any risk of finding themselves in it. Or else they think that it is a matter independent of the rites of the Church. The destiny of the souls of those who have already died does not seem to be a matter of particular concern either: a mass for the repose of the dead person's soul is celebrated on the thirtieth day after his death and here the matter rests.

Thus the roles played by religious beliefs and practices in the lives of the people of Vila Velha fall mainly within the context of patronage. However, the results achieved through religious patronage are in many cases as limited as those of worldly patronage. People are still essentially on their own and they know it. Religion is neither the opium nor the cure for their condition.

EPILOGUE

In the course of this book I have often pointed out that land in Vila Velha is losing its value, labourers are looking for work elsewhere, and landowners are trying to sell their property. One might almost say that land hunger seems to be giving way to land disgust. Changes in the social structure of Vila Velha will take place in the years to come and it may well happen that the conflict of interests between landowners and labourers, which I took to be the keystone for a sociological understanding of Vila Velha, will become much less important than it is today, thus losing its sociological prominence.

While this aspect remains prominent, however, it is perhaps worth making some final considerations of one of the questions arising from this book: why is it that in a province where the distribution of wealth is so obviously unequal and where the mass of the population lives scarcely above subsistence level, law and order can be maintained with no apparent use of open force, and not only does social revolution seem to be as remote as the Garden of Eden but reformist attempts have been so scarce and ill-fated?

The fact that I base my answer on the study of a small area and of a small number of people may be open to two criticisms. First, the particular population studied may not be typical of the province. Secondly, the study of a small community may lead the student to place an exaggerated emphasis on the particular aspects that enhance its individuality at the expense of those that make it part of a larger society. The first criticism could be met fully only after an anthropological survey of a statistically significant number of rural communities in the south of Portugal had shown that these communities did not differ in any significant respect from Vila Velha. In the absence of such comparative evidence, however, I can only say that I have no reason to think that Vila Velha is in any way a striking exception among the rural parishes of Alentejo, and that I do have several reasons to think that it is much like many others. The second criticism may be repudiated by the fact that I did not study a single village, but a group of villages and the areas of land which encompass them.[1] The limits of this area—which correspond almost entirely to the limits of the freguesia—enclose what French rural sociologists have called the 'village working area', i.e. the area in which villagers sell their labour to landowners. A working area reproduces, on a smaller scale, the structure of property and the pattern of working relations of the wider region of which it is a part.

This approach prevents consideration of any village or town as an isolated whole, opposed to the rest of the world, living by its own localistic values, which help to solve the class struggle within its walls. In the case of Vila Velha localistic feelings do exist, towards the next village, the next freguesia, Vila Nova, Lisbon, Spain, but they are expressed for the benefit—or rather to the detriment—of outsiders. They do not correspond to strong cohesive feelings within each village or within the freguesia as a whole. Such feelings do not exist for most purposes and certainly do not bind labourers and landowners in a united front against the outside world. In some critical periods landowners have been at cross purposes with landowners (or employers) from other regions by attempting to prevent labourers from leaving Vila Velha, while local labourers have taken a stand against labourers from other regions by objecting to their coming to Vila Velha. In local terms, however, each group was obviously in opposition to the other as well.

However, the importance of the cleavage established by this opposition can only be assessed properly if the cleavage is seen in the context of many other aspects of the society. This can best be done by anthropological methods and, therefore, in a limited area. A sociological study of the relationship between labourers and estate owners would almost certainly cover a wider area, but it would probably exclude other groups of the population and make use of questionnaires specifically designed to elucidate the relationship. There is always a vast difference between what sociological interviewers are explicitly told and the ways in which in their daily lives people really go about the matters on which they are being interviewed. When sensitive areas are touched upon, as in the case of questions about attitudes towards present

[1] In a region of latifundia an anthropologist must spend as much time in the fields as he spends in the towns and villages.

patterns of land distribution or duties towards their fellow labourers (or fellow landowners), it can be expected that the gap will be very wide. It would appear, therefore, that while, on the one hand, an analysis of one village in accordance with the strict tenets of functional anthropology would underestimate the conflicting positions of landowners and labourers, a sociological survey of this conflict conducted over a much wider area would give it an exaggerated emphasis. Although reporting true aspects of reality, both studies would have distorted the problem.

The evidence each would claim in its support is familiar. In Vila Velha we do not find many instances of what could be described as open conflict between labourers and landowners: there are no strikes, no wilful destruction of a rich man's property by the poor, labourers politely salute landowners in the street, and landowners respond with superior paternalistic kindness. Hatred and suspicion along class lines do not have visible, let alone violent, expression. But anyone more than slightly acqainted with the labourers knows that they hold strong views about the way in which land is distributed at present. The alternative arrangements they suggest vary according to their degree of political sophistication, but they unanimously agree that at least the big latifundists should be systematically deprived of most of their land. Why are these feelings, almost universally expressed in private, so little reflected in the fabric of social relations? Again, two different explanations might be provided. One submits that privately expressed feelings are not really deep, except in so far as man is always discontented with his lot, and that relationships of kinship, neighbourhood, spiritual kinship, other forms of patronage and shared religious beliefs, which cut across several strata of society, do in fact provide 'vertical' relationships which bind a society together, neutralizing its class divisions and even calling into question the usefulness of the concept of 'class' in any analysis of this type of society. The alternative explanation implies that the repressive machinery of the State, relying on the forces of fear and intimidation, is responsible for the present social structure by keeping the labourers in their place.

The truth lies somewhere between these two extreme views. The dichotomy between landed and landless is not as clear-cut as it would be if one considered only latifundists and landless labourers. Sharecropping families with some land and *concertados* who eventually become managers, are closer to small proprietários than to landless labourers, and small proprietários are closer to the local *lavradores* than the latter are to the latifundists. The members of these intermediate groups—those who could either join or oppose a revolution in Lenin's classification—act as a buffer between the latifundists and the labourers, not only on account of their numbers and their mixed beliefs about the present pattern of land tenure, but also, and perhaps mainly, because they illustrate the fact that not all landowners are the idle and ruthless exploiters of other men's labour—the view of the latifundists which is held by the labourers. This accounts for the preferential treatment—in terms of productivity—which labourers give to proprietários. It also makes it more difficult for labourers to envisage a complete transfer of property from the landed group to the landless. Finally, because there is a widespread belief that the small landowners make better use of their land than the big ones, it is easier to see why labourers insist that the big estates should be divided among them (an uneconomical proposition in local ecological and technological conditions) rather than collectively owned.

Nevertheless, the fact remains that the striking difference in wealth, the conflicting interests of the rich landowners on one side and the poor labourers on the other, and the plight of the latter over the last hundred years, abundantly illustrated by the description of the unemployment crises, have created in the labourers' minds an entrenched conviction of the unfairness of the society in which they live and a deep, if rarely outspoken, hatred of the latifundists: the 'buffer' group of the small landowners is not sufficient to explain why this hatred has not found more open and organized expression.

Kinship obligations do not play any important role here. There are few close kinship relations between the several groups we have considered (labourers, seareiros, proprietários, latifundists) and none between labourers and latifundists. Obligations of neighbourhood do impose codes of conduct which imply a general restraint on violent or disruptive behaviour. But latifundists do not live in the freguesia and they are not neighbours (*vizinhos*) to their labourers. The close nature of the settlements encourages the spread of ideas (including subversive ideas) amongst the inhabitants and tends to unite the more dissatisfied elements against the latifundists. At the same time, however, it makes it extremely difficult to keep any proposed conspiracy secret. The neighbourhood tends, therefore, to act both as a stimulant to revolutionary feelings and as a hindrance to their chances of materializing in the form of concrete action. But in times of social unrest (as in 1911 and again in 1962) it has permitted a quick and effective mobilization of the labourers. Neighbourhood values, therefore, do not provide an answer to the question.

Nor do religious beliefs. The most important part of the religious life of Vila Velha consists of a set of personal bargains made between individual believers and individual saints in which the order of society is neither exalted nor condemned. The wealthier group attempts to impose regular religious practice on the poor, mainly so that they can be taught to be content with their lot in this world, but this attempt has not proved very successful.

Social unrest has been prevented, to a certain degree, by the operations of patronage described in this book. Patronage operations in themselves have not, however, been a major deterrent, for reasons that are easily understandable. Patronage, by its very nature, can only benefit a small number of people. Those who are unable to obtain privileged protection become increasingly dissatisfied and malcontent. The withdrawal of bargaining power from the lower groups, with the collapse of parliamentary democracy and its associated forms of political patronage, has further emphasized the limited importance of patronage as a means of alleviating the social disparities resulting from the distribution of land. Even during the time of stable parliamentary political life (in the last decades of the nineteenth century) the absence of conspicuous political and social unrest among the labouring masses, owed more perhaps to lack of revolutionary political indoctrination (which, in the region under study, does not appear to have begun before the first years of this century) than to the effectiveness of political patronage or to the 'paternalistic' practices of landowners which have since withered away. Patronage, in its widest sense, does play a role in helping to maintain order but it cannot, either in itself or in combination with the other institutions reviewed so far, account satisfactorily for this lack of unrest.

The solution to the problem has to be found in the political structure: both in the administrative and corporative framework discussed and in the characteristics of political life in a more general sense. The political structure, however, prevents rather than represses unrest. Repression does take place, of course—and anyone who has seen Republican Guards dealing with rural strikers or, for that matter, with alleged criminal offenders, knows that it is not a pleasant affair. But the remarkable point is that it is very seldom needed.

In order to understand why this is so, a few critical points should be stressed. First, key posts in the administration (Civil Governor, mayor) are not elective. Aldermen (*vereadores*) are elected by a municipal council that is itself appointed; the Junta de Freguesia is elected by heads of families, but its limited powers, the antipathy expected from the higher authorities in the event of any hypothetical list of alternatives to the official candidates, and the absence of free political parties transform these elections into virtual appointments. As a consequence, people are not used to making choices and to taking responsibilities in matters of local government, nor, for that matter, in those of central government either.

The absence of legal political parties has largely contributed towards the maintenance of widespread political ignorance and apathy. The União Nacional, which is often described as the government party, is not exactly a political party and its structure is so firmly manipulated and controlled from above that it does not invite the rank and file to express more than dutiful obedience to the dictates of its executive committee. The republican parties have disappeared or exist only in name. The only true political party left is the illegal Communist Party. Adherence to this underground party springs more from semi-religious belief than from rational political argument or pragmatic concern, and in any case it does not seem to have had any sustained effect in Vila Velha. The inhabitants of Vila Velha who consider themselves to be politically minded are divided between those who are *da situação*, i.e. who support the Government (these include the latifundists, most proprietários, and a few other men) and those who are *da oposição* i.e. against the Government (these are found mainly among the labouring and sharecropping groups, shopkeepers, and artisans, and also a few clerks and professional men from Vila Nova). Little political sophistication is involved in these choices: having the cake or wanting to have it often provides the clue to the position taken. Government supporters may become involved in political action—they may become mayors, aldermen, or active members of the União Nacional—but government opponents, except for the very few who have joined the Communist Party, limit themselves more or less to private talk.

To most of the population of Vila Velha, however, politics are an alien and potentially dangerous activity. The people are generally politically ignorant and respond in a lukewarm fashion to appeals from both the Right and the Left. They allow their lives to be controlled politically by the authorities in power and are sceptical about any possibility of influencing these authorities, let alone of changing them.

This general feeling of political indifference and powerlessness is reinforced by the nature of industrial relations in the corporate state. Its most relevant feature from a political viewpoint is that it prevents the unionization of rural labourers. Independent labourers' unions would have provided an institutionalized channel for voicing collective grievances, and would have represented a bargaining power with which landowners would have had to reckon. Corporative organization has only served to provide limited welfare benefits and alternative employment. The combined effect of corporative measures has been to keep labourers on the land but not to raise their wages or improve their working conditions, and they have not contributed towards fostering the labourers' awareness of their interests and rights as a group.

Over the last forty years these factors—the characteristics of the administrative and corporate systems and the characteristics of political life in a wider sense—seem to me to be mainly responsible for the absence of organized and sustained attempts by labourers to subvert the present order of social stratification or, alternatively, to mitigate in any substantial way its most blatantly inequitable features.[2] The outward acceptance of the

[2] This does not explain why subversion or reform did not take place before: we know that, at least since 1911, labourers' grievances were widespread throughout the

social order thus finds an explanation in the nature of the political system. Nothing can be organized locally to call into question the present order and very little can be done from outside.[3]

It might be argued that I am giving undue emphasis to the political system as a cause of the labourers' lack of organization. Indeed, a general feature of this society—and not only of the labouring group—is that it is very difficult for associations of any kind to succeed. Some will tend to attribute this to proclivities of the Portuguese character, others, with less simplism, to a system of values that places little obligation on the individual beyond the close circle of his family and friends. This system of values does exist and some of its main characteristics are similar to those found in other mediterranean societies under different political systems. In the course of this book I reviewed many cases in which such a system of values was obviously in operation and it cannot be said that the present political system gave rise to such values. Nor do I claim this to be so. What is relevant to the point at issue is that the political system has allowed the traditional system of values to remain in force, as it were, by opposing modern forms of social organization, such as independent trade unions and free political parties,[4] that would neces-

province and could be articulately expressed at times, while the New State came to power only in 1926. The parliamentary republic, judging by its repression of the massive rural strikes in 1911 and 1912, had little sympathy with the claims of the rural masses of the south, yet conditions for political propaganda were incomparably freer during those years—as indeed during the years of the parliamentary monarchy—than they have ever been since. This freedom was not exercised in Vila Velha—the politically minded labourers were always few and their impact was slight. As far as we can circumscribe the problem to this small area, therefore, the ideological premises and the institutional machinery on which articulate reformist claims and revolutionary aspirations are based were lacking, and only general movements, spreading from the outside, were able to give direction and momentum to labourers' discontent. Why such movements were apparently so few and what their exact nature was before 1926 are different problems which cannot be solved without adequate research yet to be undertaken.

[3] The exceptional case of the 1962 strikes should not mislead one into erroneous assumptions: the labourers' claims were very limited and many people in the administration considered them to be long overdue; the Government, at odds with the big landowners over cereal farming policies, did not see the need to crush the strikers. Only a few ringleaders were arrested in the province, but this action was enough for the agitation to subside once the immediate claims were met.

[4] This does not apply only to political parties or trade unions: any private association has to have its statutes approved by the Government and its elected directors cannot take office without government sanction.

sarily come into conflict with some of the traditional values and restrict their scope of action. In Vila Velha this has obviously had much more damaging effects on the labourers than on the landowners. It is not the proud independence of the honourable Mediterranean man that accounts for the isolation of the poor labourer—it is rather his isolation that may lead him to try to find some comfort in the thought that he is both independent and proud.

APPENDIX I

POPULATION

Years	*Freguesia of Vila Velha*	*Distrito of Evora*	*Portugal*
1864	1,380	102,148	3,927,392
1878	1,410	113,948	4,303,664
1890	1,563	121,625	4,713,319
1900	1,557	128,842	5,039,744
1911	1,909	150,020	5,586,053
1920	1,769	155,918	5,668,232
1930	2,161	179,036	6,334,507
1940	2,526	209,956	7,218,882
1950	2,455	221,881	7,921,913
1960	2,161	219,916	8,292,975

APPENDIX II
POPULATION RATES

FREGUESIA OF VILA VELHA

Periods	*Births*	*Deaths*	*Natural net increase*
1865–1878	780	695	85
1879–1890	590	423	167
1891–1900	506	396	110
1901–1911	714	371	343
1912–1920	593	401	192
1921–1930	606	367	239
1931–1940	635	276	359
1941–1950	450	250	200
1951–1960	410	200	210

RATES PER THOUSAND

1865–1878	39·94	35·58	4·36
1879–1890	33·10	23·72	9·28
1891–1900	32·43	25·38	7·05
1901–1911	41·20	21·41	19·79
1912–1920	32·02	21·65	10·37
1921–1930	30·64	18·55	12·09
1931–1940	27·10	11·78	15·32
1941–1950	18·07	10·04	8·03
1951–1960	17·76	8·66	9·10

DISTRITO OF EVORA

Periods	*Births*	*Deaths*	*Natural net increase*
1921–1930	53,406	28,753	24,653
1931–1940	54,458	27,386	27,072
1941–1950	47,599	26,759	20,840
1951–1960	40,239	21,655	18,584

RATES PER THOUSAND

1921–1930	31·8	17·1	14·7
1931–1940	28·1	14·7	13·4
1941–1950	22·1	12·4	9·7
1951–1960	18·6	9·8	8·8

PORTUGAL

1921–1930	1,889,244	1,136,763	752,481
1931–1940	1,859,366	1,101,345	758,021
1941–1950	1,860,238	1,091,372	768,866
1951–1960	1,902,573	917,000	985,573

RATES PER THOUSAND

1921–1930	31·4	18·9	12·5
1931–1940	28·9	16·1	12·8
1941–1950	24·5	14·4	10·1
1951–1960	24·6	11·2	13·4

APPENDIX III
MIGRATORY MOVEMENTS

FREGUESIA OF VILA VELHA

Periods	*Net natural increase*	*Actual change in population*	*Net migration*
1864–1878	85	+ 30	− 55
1878–1890	167	+153	− 14
1890–1900	110	− 6	−116
1900–1911	343	+352	+ 9
1911–1920	192	−140	−332
1920–1930	239	+392	+153
1930–1940	359	+365	+ 6
1940–1950	200	− 71	−271
1950–1960	210	−294	−504

DISTRITO OF EVORA

1920–1930	24,653	+23,118	− 1,535
1930–1940	27,072	+30,920	+ 3,848
1940–1950	20,840	+11,925	− 8,915
1950–1960	18,584	− 1,965	−20,549

PORTUGAL

1920–1930	752,481	+666,275	− 86,206
1930–1940	758,021	+884,375	+126,354
1940–1950	768,866	+703,031	− 65,835
1950–1960	985,573	+371,062	−614,511

APPENDIX IV

YIELDS OF CEREALS IN SOUTHERN EUROPE AVERAGE 1957–63

Quintals per hectare

	Portugal	*Spain*	*Greece*	*Yugoslavia*	*Italy*	*France*	*Average OECD Europe*
Wheat	8·1	10·3	15·4	16·7	18·4	25·3	17·6
Rye	6·3	8·8	9·4	10·4	15·2	13·9	18·2
Barley	5·2	13·0	12·7	14·3	12·7	25·2	22·2
Oats	3·3	8·8	11·7	10·8	13·3	18·7	19·7
Maize	10·5	22·8	13·4	21·4	31·1	28·5	23·1

(Source: OECD, Agricultural and Food Statistics, Economic Surveys, PORTUGAL (Paris), December: 1966.)

APPENDIX V

WHEAT

CONCELHO OF VILA NOVA 1911–65

	Sowing			Production		
	Weights of seed sown (q.)		Area sown		Yields	
Year	*Total*	*Per ha.*	*ha.*	*Total*	*Per q.*	*Per ha.*
1911*	4,309	0·67	6,471	47,196	10·95	7·29
2						
3						
4						
5	6,403	0.71	9,006	36,780	5·74	4·08
6				36,788		
7				35,465		
8	5,344	0·70	7,634	34,795	6·51	4·56
9	5,579	0·70	7,970	26,788	4·80	3·36
1920	5,773	0·70	8,247	41,200	7·14	5·00
1	5,318	0·70	7,597	34,567	6·50	4·55
2	5,651	0·70	8,073	28,256	5·00	3·50
3	5,886	0·70	8,409	70,636	12·00	8·40
4	6,198	0·70	8,854	53,413	8·62	6·03
5	6,676	0·70	9,537	66,766	10·00	7·00
6	6,785	0·70	9,693	40,060	5·90	4·13
7	6.671	0·70	9,530	50,075	7·51	5·25
8	6,728	0·70	9,611	33,633	5·00	3·50
9	6,562	0·70	9,374	52,494	8·00	5·60
1930	6,645	0·70	9,439	66,449	10·00	7·00
1	7,752	0·90	8,613	46,514	6·00	5·40
2	8,915	0·90	9,906	89,153	10·00	9·00
3	7,244	0·90	8,049	45,274	6·25	5·62
4	7,327	0·90	8,141	109,655	14·97	13·47
5	7,110	0·87	8,182	95,176	13·39	11·63
6	7,133	0·88	8,083	32,100	4·50	3·97
7	6,137	0·88	6,974	51,346	8·37	7·36
8	6,191	1·01	6,132	43,379	7·01	7·07
9	5,571	0·90	6,190	71,456	12·83	11·54
1940	5,469	0·90	6,077	30,403	5·56	5·00
1	5,967	0·90	6,630	56,092	9·40	8·46
2	6,193	1·00	6,181	83,878	13·54	13·57

* In 1869 the Câmara had estimated the production of the Concelho in 1,200,000 Kg. (12 Sept.).

Year	Sowing: Weights of seed sown (q.) Total	per ha.	Area sown ha.	Production: Total	Yields per q.	per ha.
3	5,445	0·90	6,050	43,728	8·03	7·23
4	7,792	0·90	8,658	38,962	5·00	4·50
5	6,730	0·90	7,478	23,091	3·43	3·09
6	7,747	0·90	8,610	72,395	9·34	7·53
7	6,934	0·90	7,704	48,954	7·06	6·35
8	7,432	0·90	8,258	40,950	5·51	4·96
9	8,188	0·90	9,098	41,759	5·10	4·59
1950	7,369	0·90	8,188	75,901	10·30	9·27
1	8,106	0·90	9,007	75,399	9·30	8·37
2	9,350	0·90	10,389	75,100	8·03	7·23
3	11,220	0·90	12,467	89,970	8·02	7·22
4	11,650	0·90	12,944	98,465	8·45	7·61
5	12,456	0·90	13,850	62,315	5·00	4·50
6	10,900	0·90	12,111	72,800	6·68	6·01
7	11,230	0·90	12,478	103,930	9·25	8·33
8	11,820	0·90	13,133	115,000	9·70	8·73
9	11,900	0·90	13,222	88,500	7·44	6·69
1960	11,585		10,532	87,505		
1	9,500		8,636	44,590		
2	12,430		11,300	75,090	6·04	6·65
3	10,740		9,764	74,580	6·94	7·64
4	10,650		9,682	57,775	5·42	5·97
5	9,471		8,610	65,833	6·99	7·65

(Source: National Institute of Statistics, Lisbon.)
q = quintal.

APPENDIX VI
MIRACLES

Some of the miracles performed by Our Lord of the Cross have been recorded in small wood paintings found in the church and they cover two centuries:

'Miracle of the *Senhor dos Passos* performed towards José Fialho Recto, whom, being seriously ill, the Lord in His Mercy saved from danger. May so good a Lord be praised forever.' (No date—but probably from the beginning of the eighteenth century.)

'Vow of Joana Maria to the *Senhor Jesus dos Passos* in a malignant fever that assailed her in the year 1736.'

'Mercy shown by the *Senhor dos Passos* of the town of Vila Velha towards the Rev. Vicar of the town of Terena, whom the Lord restored to perfect health after a serious illness in the year 1780.'

'Visible miracle that the *Divino Senhor Jesus dos Passos* mercifully granted to José Maria Pereira de Miranda, physician in this town, whom he saved from impending death after all the resources of the art of medicine had been exhausted, on 15 July 1855.'

'Miracle of the *Senhor dos Passos* towards Mariana Lopes Godinho, residing at Monte do Duque, parish of São Pedro do Corval, who, being seriously ill, was saved by him from death on 21 August 1908, in answer to the prayers of her husband Francisco Correia Caeiro, of Joana Lopes Godinho, Micaela Lopes Godinho, Domingos Lopes Bulhão, and other persons who accompanied her.'

APPENDIX VII

UNEMPLOYMENT IN THE FREGUESIA, 1956–65

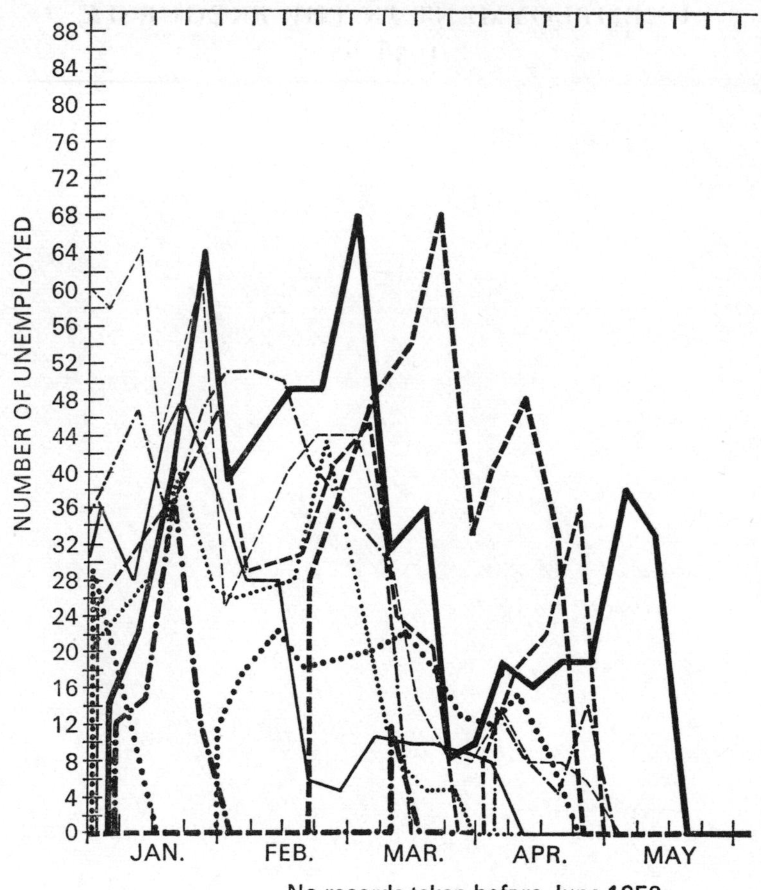
NUMBER OF UNEMPLOYED
88
84
80
76
72
68
64
60
56
52
48
44
40
36
32
28
24
20
16
12
8
4
0
JAN.
FEB.
MAR.
APR.
MAY
No records taken before June 1956

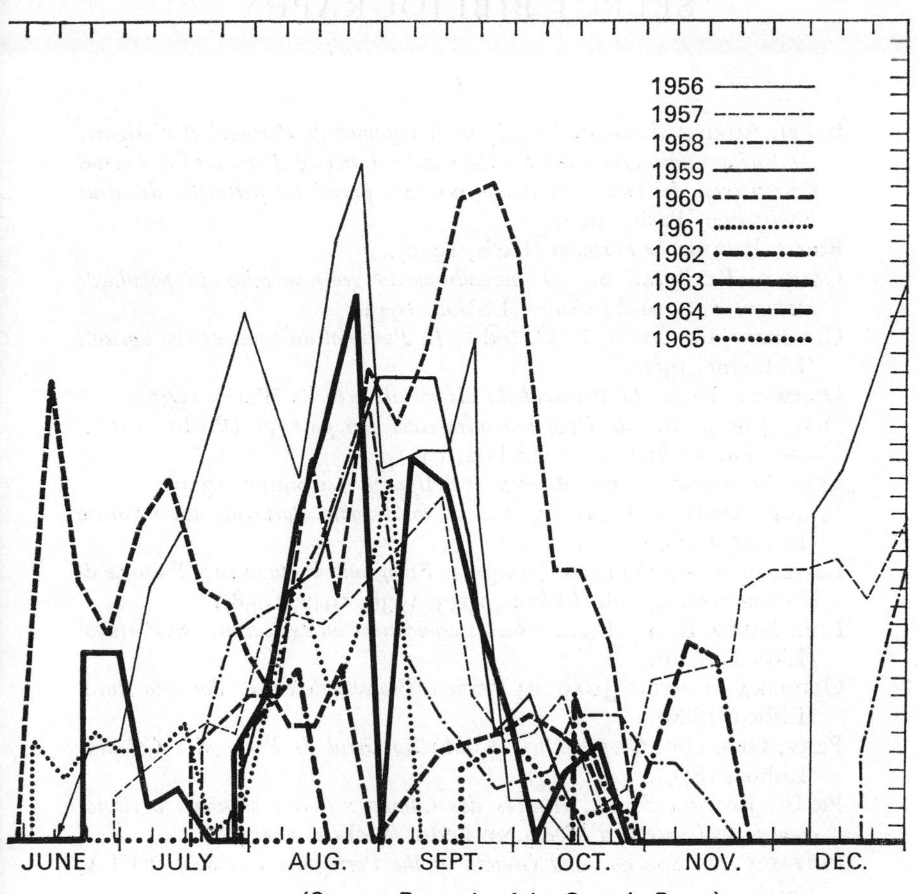

(Source: Records of the Casa do Povo.)

SELECT BIBLIOGRAPHY

I

BALBI, ADRIEN, *Essai statistique sur le royaume de Portugal et d'Algarve comparé aux autres états de l'Europe et suivi d'un coup d'oeil sur l'état actuel des sciences, des lettres, et des beaux arts parmi les portugais des deux hémispheres* (Paris, 1822).

BIROT, PIERRE, *Le Portugal* (Paris, 1950).

CAMPOS, EZEQUIEL DE, *O enquadramento geo-económico da população portuguesa atraves dos séculos* (Lisboa, 1943).

CINCINATO DA COSTA, B. C. (ed.), *Le Portugal du point de vue agricole* (Lisbonne, 1900).

DESCAMPS, PAUL, *Le Portugal, la vie sociale actuelle* (Paris, 1935).

DIAS, JORGE, *Rio de Onor-comunitarismo agropastoral* (Porto, 1953).

——— *Ensaios Etnológicos* (Lisboa, 1961).

FEIO, MARIANO, *Le Bas Alentejo et l'Algarve* (Lisbonne, 1949).

JUDICE, ANTONIO TEIXEIRA (ed.), *Notas sobre Portugal*, 1st volume (Lisboa, 1908).

LEITE, DE VASCONCELLOS, JOAQUIM, *Etnografia Portuguesa: Tentame de sistematização* (4 vols. Lisboa, 1933, 1936, 1942, 1958).

LIMA BASTO, E. A., *Alguns aspectos económicos da agricultura em Portugal* (Lisboa, 1936).

OLIVEIRA MARTINS, JOAQUIM PEDRO, *Projecto de Lei de Fomento Rural* (Lisboa, 1886).

PERY, GERALDO, *Geographia e Estatística Geral de Portugal e Colonias* (Lisboa, 1875).

PICÃO, JOSÉ DA SILVA, *Através dos Campos: usos e costumes agrícolo-alentejanos (concelho d'Elvas)*, 2nd edn. (Lisboa, 1947).

PINTADO, X., *Structure and Growth of the Portuguese Economy* (EFTA, 1964).

RIBEIRO, ORLANDO, *Portugal, o Mediterraneo e o Atlântico* (2nd edn., Lisbon, 1963).

Portugal, tome V in *Geografia de España y Portugal* (Barcelona, 1955).

SERGIO, ANTÓNIO, *Introdução geográfico-sociológica à história de Portugal* (Lisboa, no date).

SILBERT, ALBERT, *Le Portugal méditerranéen à la fin de l'Ancien Régime* (2 vols. Paris, 1966).

——— *Le problème agraire portugais au temps des premières Cortès libérales* (Paris, 1968).

II

BAROJA, J. C., 'Honour and Shame: A historical account of several conflicts', *Honour and Shame: The Values of Mediterranean Society* (ed.) Peristiany (London, 1965).

BOISSEVAIN, J., *Saints and Fireworks: Religion and Politics in Rural Malta* (London, 1965).

——— 'Patronage in Sicily,' *Man*, 1 (1965).

BOURDIEU, P., 'The Sentiment of Honour in Kabyle Society', trans. by Sherrard, *Honour and Shame: The Values of Mediterranean Society*, (ed.) Peristiany (London, 1965).

CAMPBELL, J. K., 'The Kindred in a Greek Mountain Community', *Mediterranean Countrymen*, (ed.) Pitt-Rivers (The Hague, Paris, 1963).

——— *Honour, Family and Patronage: A study of institutions and moral values in a Greek mountain community* (Oxford, 1964).

——— 'Honour and the Devil', *Honour and Shame: The Values of Mediterranean Society*, (ed.) Peristiany (London, 1965).

FRIEDL, E., 'The Role of Kinship in the Transmission of National Culture to Rural Villages in Mainland Greece', *American Anthropologists* Lxi (1959).

——— *Vasilika, A Village in Modern Greece* (New York, 1962).

GELLNER, E., 'Saints of the Atlas', *Mediterranean Countrymen*, (ed.) Pitt-Rivers (The Hague, Paris, 1963).

KENNY, M., *A Spanish Tapestry, Town and Country in Castille* (London, 1962).

——— 'Patterns of Patronage in Spain', *Anthropological Quarterly*, 33 (1960).

LISON-TOLOSANA, C., *Belmonte de los Caballeros, A Sociological Study of a Spanish Town* (Oxford, 1966).

PETERS, E., 'Aspects of Rank and Status among Muslims in a Lebanese Village', *Mediterranean Countrymen*, (ed.) Pitt-Rivers (The Hague, Paris, 1963).

PITT-RIVERS, J., *The People of the Sierra* (London, 1954).

——— 'Honour and Social Status', *Honour and Shame: The Values of Mediterranean Society*, (ed.) Peristiany (London, 1965).

SILVERMAN, S., 'Patronage and Community-Nation Relationship in Central Italy', *Ethnology*, 4 (1955).

INDEX